A COMPARATIVE STUDY OF BELLARMINE'S DOCTRINE ON THE RELATION OF SINCERE NON-CATHOLICS TO THE CATHOLIC CHURCH

JOHN A. HARDON, S.J.

Doctoral Dissertation

PONTIFICAL GREGORIAN UNIVERSITY

ROME 1950

A COMPARATIVE STUDY OF BELLARMINE'S DOCTRINE
ON THE RELATION OF SINCERE NON-CATHOLICS TO
THE CATHOLIC CHURCH

by John A. Hardon, S.J.

Imprimatur:
    Reverend Joseph E. Kurtz, D.D.
    Archbishop of Louisville
    September 12, 2008

ISBN 978-1-931101-03-5

Printed and Published in
the United States of America by

ETERNAL LIFE ®
902 W STEPHEN FOSTER AVENUE
BARDSTOWN, KY 40004
800-842-2871

TABLE OF CONTENTS

Foreword

The Servant of God, Fr. John A. Hardon, S.J., (1914-2000) was one of the most distinguished theologians and catechists the Catholic Church in America has produced. The prolific author of over 200 books and countless articles explaining and defending Catholic teachings, the Jesuit theologian was a true Confessor of the Faith who strengthened the faith of many during the "Crisis of Faith" that would afflict the Church in the United States and Western Europe. He was indefatigable in assisting many lay apostolates such as "Eternal Life" (headed by the saintly layman, William J. Smith) whose annual "The Church Teaches Forum" Fr. Hardon graced with his holy presence. Faithful to the charism of the Society of Jesus to "think with the Church" (*"sentire cum ecclesia"*), he fearlessly and uncompromisingly defended the moral teachings of the Vicars of Christ affecting marriage and the family, thereby winning the admiration and love of millions of Catholic laity beset by the spread of dissent following the rejection of Pope Paul VI's prophetic 1968 encyclical "Humane Vitae". Throughout his long priestly life he proved to be a true son of **"my father, St. Ignatius Loyola"**, in declaring "in season and out of season" that **"Faith in Christ is shown by Loyalty to the Pope …We can be united among ourselves as Christians on one condition: there is one center of unity in the world and that is in the Vicar of Christ."**

A champion of religious life, the Jesuit theologian was the leading force in the creation of the Institute of Religious Life, and encouraged the formation of lay groups involved in Catechesis such as Catholics United for the Faith (CUF) and The Marian Catechists. He was especially conscious of the need to foster the use of every kind of Media to spread Catholic Truth, and spent his life lecturing, writing, counseling and teaching priests, religious, and laity to remain steadfastly obedient to the Magisterium of Holy Church. His **"The Catholic Catechism"** (1974) remains a classic work of profound erudition reflecting the authentic teachings of Vatican II that were being undermined by corrosive influences in the Church which had succumbed to the siren songs of contemporary rationalism, relativism, and secularism.

From 1949 to 1951 Fr. Hardon studied at the Gregorian University in Rome, writing his doctoral dissertation on the thought and writings of

St. Robert Bellarmine, Doctor of the Church, and the greatest ecclesiolo-
gist (one who studies in depth the nature of the true Church) in the history of the Church. It is this 1950 dissertation **"A Comparative Study
of Bellarmine's Doctrine On the Relation of Sincere Non-Catholics
To the Catholic Church"** that would evidence Fr. Hardon's own superb
grasp of the nature of the Church and his coming to grips with the serious errors being committed by theologians who, before and after Vatican
I, tended to obscure the visible identification of Christ's true Church,
a phenomenon, it must be sadly admitted, that persists after Vatican II
into our own day. It is St. Robert Bellarmine's teaching on the visible
organization of the Catholic Church as the "one, holy, Catholic, and apostolic Church" professed in the Nicene-Constantinopolitan Creed (431
A.D.) and as the Mystical Body of Jesus Christ which Fr. Hardon in
1950 saw as the antidote to false and erroneous teachings that continued
to be perpetrated, even by orthodox scholars. Fr. Hardon will be seen to
have been remarkably astute in noting the perennial validity of Cardinal Bellarmine's core-ecclesiology that would, in fact, receive modern
confirmation in the teaching of 19th and 20th century Popes and eventually find its honored place in the documents of Vatican II, especially
it's "Dogmatic Constitution on the Church" (**Lumen Gentium**). It is,
moreover, "Bellarminism" that is reflected in the ecclesiology of "**The
Catechism of the Catholic Church**".

Fr. Hardon's masterful work constituted a scholarly examination of
the centuries' old theological attempts to find an adequate definition of
the Church that would be faithful to the import of Scripture and Apostolic Tradition, and serve the apologetical needs of the faithful. He noted Cardinal Bellarmine's overriding concern to safeguard the doctrine
of the true Church's essential visibility - a doctrine found in Scripture
and Tradition, but sharply challenged by the Protestant reformers who
viewed the Church as essentially an invisible assembly or grouping of
the saved or the predestined elect, or who insisted that only those in the
state of grace were really members of the true Church. This denial of
the Church as a visible society, of its visible and hierarchical nature,
meant that the true Church was an invisible entity whose members could
be known with certainty by God alone. The greatest Controversialist of
the Counter-Reformation, St. Robert bent every effort and used his vast
erudition to defend the visible nature of the historic Catholic Church and
to refute the novel errors and heresies of Luther and Calvin and their
followers which prevented sincere seekers of truth from finding Christ's
one Church. This he did by demonstrating in his classic work "**De Ecclesia Militante**" that the "congregation of the faithful" ("congregatio fidelium") and the "Church of the Saints" ("ecclesia sanctorum") founded

by Christ as His Church, was in fact a visible, social body, an actual visible society, whose members were bound together by both internal and external bonds and was easily identifiable by its visible structure. Moreover, since membership in the true Church was necessary for salvation, theologians had the special obligation to provide a definition of the Church that would enable both the "plain man" and the most erudite to discover easily that one Church of Christ which was described in Holy Scripture as the "Body of Christ" and the "One Fold", and indeed the sole "Ark of Salvation".

However, it was not only Protestants who had failed to provide a valid definition of the true Church. St. Robert would criticize the orthodox theologians of his period whose definitions of the Church were inadequate, ambiguous, or outrightly erroneous, and which appeared to support Protestant notions of the invisibility of the Church. Such theories obscured the visibility of the Church in such manner as to make the Church an amorphous entity whose membership was made up of men and women who were not visibly within its hierarchical communion. **The crucial question of who is an actual member of the Church** (to which St. Robert Bellarmine would give the key solution) would, nevertheless, continue to trouble Catholic theology from his time to ours as some theologians persisted in giving "definitions" of the Church which dissolved the boundaries of the Church to include those who were not actual members in full communion with the Successor of Peter, the visible head of the Church Militant. In the present "Crisis of Faith" the Church remains disturbed by the popular writings of Catholic journalists and those of dissenting theologians who have not hesitated to declare non-Catholic Christians "members of the Church" or "parts of the Church" or "partial members" or "initial members" or "incomplete members" or "invisible members". The result is that the very term "member" is rendered vague and without specific meaning. With such misleading language the boundaries of the Church, as Pope Pius XII observed, "dissolve into nothingness" and "leave the Mystical Body of the Redeemer in such obscurity and so maimed, that those seeking the haven of eternal salvation cannot see it and cannot find it." (*Mystici Corporis,* n. 43).

Fr. Hardon's excellent study revealed the outstanding merit of Cardinal Bellarmine's ecclesiology which lay in his demonstrating that an actual member of the Church was the man or woman joined to Our Lord by a **threefold external bond**: who are baptized and profess the true faith; share in the communion of the same Sacraments; and are under the Church's legitimate rulers, the Bishops united to their visible head, the Roman Pontiff. Non-Catholic Christians could well possess faith and sanctifying grace, but lacking any of the above external bonds could not be regarded as **actual or real members** or **"parts"** of the Church. From the 18th to the 20th century, moreover, further confusion had resulted from misuse of the terms "body and soul of the Church". St. Robert showed that any attempt to define a member of the Church as one belonging to the soul of the Church and not to the visible body was but another faulty explanation leading to the error of a "spiritual or invisible Church" distinct from the actual visible Church Christ founded. To speak of the "soul of the Church" as an invisible society (as some later theologians would attempt) was to thoroughly distort St. Robert Bellarmine's theology of the Church which would receive support and confirmation in Magisterial documents.

Another remarkable contribution to Catholic theology by St. Robert Bellarmine is stressed in Fr. Hardon's impressive volume. This was Bellarmine's explanation that the traditional formula "**Nulla Salus Extra Ecclesiam**" did not mean that one had to be a visible member of the Catholic Church to arrive at salvation (as some erring rigorists continue to allege to this day). Drawing upon the writings of previous theologians, the Saint taught that one could be saved as an actual member of the Catholic Church while a non-Catholic Christian in good faith could be saved as a **member "in voto", that is, one in intention, desire and resolution.** His basic doctrine was that, at the very least**, voto membership** in the one, visible Church is necessary for salvation. As Fr. Hardon observed, "This distinction between membership in the Church **in re** (in reality) and **in voto** (in desire) represents a milestone in Catholic ecclesiology." The Church would increasingly accept the thesis that baptized non-Catholic Christians in good faith have indeed been incorporated into Christ and His Church, and are thus mysteriously "within it"; however, as long as they remain separated from its visible structure and framework, they cannot be termed real members of the Catholic Church.

Fr. Hardon's volume traces the remarkable development of doctrine that has taken place in the Church's understanding of membership in the visible Church of Christ.

Because, however, **membership in re or in voto** led to continual disputes among theologians dealing with ecumenical matters and who preferred to speak of "**degrees of membership**", Vatican II would avoid the term "member" and speak instead of "**full incorporation" in the visible Body of Christ**. However, according to the teaching of the Ecumenical Council, the "fully incorporated" person is clearly the actual member of the visible society of the Catholic Church which **is** the Mystical Body of

Christ. There are not "degrees of membership" in the Church (as some theologians, influenced by a false irenicism, had attempted to popularize). The same theologians had also sought, mistakenly, to distinguish members of the Catholic Church from the members of the Mystical Body of Christ). In teaching instead that there are "**degrees of incorporation**" in the true Church, Vatican II noted that Protestants and Eastern Orthodox are partially incorporated in the Church and so in various degrees enjoy an imperfect communion with the Catholic Church. Thus, Vatican II documents declare separated Christians by their baptism do belong to the Church in some way; they are joined to or linked to the Catholic Church, but they still lack that "full incorporation" in the visible Church which, for his part, though not using the term "full incorporation", St. Robert Bellarmine had identified with "actual membership".

Contrary to the view of dissenter theologians giving vent to the questionable "spirit of Vatican II, there was no rejection of Bellarminian ecclesiology by Vatican II. There was no Vatican II "Copernican Revolution" which changed the traditional conditions for being a member of the Catholic Church. No one understood the teaching of Vatican II regarding the situation of non-Catholic Christians more than the Supreme Pontiff who presided over its last sessions and approved its documents. In his General Audience of May 15, 1974, Pope Paul VI asked:

"Do not the baptized all belong to the Church? And is not the Church one only? Yes, the Council answers, but membership in the Church requires other conditions, as well as baptism, such as identical faith (cf. Eph. 4:51; Jn. 10:16), and unity of [hierarchical] communion (Lumen Gentium, 15; Unitatis Redintegratio, 2, 3, etc.), so that, as the Council teaches, that only by means of the Catholic Church of Christ, which is the general instrument of salvation, is it possible to obtain the fullness of salvific means…"

Vatican II in its magnificent "Dogmatic Constitution on the Church" **(Lumen Gentium)** declared:

"Fully incorporated into the Church are those who, possessing the Spirit of Christ, accept all the means of salvation given to the Church together with her entire organization, and who - by the bonds constituted by the profession of faith, the sacraments, ecclesiastical government, and communion - are joined in the visible structure of the Church of Christ, who rules her through the Supreme Pontiff and the bishops. Even though incorporated into the Church, one who does not, however, persevere in charity is not saved …The Church knows that she is joined in many ways to the baptized who are honored by the name of Christian, but who do not, however, profess the Catholic faith in it's entirety or have not preserved unity or communion under the successor of Peter." (nos. 14, 15)

No greater honor could have been accorded St. Robert Bellarmine than to have his teaching concerning the essential conditions for membership in the Catholic Church (and the acute importance of such membership) vindicated by the Church's latest Ecumenical Council.

Fr. John Hardon, S.J.'s, scholarly research tracing the history of St. Robert Bellarmine's doctrine concerning membership in the Catholic Church from the 16th century into the reign of Pope Pius XII gives a fascinating insight into the mind, heart, and thought of a Doctor of the Church, and remains an indispensable work for the study of how doctrine concerning the nature of the Catholic Church developed historically.

-James Likoudis
president emeritus, Catholics United for the Faith (CUF)

INTRODUCTION

Bellarmine represents a landmark in the history of Catholic theology. His life of seventy-nine years, from 1542 to 1621, spanned the time immediately following the Protestant Revolt. Luther died in 1546, Henry VIII in 1547, Melanthon in 1560, Calvin in 1564. St. Robert was therefore a contemporary of the original rebels against the authority of the Church and historically became the first comprehensive exponent of Catholic doctrine against the attacks of the Protestants. This fact is important to keep in mind in studying his doctrine on the relation of non-Catholics to the Church. Living during the period of a mass rebellion against papal authority and having personal experience for many years in Northern Europe with first generation apostates from the faith, it was inevitable that his attitude toward non-Catholics should be one of uncompromising rigor in opposing their errors, softened only by his love for them as "the straying sheep" with whom he pleaded to return, at the cost of salvation, to their Father's house.

We are particularly interested, in the present study, in one phase of Bellarmine's ecclesiology which has not received the attention it deserves; namely, his doctrine on the membership of non-Catholics in the Catholic Church. His distinction between the body and soul, of the Church, and between *re* and *voto* membership in the Church have become the standard method of explaining the salvation of non-Catholics who die outside the Catholic Church. Unfortunately, these distinctions are often misused, because they have not been examined in their proper context. The first purpose of this study, therefore, is to supply the context and, consequently, explain the distinctions. Moreover, Bellarmine's doctrine has been confirmed by the Church and somewhat refined, notably in the last century. So the second purpose of this study will be to compare his doctrine on non-Catholic membership in the Church with the corresponding doctrine of recent popes, starting with Pius IX and the Vatican Council. Finally, certain basic elements in Bellarmine's teaching, like his *body-soul* and *re-voto* distinctions, have been misapplied because they have not been understood. The third purpose, therefore, will be to examine these misinterpretations of St. Robert, limiting our analysis to modern Catholic writers in the United States.

The order of procedure in handling the problem will be different for the different sections. In the expository part, the sequence will be the same as that which Bellarmine follows in *De Ecclesia Militante*, where he deals with the subject of Church membership. In the comparative section, the order will be chronological, from Pius IX to Pius XII. In the last part, the critical analysis will cover the period, roughly, from 1900 to the present day.

A final point to be noted is that the writer does not intend to examine the question of the salvation of those who die outside the visible unity of the Church. Where the question is treated at all, it will only be incidentally, in its bearing on the main theme of this study, namely, whether and to what extent, in the light of Bellarmine's principles, non-Catholics *in bona fide* may be considered members of the Roman Catholic Church. Moreover, for the sake of conciseness, not all such non-Catholics are the subject of our examination, but only heretics and the unbaptized, whether they desire to enter the Catholic Church or not.

PART ONE

EXPOSITION OF BELLARMINE'S DOCTRINE

CHAPTER 1

GENERAL PRINCIPLES ON CHURCH MEMBERSHIP

I. DEFINITION OF THE CHURCH

In opposition to Calvin's theory of two Churches founded by Christ, the one interior and invisible, the other exterior and sensibly perceptible, Bellarmine declares that, "According to our doctrine, there is only one Church, not two. And this one and true Church is the assembly of men, bound together by the profession of the same Christian faith, and by the communion of the same Sacraments, under the rule of legitimate pastors, and in particular of the one Vicar of Christ on earth, the Roman Pontiff."[1]

Bellarmine's whole ecclesiology is synthesized in this formula, consequently also his doctrine on the problematical membership of non-Catholics in the true Church. "From this definition," he observes, "we can easily decide what people belong to the Church and what people do not. For there are three parts to this definition, namely:

- Profession of the true Faith,
- Communion of Sacraments, and
- Subjection to the Roman Pontiff, the legitimate Pastor.

"By reason of the first part are excluded all unbelievers, as well as those who were never in the Church, like the Jews, Pagans and Turks, as those who were formerly in the Church but have left it, like heretics and apostates.

"By reason of the second part are excluded catechumens and those who are excommunicated; the first because they have not been admitted to a participation of the Sacraments, the second because they have been debarred from them.

"By reason of the third part are excluded schismatics, who have the Faith and the Sacraments, but are not subject to the legitimate Pastor; and therefore, they profess the Faith and receive the Sacraments outside (the true Church)."[2]

1

St. Robert visualizes no other possibilities. "All other people," he says, "even when they are wicked and abandoned criminals, are included" as members of the Church.[3]

Since so much depends on a proper understanding of this definition, it will help to compare it with another less familiar formula to be found in Bellarmine's *Dottrina Cristiana*, published in 1597-1598, about ten years after the appearance of the first volume of the Controversies.

In answer to the question: *What do we mean by the Church?*, he explains, "By the Church we mean a convocation and congregation of men, who are baptized and make profession of the faith and laws of Christ, under obedience to the supreme Roman Pontiff." *Why is it called a convocation?* "Because we are not born Christians as we are born Italians or Frenchmen or of any other nationality. But we are called by God and enter into this congregation by means of Baptism which is, as it were, the door of the Church. However, it is not enough to be baptized to be in the Church. It is also necessary to believe and confess the holy faith and laws of Christ, as the pastors and preachers of the Church teach us. Nor is even this enough; it is also necessary to be subject in obedience to the supreme Roman Pontiff, as the Vicar of Christ, which means to recognize and regard him as the highest superior in place of Christ."[4]

If we analyze this second definition, it will be seen to break down again into three elements, as follows:

The Church of Christ is composed of all those

- Who are baptized,
- Who profess the faith and laws of Christ, that is, who believe internally and confess externally the Christian faith and laws, not as subjectively conceived but as taught by the official pastors and teachers in the Church,
- Who make this profession or confession under obedience to the Pope, because they recognize in him the Vicar of Christ, and the Supreme Ruler in spiritual matters, in place of Christ.

II. DIFFERENCES BETWEEN THE CATHOLIC AND HISTORICAL DEFINITIONS OF THE CHURCH

The fundamental "difference between our definition (of the Church)," says Bellarmine, "and all others, is that all the rest require only internal virtues to constitute a person in the Church, and therefore, they make the true Church something invisible. Whereas we also believe that in the Church are found all the virtues: faith, hope and charity, and all the rest. However, for anyone to be called in some sense a part of the true Church of which the Scriptures speak, we do not think that any internal virtue is required, but only an external profession of faith and communication of the Sacraments, which can be perceived by the senses themselves. For the Church is an assembly of men, as visible and palpable as the assembly of the Roman people or the Kingdom of France or the Republic of the Venetians."[5]

Two things are to be noted in the comparison which Bellarmine makes between the orthodox and heterodox definitions of the Church. First is that he omits mentioning submission to the Pope, in repeating the elements of the true Church. Instead, he identifies, or absorbs, obedience to the Pope in the profession of the true faith. But this is not significant because submission to the Pope is only one part or phase of profession of the faith, although, in Bellarmine's time, it was the most practically important part.

The second item is that Bellarmine places the specific difference between the correct and false conception of the Church in what looks like a minor detail: *external* profession of faith and *external* participation in the Sacraments. However, to call this a minor detail is to belie the true nature of the Church and, finally, the true nature of man. For Bellarmine, external profession of faith and sharing of the Sacraments is as essential to the Church as man's body is essential to man. To explain: "The Church is a definite society, not of angels or of souls, but of men. Now, it cannot be called a society of men unless it consists in (is united by) external and visible signs. For it is not a society unless those who belong to it can mutually recognize each other as members; but, being men, they cannot recognize each other unless the bonds of the society are visible and external, which is confirmed from the practice of all human societies, where men are ascribed (for example) to an army or a city or a kingdom ... in no other way than by means of visible signs. Hence St. Augustine says that, 'Men cannot be united in the name of any religion, be it true or false, unless they are somehow bound together in the community of visible sacraments or signs.'"[6]

To recapitulate: there must be external profession of faith and sharing of the Sacraments to constitute the Church as a visible society, composed of visible members who, except for these signs, would not know which people, including themselves, belong to the Church and which do not.

But this is not all. Beyond the mere static *visibility* of the Church, which is postulated by its having visible members, the Church has also, and especially, an active and dynamic *unity*, such that

1. There is a subordination of subjects to superiors, finally culminating in subjection to one single head, the Pope;
2. There is coordination of the subjects among themselves, cooperating with each other in mutually working out their salvation within the framework of the Church.

Now, this kind of vital unity cannot exist among men in the present disposition of Providence, unless it is entered into, manifested, and preserved by means of common, unifying, *external* symbols and signs.

The unity of the Church is one of subordination of inferiors to superiors, and the dispensation of grace is determined by the sincerity of this subordination. But how can subjects recognize their superiors and superiors their subjects, unless there is some visible sign

- That subject and superior belong to the Church in the first place,
- That the position of two different people in the Church is not one of equality but a relation of subjection and authority,
- That in a given instance a superior is exercising his authority, as superior, on this particular subject, as his subject?

Unless a person receives Baptism, for example, which is an external rite, how is a man to know whether he is subject to the Pope, and therefore should obey him; and how is the Pope to determine whether he is the man's superior, and therefore should command him?

The unity of the Church is also one of coordination, and, again, grace is dispensed according to the degree of charity which binds the members of the Church to one another. But how can two persons cooperate with one another unless they first recognize each other as fellow members in the same Church?

The objection of the Protestants is that unity of faith, invisible and interior, is enough for the Church. It could be, Bellarmine admits, if Christ had so willed. Absolutely speaking, Christ might have instituted a Church in which only invisible bonds of unity prevailed. But then, St. Robert suggests, He would have had to change the nature of man, which is bodily and visible, and, therefore, limited in its perception of the spiritual in others to its manifestation in visible signs. Given a society of angels or pure spirits, then, we can talk about invisible, and only invisible, bonds of unity; that is, invisible to us but visible to them.[7]

But given a society of men, unless by a miracle of grace we could read the minds of others to tell what they believed and whether they believed the same as we do, there must be external profession of internal conviction. Otherwise the society does not even begin to exist, much less increase and perfect itself in that unity which is the special mark of its Divinity.[8]

III. THE BODY AND SOUL OF THE CHURCH

Analysis of the Concepts

Bellarmine realized that his definition of the Church was liable to misunderstanding. Even Catholics would be scandalized to think of their Church as a mere juridical institution whose membership was conditioned by external profession of faith and a token reception of the Sacraments, more of a lifeless skeleton than the vibrant organism of Christ's Mystical Body which it really is.[9]

Immediately after giving his definition, therefore, St. Robert explains himself, in a kind of apologia, on the body and soul of the Church. He is credited with having invented this doctrine, at least his formulation of it is supposed to be an innovation in Catholic theology. The fact is, it was meant to serve only one purpose: to show that the definition of the Church previously given represents the absolute minimum required for valid membership, that it is not, and does not pretend to be, a comprehensive description of the nature of the Church.

"We must note, however," he says, after defining the Church, "that, according to Augustine, the Church is a living Body, in which there is a body and a soul. The soul are the internal gifts of the Holy Spirit; faith, hope, and charity, and the rest. The body are the external profession of faith and communication of the Sacraments. From which it follows that some people belong to both the soul and the body of the Church, and are, therefore, united to Christ, the Head, both interiorly and exteriorly. And these are most perfectly in the Church. They are like living members in the body, although among them, too, some participate more and some less in the life (of the body), and some have only the beginnings of life, having, as it were, sensation without movement, like those who have faith without charity. Others, however, are of the soul but not of the body (of the Church), as Catechumens and those who have been excommunicated, who may have faith and charity which is possible. Finally, some belong to the body and not the soul (of the Church), like those who have no internal virtue, but yet, out of hope or (moved) by some temporal fear, they profess the faith and share in the Sacraments, under the rule of legitimate pastors."[10]

If we analyze the various elements of this doctrine, we have:

The Church is a living Organism, composed of body and soul. This composition means:

in general:

That the soul is the gifts of the Holy Spirit that is, faith, hope, charity, and the internal, infused virtues

That the body is the external profession of faith, including submission to the Pope and participation in the same Sacraments.

In specie:

That some people belong to the body *and* the soul of the Church, which means that:

- They are united to Christ, the Head, interiorly by the virtues and exteriorly by professing the faith and sharing in the Sacraments.
- They belong most perfectly to the Church.
- They are like living members in the human body.
- They are subdivided into three classes:
  - Those who have more of the life of the Church in their souls, because they have more faith and charity.
  - Those who have less of this life because they have less faith and charity.
  - Those who have only the beginning of this life, because they have only faith, internal and external, and no charity, that is, sanctifying grace.

Others belong to the soul and not to the body of the Church, like catechumens and those who are excommunicated. However, not all catechumens or excommunicates are in this class, but only those who have both internal and external faith, and charity, or sanctifying grace.

Others, finally, belong to the body but not to the soul of the Church, as those who have no *internal* virtue, but yet *externally* profess the true faith and share in the Sacraments, under subjection to the Pope, from hope or fear or some other temporal motive.

"Our definition," Bellarmine concludes, "comprehends *only* this last mode of being in the Church," that is, of those who have been baptized, who are not in the grace of God, and yet, who externally profess the true faith and approach the Sacraments, under external obedience to ecclesiastical authorities. Why the limitation? In order to show what is "the minimum required for anyone to be called a part of the visible Church," i.e. simply, a part of the Church, because there is only one Church, and that is visible.[11]

Basis for the Doctrine in Christian Tradition

Without going into a long defense of St. Robert's distinction between the body and soul of the Church, one point at least should be explained as a basis for his complete doctrine on membership in the Church. The point is whether he was justified in identifying the soul of the Church with the created internal gifts of the Holy Spirit, when traditionally the uncreated Spirit of Christ Himself has been considered the Soul of the

Church. Thus, St. Augustine, "For what the soul is to the body of a man, that, the Holy Ghost is to the body of Christ, which is the Church. What the Holy Ghost does in the whole Church, that, the soul does in all the members of one body."[12] And again, "What our spirit — that is, our soul — is to our members, that, the Holy Ghost is to the members of Christ, to the body of Christ, which is the Church. Therefore, the Apostle, when he had spoken of the one body, lest we should suppose it to be a dead body, says, 'There is one body.' I ask: Is this body alive? It is alive. Whence? From the one Spirit. 'There is one Spirit.'"[13] So later on, St. Gregory; "The holy universal Church is one body, constituted under Christ Jesus its Head. ... Therefore, Christ, with His whole Church, both that which is still on earth and that which now reigns with Him in heaven, is one Person; and as the soul is one which quickens the various members of the body, so the one Holy Spirit quickens and illuminates the whole Church. For as Christ, who is the Head of the Church, was conceived of the Holy Ghost, so the Holy Church, which is His body, is filled by the same Spirit that it may have life, is confirmed by His power that it may subsist in the bond of one faith and charity... of this Spirit the heretic does not live, nor the schismatic, nor the excommunicated, for they are not of the body; but the Church has a Spirit that gives life, because it inheres inseparably to Christ its Head: for it is written, "He that adheres to the Lord is one spirit with Him.'"[14]

Very simply, Bellarmine made no secret of professing the traditional doctrine. For example, in defending the Church's infallibility, he argues from the Divinity of its Head and Soul to the inerrancy of its body. "The Church," he says, "is governed by Christ as its Spouse (and) Head, and by the Holy Ghost as its Soul....Consequently, if the Church could err in dogmas of faith and morals, error would be attributed to Christ and the Holy Spirit, whereas the Lord said, 'The Spirit of truth will teach you all truth.'" John 16-13.[15] Again, in defending the function of sinful members as instruments of grace in the Church of God, he has recourse to the operation of the Holy Spirit as the Soul of the Church. "An evil bishop," he explains, "a wicked priest, a bad teacher, are dead members of the Body of Christ, and therefore not true members, if we understand 'member' in its essential meaning as a certain part of the living body. However, they are very true members if we consider them as instruments (of activity within the Church); so that the Pope and bishops are real heads, the teachers are real eyes and a real tongue of this Body. And the reason is that persons are constituted its living members through charity, which the wicked do not have. But the instruments of operation (in the Church) are constituted through the power of orders or of jurisdiction, which can be had even without grace. For although in a natural body, a dead member cannot be a true instrument of operation, yet in the Mystical Body it can be. For in a natural body, its action depends on the soundness of the instrument, because the soul cannot operate well except through good instruments, nor can it exercise the vital functions except through living instruments. But in the Mystical Body, the functions do not depend on the soundness or life of the instrument. For the Soul of this Body, that is, the Holy Spirit, can operate as well through good instruments as through bad, through those which are living as through those which are dead."[16]

The most that could be said against Bellarmine's position is that he may be inconsistent: once he calls the soul of the Church the Holy Spirit, and then he calls it the gifts of the Spirit. Which does he mean? A reasonable answer is that he means both, namely, that the soul of the Church is the Spirit of Christ, in so far as He brings with Himself the created gifts of His grace. This solution reconciles the apparently contradictory passages in Bellarmine, and also gives an answer to the problem arising from his conception of the soul of the Church on a graduated scale. For, according to Bellarmine, there are degrees of attachment to the soul of the Church, until finally the only ones to whom he denies any membership in the *"anima Ecclesiae"* are those who have no internal virtue whatsoever. This becomes intelligible if we understand St. Robert to mean that the Holy Spirit bearing his gifts is the soul of the Church. For while it is one and the same Spirit who operates on all the members of the Church, yet, the degree of His operation, the amount of His grace, and the number of His gifts will be proportioned to the intimacy with which individuals are joined to the body of the Church, and the importance of the function and office which they hold in its body.

Consequently, it is significant that Bellarmine uses the expression "*de anima Ecclesiae*," in describing the relationship of various peoples to the soul of the Church. This allows him, even grammatically, to speak of varying degrees of association to the Church's soul, conditioned by the degree of participation in the grace of God. So that the highest degree is possessed by those who are actually in the state of grace, the lowest by those who have only a vestige of supernatural faith, once possessed and now lost. It also allows him to consider those who are not actual members of the body of the Church, to belong to its soul, which is the Holy Spirit, in as much as they are directed by this Spirit towards eventual incorporation in the Mystical Body, by actual profession of the Catholic faith.

To summarize, therefore, Bellarmine's identification of the soul of the Church, now with the Holy Spirit, now with His gifts, is justified if we understand that in the latter case he is taking the soul of the Church not objectively but subjectively, not causally but effectively, affecting the Church not collectively but individually. Thus, the uncreated Holy Spirit is the Soul of the Church, in so far as He objectively causes the society of human beings who form the Body of Christ to live the life of the grace in union with Christ their Head. But in so far as they are participating in this life, it is equally correct to speak of the created gifts of the Holy Spirit as the soul of the Church, considering these gifts individually and subjectively as the effect of the Holy Spirit in the souls on whom he operates.

St. Robert does not deny that the Holy Spirit Himself animates the soul of the Church. In fact, he affirms it when he also calls the gifts of the Holy Ghost the soul of the Church. Metaphysically, the soul and body are correlatives. Their exact meaning can only be determined by the relation in which they stand to each other in any given context.

Consequently:

With relation to the collectivity of human beings, who are only lifeless matter, supernaturally, before being affected by the Spirit of God, the Holy Ghost is the Soul of the Church. Here the correlative terms are:

<u>The society of human beings in the Church</u>
The Spirit of God which animates them

But with relation to man's individual, personal share in the process of sanctification, namely, his profession of faith and approaching the Sacraments, the internal gifts of the Holy Spirit are the soul of the Church. And here the correlative terms are:

<u>Personal human effort in the members of the Church</u>
Gifts of the Holy Spirit, animating this effort by grace

CHAPTER II

APPLICATION OF PRINCIPLES ON CHURCH MEMBERSHIP

I. MEMBERSHIP OF THE UNBAPTISED

Unbaptized Infidels

Following on his definition of the Church, the first class of people whose possible membership in the Church Bellarmine investigates are those who have never been baptized, whom he divides into two categories, covered by the generic terms: infidels and catechumens. The infidels are all those "who have not given their names to Christ by Baptism, but follow some other kind of religion."[17] Concretely, they are "the Jews, Moslems (Turcae) and Pagans."[18] It might be objected that catechumens also have not yet given their names to Christ by Baptism and should therefore be numbered among the infidels. But they *are willing* to give their names to Christ, and for that reason are properly distinguished from rank unbelievers.

Are infidels then, members of the visible Church of Christ ? Simply not. St. Robert uses exactly two sentences and less than forty words to dismiss them from further consideration. "Unquestionably," he says, "Paul was speaking of the non-baptized infidels when he said: 'What have I to do with those outside?'" (I Cor. 5-12). Consequently, they are "all outside" who are unbaptized unbelievers, and not members of the true Church.[19]

Unbaptized Catechumens

Statement of the Problem

However, it is not so easy to decide whether catechumens are members of the Church, although, like the infidels, they are also not baptized. The difficulty is that, "they are believers and can be saved if they die in their condition (as catechumens), and yet, no one is saved outside the Church... Now it is certain that catechumens are not actually and properly in the Church but only potentially, like a man who is conceived but not yet developed and born is not said to be a man except potentially."[20] How then, can they be saved, if they are not really members of the Church? But they are saved if they die before Baptism. Hence the problem which, briefly, can be put thus:

1. Membership in the Church is necessary for Salvation.
2. But catechumens are not members of the Church.
3. Therefore, they should not be saved.
    *   But catechumens may be saved, if they die before Baptism.
    *   Consequently, how explain their salvation?

Bellarmine examines three possible solutions of the problem, two of which he rejects as untenable, and the third he proposes as his own:

The first explanation solves the problem by denying its existence, declaring that catechumens are not saved.

The second explanation distinguishes the term "Church" in the basic proposition, by saying that membership in at least the Church of the Faithful is necessary for salvation, and, because catechumens belong to *this* Church, they can be saved.

The third explanation, which is Bellarmine's, distinguishes the term "membership" in the same proposition, saying that membership, either actual or in desire, is necessary for salvation. And since catechumens belong to the Church at least in desire, therefore they can be saved.

Membership in the Church is Necessary for Salvation

According to Bellarmine, we can prove from the constant tradition of the Church that membership in the Church of Christ is absolutely necessary for salvation. Thus, he says, in the Apostles' Creed we join together the Catholic Church with the remission of sins. For we say: "I believe in the Holy Catholic Church, the Communion of Saints, the forgiveness of sins."[21] "For which reason," he continues," "the Church is compared with the Ark of Noe; because just as during the deluge, everyone perished who was not in the ark, so now those perish who are not in the Church, as Jerome says in his letter to Damasus."[22] The words of St. Jerome are as follows: "I, following no leader save Christ, am associated in fellowship with Your Beatitude, that is, with the See of Peter. On that rock I know the Church was built. Whosoever eats that Lamb outside that house is profane. If anyone shall be outside the Ark of Noe, he shall perish when the flood prevails."[23]

"The same testimony," says Bellarmine, "is given in that celebrated dictum of Cyprian on the unity of the Church, when he says: 'He cannot have God for his Father who has not the Church for his mother.'" In context, the full passage reads: "The bride of Christ cannot be falsified;

she is chaste and incorrupt. She knows but one home; she with scrupulous chastity keeps inviolate her one bride-chamber. She it is who preserves us for God; she finds places in the Kingdom for the children she has begotten. Whosoever separates himself from the Church is joined to an adulterer and has cut himself off from the promises made to the Church; no one who quits the Church of Christ will attain to the rewards of Christ. He is a stranger, profane, an enemy. He cannot have God for his father who has not the Church for his mother. If anyone was able to escape who was outside the Ark of Noe, then whosoever is outside the Church escapes."[24]

"See also Augustine," says Bellarmine, "in the first chapter of his fourth book *De Baptismo*," where we read: "The Church is compared to Paradise (by St. Cyprian), which shows us that men can indeed receive its (the Church's) Baptism even outside her fold, but that no one attains to or possesses the salvation of beatitude outside of her ranks."[25]

However, the best evidence for the necessity of the Church as a means of salvation, to which St. Robert frequently recurs, is the doctrine of the Fourth Lateran Council which says that: "There is one universal Church of the faithful, outside of which no one at all is saved."[26]

Catechumens are Not Actual Members of the Church

Christian tradition, says St. Robert, has consistently denied actual membership in the Church to catechumens.

Summarily, there are three sources of evidence for this fact:

- Baptism is necessary for membership in the Church. But catechumens are not baptized.

- Members of the Church have been traditionally called "the faithful" or *fideles*. But catechumens are traditionally denied this title.

- Members of the Church have a right to share in the Sacraments and other privileges common in the Church. But catechumens are specifically excluded from this participation.

However, the last two arguments are reducible to the first, so that catechumens are not called *fideles* and are denied the common privileges of the Church because they are not baptized. Consequently, it will be enough to review only the first argument in detail: catechumens are not in the Church because they have not been baptized.

In common with Catholic tradition, Bellarmine looked upon Baptism as the entrance to the Church. Thus, in the *Dottrina Cristiana*, "We are called by God and enter into this congregation (of the Church), by means of Baptism which is, as it were, the door of the Church."[27] He also argued from the necessity of entering the Church in order to be saved, to the necessity of infant Baptism; otherwise the unbaptized infants could not attain to salvation. But the question here is not whether unbaptized infants, but whether catechumens, who are adults, are in the Church before they receive Baptism of water. In other words, is actual Baptism necessary for actual membership for everyone? According to Bellarmine, Baptism is the *only* door of the Church, without which there is no actual membership in the visible Church for anyone.

If we go back to the first Pentecost when St. Peter preached to the assembled multitude in Jerusalem, we read that, "They that received his (Peter's) word were baptized; and there were added that day about three thousand souls." *Acts 2-41*. There is no question here of infants but of adults, yet, on the word of the Scriptures, only after having been baptized were the converts received into the Church. So that, says St. Robert, "We see that to be baptized is nothing else than to enter the Church," whether the neophyte be an infant or an adult. "Consequently, the Fathers unanimously distinguish catechumens from the faithful, and teach that those who have not received Baptism are not yet within the Church."[28]

Also, according to the Council of Florence in its instruction for the Armenians, we begin to belong to the body of the Church only on receiving Baptism.[29] For which reason, says the Council, "Holy Baptism holds the first place among all the Sacraments, which is the door of the spiritual life: through it we are made members of Christ and of the body of the Church."[30] The statement is absolute and universal. All without exception must be baptized to enter the Church.

Solutions of the Problem

Unsatisfactory: Catechumens are not saved

The problem is to decide on the fate of those adults who wished to receive Baptism but who died before they could receive the Sacrament and, consequently, before they entered the body of the Church. "Catechumens do not, therefore," in view of what has been seen, "actually and properly belong to the Church. How then, you ask, are they saved if they are outside the Church?"[31]

St. Robert examines the first answer offered, namely, that catechumens do not enter heaven. This rigorist doctrine, he finds, appeared in "a book called *De Ecclesiasticis Dogmatibus*, falsely attributed to Augustine, in which he definitely states that a catechumen is not saved even if he practiced good works, unless he had been cleansed by the Baptism of water or of blood."[32]

Bellarmine very prudently suspected the authenticity of a work which, in many codices and manuals of theology, for example, Peter Lombard's *Book of Sentences*, was credited to St. Augustine. But St. Thomas, and after him most modern editors, correctly assign the spurious work to Gennadius of Marseilles, against whom the Second Council of Orange was convened.[33]

The chapters of *De Ecclesiasticis Dogmatibus* are hardly more than sentences. There are fifty-five of them in four pages of Migne.[34] Chapter XLI treats of Baptism, and reads, "We believe that only the baptized are on the road of salvation. We believe that no catechumen has life everlasting, although he has died in good works, excepting martyrdom, in which all the sacred elements (*sacramenta*) of Baptism are contained."[35]

Years later, in the twelfth century, the doctrine was resuscitated, and, Bellarmine notes, was condemned by St. Bernard in one of his letters to Hugh of St. Victor. The latter had written to Bernard, inquiring his opinion on the doctrine of some person who taught that actual Baptism by water, or martyrdom, was necessary for the salvation of everyone. Bernard answers, "You write that a certain individual — I do not know who he is because you do not mention his name — on reading the words of the Lord, 'Unless a man be born again of water and the Holy Ghost, he will not enter into the Kingdom of heaven,' *John 3-5*, claims that no one can possibly be saved unless he has actually received this visible Sacrament (of Baptism), or, in its place, has suffered martyrdom. (According to the anonymous adversary) even though a person has perchance desired (Baptism) with true faith and contrition of heart, yet was prevented by death to attain what he wanted, he is still certainly damned."[36]

Bellarmine regards this attitude as too harsh (*nimis durum*). Catechumens are evidently saved if they die in the grace of God, as Catholic tradition has always believed. "Certainly Ambrose, in his oration at the funeral of Valentinian, expressly declares that catechumens can be saved, in whose number was Valentinian at the time of his death."[37]

In context, St. Ambrose said to his audience, "I hear that you grieve because he (Valentinian) had not received the Sacrament of Baptism. Tell me, what else is in our power except our will and desire. For a long time, and even before he came to Italy, he had this desire to be received (into the Church) and indicated that he wished to be baptized by me in the near future, and therefore considered inviting me (to receive him into the Church) before attending to other business. Did he, then, not have the grace which he desired? Did he not have what he sought? Undoubtedly he received what he looked for. Hence we read: 'The just man, whatever kind of death may have prevented him, shall be in rest.'" *Wisdom 4-7.*[38]

In treating the subject of Baptism, St. Robert also examines the opinion which denies the possibility of sanctifying grace to anyone who has not been baptized. He admits that, "among the ancients this proposition was not so certain at first as later on: that perfect conversion and repentance is rightly called the Baptism of desire and supplies for Baptism of water, at least in case of necessity."[39] He continues, "As far as I know, none of the ancients questioned that martyrdom satisfies for Baptism of water, but there were not lacking those who denied that conversion and repentance does the same." Then he quotes the spurious work of Augustine and St. Bernard's letter, as seen before, and concludes, "it is certainly to be believed that true conversion supplies for Baptism of water when it is not from contempt but through necessity that persons die without Baptism of water."[40]

To prove this proposition, four authorities are mentioned but without giving their doctrine, namely: Sts. Augustine and Bernard, Innocent II and the Council of Trent. Going back to the sources quoted by Bellarmine, we have first a passage from St. Augustine, in which he says, "I have no doubt that a Catholic catechumen, possessed of Divine charity, is better than a heretic who has been baptized. In fact, even within the Catholic (Church), we prefer a good catechumen to a wicked person who is baptized. However, we commit no injustice against the Sacrament of Baptism which the one has and the other has not yet received, nor do we think that the Sacrament of a catechumen is preferable to the Sacrament of Baptism, when we consider a particular catechumen more faithful and more virtuous than a particular baptized individual. For the Centurion Cornelius, not yet baptized, was better than Simon (Magus), already baptized; since the former was filled with the Holy Spirit before Baptism, while the latter, even after Baptism, was inflated with the spirit of evil ... Certainly the Blessed Cyprian takes as very good evidence that suffering sometimes fills the place of Baptism, from what was said to the thief who was not yet baptized: 'This day thou shalt be with Me in Paradise.' *Luke 23-43.* The more I think about it, the more I believe that not only suffering for the name of Christ but also faith and conversion of heart can supply for what is lacking on the part of Baptism if, perchance, for lack of time (*in angustiis temporum*), the mystery of Baptism cannot be approached."[41]

St. Bernard also leans on the authority of Augustine and Ambrose, but somewhat extends the conditions under which conversion and repentance can make up for actual Baptism. "With these" (Augustine and Ambrose), he says, "I am willing to err or to be right, believing that a man with the desire of receiving the Sacrament (of Baptism), can be saved by faith alone, if death should prevent him from fulfilling his desire, or any other invincible force stands in the way. Was not this perhaps why the Savior, after He had said, 'He that believes and is baptized, shall be saved,' carefully and prudently did not add, 'but he that is not baptized,' but only, 'he that does not believe, shall be condemned'? *Mark 16-16*; suggesting that at times faith alone is sufficient for salvation, and that without it nothing avails. And even in martyrdom, which everyone admits can take the place of Baptism, this result is not the effect of suffering but of faith. For what else is martyrdom without faith except suffering?"[42]

The document of Innocent II mentioned by Bellarmine is a letter which he addressed to the Bishop of Cremona, who asked whether the suffrages of the Church might be offered for a "priest" of his diocese who was known to have died before receiving Baptism. "In answer to your question," the Pope said, "We answer: because the priest, who as you say in your letter died without the water of Baptism, persevered in the faith of Holy Mother Church and in the confession of the name of Christ, We unhesitatingly assert that he was freed from original sin and attained to the joy of the heavenly country. Read…in the 8th Book of Augustine's *City of God* where, among other things, is said: 'Baptism is invisibly administered (to the person) whom the pressure of necessity and not the contempt of religion excluded (from the number of the baptized).' Read also the book on the death of Valentinian, in which the Blessed Ambrose says the same thing. Consequently, you may consider your questions resolved by the doctrine of the Holy Fathers, and order public prayers and sacrifices to be offered to God for the aforesaid priest."[43]

Finally, the Council of Trent, in its chapter on the necessity of Baptism, describes justification as "a translation from that state in which a man is born a child of the first Adam, to the state of grace and of the adoption of the sons of God, through the second Adam, Jesus Christ our Savior. This translation, however, cannot, since the promulgation of the Gospel, be effected except through the laver of regeneration or its desire, as it is written, 'Unless a man be born again of water and the Holy Ghost, he cannot enter into the Kingdom of God.'" John 3-5[44].

On the basis of his evidence, therefore, Bellarmine concludes that catechumens can be saved, if they die before Baptism. However, also on the basis of tradition, he limits the possibility of their salvation to the fulfillment of certain conditions which, in summary, are as follows:

A catechumen may be saved, although he dies before actual Baptism of water, if —

- He is a true catechumen, that is, one who explicitly desires to be baptized.[45]
- He is so far responsive to the grace of God as to repent of his sins from a motive of charity, based on supernatural faith.[46]
- He was not deliberately contemptuous of the Sacrament of Baptism, or if he was, has since repented of this sin.[47]

Unsatisfactory: Catechumens belong to the "Church of the Faithful"

Quite clearly, it is no solution but a dismissal of the problem to say that since catechumens are not members of the Church, they cannot be saved. Closer to a solution was Melchior Cano's, who said that, "The Church can be understood in two senses: first there is (the Church) which is made up of the assembly of all the faithful from the beginning of the world to the end. In this sense, catechumens are most truly members of the Church. Then again, that is called the Church which is entered through Baptism, in the name of Christ.... and of this Church, catechumens are not a part."[48]

Bellarmine's version is that, "Melchior Cano says catechumens can be saved because, although they are not a part of that Church which is properly called Christian, they nevertheless belong to the Church which comprehends all the faithful from Abel to the end of the world." But his reaction is that, "This does not seem to be satisfactory because, since the coming of Christ, there is no true Church except that which is properly called Christian. So that if catechumens do not belong to this Church, they belong to none."[49]

It should be noted that Cano very correctly distinguishes his hypothetical Church of the faithful from the Church of Christ on the point of Baptism. Real Baptism in water, he admits, is an indispensable condition for becoming a member of the Church of Christ. In the original proposition, therefore, which says: *"Extra Ecclesiam, nulla salus,"* he qualified the term *Ecclesia*, so as to make the formula read:

"Outside the Church   -   of the faithful   -   there is no salvation.
                                     -    of Christ   -

In refusing to accept Cano's solution, Bellarmine allows him one concession but refuses to follow him on his one distinction. The concession is fundamental and bears repetition. It is, that there is no actual membership in the Church without actual Baptism. The distinction is untenable, namely that there is another Church besides the Church of Christ, that of the faithful, to which catechumens belong and as members of which they are saved.

In denying the concept of two churches, excogitated by Cano, Bellarmine was standing on the solid ground of tradition, which never allowed more than one Church founded by Christ, and outside of which one Church, founded by Christ, there is no salvation. Beyond denying Cano's theory and stating that it was against Christian tradition, St. Robert gives no more arguments against it. Nor did he have to, because it is obvious from basic principles that, to admit this Church of the faithful extending from Abel to the Last Judgment, would mean:

- To deny the real distinction between the Jewish Synagogue and the Church of Christ.[50]
- To deny the unity and unicity of the Church by Christ.[51]
- To deny its visibility.[52]

Bellarmine's Solution: Catechumens belong *Voto,* to the One Visible Church

In admitting Cano's presupposition, that Baptism is the only way to become an actual member of the Church of Christ, as distinct from the Church of the faithful, Bellarmine paved the way for his own doctrine, namely, that catechumens can be saved, even without Baptism of water or martyrdom, provided they die with a Baptism of desire.

The argument runs thus:

- Baptism is the only entrance into the Church. But Baptism can be *in re* or *in voto*. Therefore, entrance into the Church can be *in re* or *in voto*.
- The kind of membership in the Church is determined by the kind of entrance which a person has made.
  But, there are two kinds of entrance into the Church, *in re* and *in voto*.
  Therefore; if a person enters through actual Baptism, he becomes an actual member of the Church. If a person enters through Baptism *in voto*, he becomes a *voto* member of the Church.

In Bellarmine's own words, his doctrine reads, "I answer …. that when it is said that outside the Church no one is saved, this is to be understood of those who do not belong to the Church either in reality or in desire, as theologians commonly speak of Baptism. However, since catechumens are in the Church, if not really, at least in desire *(voto)*, therefore they can be saved."[53]

This distinction between membership in the Church *re* and *voto* represents a milestone in Catholic ecclesiology. Bellarmine was obviously not the first to have distinguished Baptism of water from Baptism of desire. For centuries before, theologians, and finally the Council of Trent, took account of unbaptized persons who could still be saved if they died with a Baptism of desire. But not until the *Controversies* do we have a clear application of the same distinction to membership in the Church. It was derived as a conclusion to the following process of thought:

- Baptism and membership in the Church are *objectively* related as unique cause and effect; that is, there is no actual membership in the Church without actual Baptism. This is true whether the subject of Baptism realizes it or not.
- Given a person who explicitly desires Baptism, one of two possibilities arise:

    Either he knows that in desiring Baptism, he also desires to become a member of the Church, and then, both the desire for Baptism and the desire to become a member of the Church are explicit.

    Or he does not realize that in desiring Baptism he also desires to become a member of the Church. And then, only the desire for Baptism is explicit, while the desire to become a member of the Church is implicit. However, although implicit, it is nevertheless real, because in sincerely desiring the cause, i.e., Baptism, he also desires the effect, i.e., enrollment in the Church as a member.
- Membership of Non-Catechumens who are not Infidels

In treating the possible membership in the Church of unbaptized persons, Bellarmine considers only two classes of people: infidels and catechumens. Infidels he excludes simply; catechumens, he allows, may be members *voto* or in desire. But what about those persons who are neither formal infidels nor formal catechumens: those who have no explicit desire to be baptized, for one of a variety of reasons, can they be considered members of the Church in any sense?

St. Robert does not expressly treat of this class of people anywhere in the *Controversies*. For one thing, it was beyond the evident purpose of his writings. However, his doctrine can be gathered from what he says elsewhere, on the subject of Baptism in the case of those who never explicitly desire to receive the Sacrament. The immediate question is whether they can be saved, but ultimately whether they can belong to the Church, because outside the Church, at least through membership *in voto*, there is no salvation.

Note that we here wish to see whether Bellarmine would extend his term "catechumen" to include also those who only *implicitly* desire Baptism and, therefore, implicitly "twice-over" desire to become members of the Church. Two general possibilities are conceivable:

- Where the unbaptized person does not desire the Sacrament because he knows nothing about Baptism, he is a pagan among pagans. Bellarmine answers this problem, which is posed as an objection from Scripture against the universal salvific will of God. St. Paul says, "How are they to call upon Him in Whom they have not believed? But how are they to believe Him, when they have not heard? And how are they to hear, if no one preaches? And how are men to preach, unless they be sent?" *Rom. 10:14-15*. "The beginning of salvation," it is objected, "is faith… But many do not have the help which is needed in order to believe because no one has yet preached the Gospel to them." How then can they be saved ?

  St. Robert answers: "This argument only proves that not all people receive the help they need to believe and be converted immediately. It does not, however, prove that some people are deprived, absolutely speaking, of sufficient help for salvation. For the pagans to whom the Gospel has not yet been preached, can *know* from His Creatures that God exists;[54] then, they can be stimulated by God, through His preventing grace, to *believe* in God, that He exists and that He is the rewarder of those who seek Him: and from such faith they can be inspired, under the guidance and help of God, to pray and give alms and in this way obtain from God a still greater light of faith, which God will communicate to them, either by Himself or through angels or through men."[55]

  Clearly, pagans living in ignorance of the necessity of Baptism can, with God's grace, attain to salvation. Following St. Thomas, whom he quotes,[56] Bellarmine would not require an explicit desire for Baptism as a condition for salvation, for those living in countries where the Church has not yet been established. This is confirmed by the letter of St. Bernard on which Bellarmine based his doctrine, at least in part. "How many are there throughout the world," Bernard asks, "who die in complete ignorance of what Jesus said secretly that night to Nicodemus. (Unless a man be born of water and the Holy Ghost, he cannot enter into the Kingdom of Heaven). What then? The law has not yet been promulgated, and they are already held responsible for breaking it? ... God forbid."[57]

  Logically, therefore, if desire for Baptism equivalates membership *voto* in the Church, and if, according to Bellarmine, this desire, among pagans at least, may be either explicit or implicit as a condition for salvation — then, in either case, membership *voto* in the Church is the result. Otherwise he would be saying that implicit desire is enough to be saved, but not enough to enter *voto* into the Church — which would contradict the supposit of his whole argument, namely, that at least *voto* membership is required for salvation.

- The second possibility is more delicate, and involves two contingencies: that of an unbaptized person who knows about Baptism but never receives the Sacrament because, mistakenly, he thinks he is already baptized; and that of a person who knows he is not baptized but never receives Baptism. Bellarmine treats of both cases. "An (unbaptized) child that is born and reared among Christians," he says, "on growing up, will either think that he is baptized or will know that he has not been baptized. If he believes he has been baptized, he will probably have the faith divinely infused into him, because the approval of Baptism which a man has received or thinks he received, is equal to the desire (*voto*) of Baptism and can lead him to eternal salvation." Then follows a reference to the letter of Innocent II regarding the unbaptized priest. "On the other hand, if a person knows that he has not been baptized and does not ask for Baptism, he certainly does not have the faith except, possibly, a faith that is human or not even human. For how is it possible that anyone who believes with certainty that he will be eternally lost without Baptism and yet does not desire or ask for Baptism, which is so easy to receive? Nor is it probable that anyone who has been educated among Christians and knows the faith of Christians, should never have heard of Baptism, when mention of Baptism is made in the rudiments of the faith and every day in the Church newly born infants are being baptized."[58]

To review these last two cases, it is clear that according to Bellarmine, Baptism supposedly received and believed in is equal to Baptism of desire and, therefore, reductively to *voto* membership in the Church. But his solution of the second case seems to be too strict, unless we interpret his statements in the historical context in which they were made. First we should notice that he does not speak about the objective possibility of an unbaptized person, living among Christians, having the faith and grace of God although he never asks for Baptism. It is not a question *de iure* but *de facto*, whether such a possibility is probable. Bellarmine thinks it is not.

Be it noted, however, that what Bellarmine is castigating here is not the mere deference of Baptism to adult life, or even to a short time before death. True, in his controversy with the Anabaptists, who said that only adults should be baptized, Bellarmine argued to the practice of baptizing infants from the principle that otherwise they cannot enter the Church — and membership in the Church is necessary for salvation.[59] But the custom of deferring Baptism till late in life was sanctioned by not a few ancients, and Bellarmine was too well acquainted with the Fathers to reprove absolutely and unconditionally a custom that was so common in the early Church.[60] What he condemned was the contempt for the Sacrament of Baptism as indispensable for salvation, which the Protestant reformers had engendered in the minds of the people. Thus wrote John Calvin, "It is an error to suppose that anything more is conferred by the sacraments than is offered by the word of God, and obtained by true faith... Assurance of salvation does not depend on participation in the sacraments, as if justification consisted in it. This, which is treasured up in Christ alone, we know to be communicated, not less by the preaching of the Gospel than by the seal of a sacrament, and it may be completely enjoyed without this seal."[61] Breaking with the traditional interpretation of *John 3-5*, Calvin declared that, "the phrase, 'born of water' does not refer to Baptism, but 'water and Spirit' in this passage are one and the same thing — the action of the Spirit is cleansing, like that of water."[62] It was this refusal to receive Baptism, based on a denial of the clear teaching of Christ which, to Bellarmine's mind, indicated that such a person "certainly does not have the faith, except possibly a faith that is human, or not even human."[63]

II.   MEMBERSHIP IN THE CHURCH FOR HERETICS

Formal Heretics

As regards formal heretics, that is, those who have lapsed from the true faith or who consciously persevere in their error, there is no question of their being members of the visible Church of Christ. Against Alphonsus Castro who taught the opposite, Bellarmine says his doctrine is obviously false because, for example, the Council of Nicea lays down certain conditions for the re-admission of the Paulianist heretics, "who are hastening back to the Church."[64] Evidently they could not be said to return to the Church if they had not previously been out of it by reason of their heresy. This is the common doctrine of the Fathers. "Ireneus," for instance, "says that Polycarp converted many heretics to the Church; from which it follows that they had previously been put out of the Church. And Augustine specifies in detail that, "Those who do not believe that Christ came in the flesh, of the Virgin Mary, from the seed of David, or that He arose from the dead in the same Body in which He was crucified and was buried, are certainly not in the Church."[65] This means that manifest heretics are not in the body of the Church, for, "Since the Church is a unified multitude ...or one body, and this unity consists in the profession of one faith and in the observance of the same laws and rites, it is impossible that those who have no communication with it, should be said to belong to the body of the Church."[66] However, it does not mean that they are necessarily outside the soul of the Church because, on Bellarmine's principles, even the vestige of internal faith is sufficient to belong to the Church's soul. It is true that their nexus with the *anima Ecclesiae* will be tenuous; and the more so as their external profession of heresy has devitalized their internal faith. But short of a complete evacuation of all supernatural virtue, even formal heretics will still have some connection with the soul of the Church.

It is this type of formal heretic that Bellarmine has in mind as often as he denies him any sort of communion with the visible Church of Christ. Thus, in answer to the objection that the Church can punish heretics and therefore has jurisdiction over them as her members, he says, "Although heretics are not in the Church, they should be, and therefore are related to it as sheep pertain to the sheepfold from which they have run away…The Church can pass judgment over those who are actually within as over those who certainly ought to be[67] as a shepherd can force a sheep wandering over the hills to return to the fold, and as the emperor can forcibly constrain a deserter in war, who fled to the camp of the enemy, to return to his own camp." To the objection from St. Paul: "What have I to do with judging those outside?" the answer is that, "the Apostle is here speaking of those who are outside in the sense that they had never been inside (the Church)," which, in St. Robert's conception, is not the case with formal heretics.[68]

Material Heretics

Possibility of Being in Good Faith

Bellarmine clearly distinguishes between the heresiarchs in his day, the religious and political leaders of the new gospel who were seducing the masses from the true faith or confirming them in their errors, and the simple people who allowed themselves to be thus deceived. Regarding the first group, his strictures are uncompromising. His defense of the Inquisition and the death penalty for heretics, for example, is to be referred to the leaders of heresy, as may be seen from the reasons which he gives for putting them to death: "that they may not do harm to the good…that by the punishment of a few, the many may be corrected…because it is often useful to those who are put to death to be executed, that is, when they become steadily worse and there is no prospect of their returning to their (former) sanity of mind." In fact, "it is a benefit to obstinate heretics to be taken from this life, for the longer they live the more errors they concoct, and more people they pervert, and the worse condemnation they prepare for themselves."[69]

Even where he seems to be less uncompromising, Bellarmine still shows no inclination to excuse the heresy of those who, because of their position and talent, ought to know that there is only one true faith, in the Catholic Church. Thus, in his controversy with James I of England, although the king was persecuting the Church, St. Robert does not directly accuse him of malice. However, this should be regarded as only prudent diplomacy. For in answer to James' statement that he wished for all Catholic kings and princes to become what he was — a confirmed Calvinist, Bellarmine replied, "Why may not, and with better reason, so many great kings and other orthodox princes desire that King James should become what they are and what all his predecessors…the Kings of Scotland were? For it is well known that, by a special blessing of God, successive generations of Scottish kings for a thousand and three hundred years were Catholics, with the one exception of James VI who, by a misfortune of fate, was deprived of the care of God-fearing parents, fell into the hands of heretical guardians and, through the training which he received from them, turned away from the path of his ancestors."[70]

If this seems to be excusing James on the score of his Protestant training, Bellarmine made it quite clear later on that the king was obviously in bad faith. St. Robert compares him with the Arians, of whom St. Antonianus said that they were not even Christians. James is another Julian the Apostate. For the Roman Emperor seduced the Christians into practicing idolatry by picturing together a portrait of himself and of Jupiter, so that unwary people would be deceived into adoring the pagan god while paying their legitimate respects to the emperor. "This is exactly what the English king has imitated. For he has proposed (for acceptance by Catholics) an oath in which, under the semblance of civil obedience in temporal matters properly due to the king, there should also be expressed sacred obedience to the same king as supreme ruler in spiritual matters, while denying this obedience to the legitimate ruler of the whole Church."[71]

However, when he comes to deal with the uneducated heretical masses, Bellarmine more often lays the blame for their perseverance in error, not on malice or hardness of heart, but on their native stupidity and lack of education, the deceits of the devil, the false teachings of the Protestant ministers, and, especially, on the bad examples of not a few Catholics. "If there are many," he observes, "who …hate our law and violently reject it, the first reason is the corrupt and depraved morals of not a few Christians.…Because we are living immoral lives, those who do not understand our law believe that what we are doing contrary to the law is being done with its connivance and permission and, consequently, they detest it as the source and root of our crimes. Another reason is the countless lies which the devil is used to disseminate by his ministers. Why (for example), in the early years of the newborn Church did some people persecute the Christians with such fury? Because, under the inspiration of the devil, the masses were made to believe that Christians adored the head of an ass and were therefore idolaters. Why do many simple heretics today execrate the Pope as Antichrist and the Church as Babylon? Because the preachers of the new gospel persuaded the wretched people that we have discarded the Gospels, that we explain everything in terms of human wisdom and the subtleties of sophists, that we have abandoned God and invoke the saints instead, that we contemn the Passion of Christ…all of which are the most obvious and stupid kind of lies…but they have become so deeply fixed and firmly rooted in their hearts, that, although they hear us shout and swear that we do not believe these things, that this is not Catholic doctrine, that all these charges are lies; although they see us prove our dogmas with countless testimonies of the Scriptures and the Fathers and reason, still they do not believe, but prefer to accept, instead of our word, what those who are deceiving them say about us."[72]

Bellarmine might seem to be excusing their errors as the result of mere ignorance and mal-persuasion, until we see to what he attributes their loss of faith. "By what means," he asked his listeners on one occasion, "is the faith preserved? Through good works … By what means, then, is it lost? Through evil works, crimes, sins, unchastity, drunkenness and avarice. Of course I do not say, as the Lutherans madly suppose, that every sin is one of unbelief and that there can be no faith in sinners. This I do not say because I know that the Church is a net which is filled with good and bad fishes; nor do I deny that no one can be in the Church without faith. What then are we saying? Simply that a multitude of sins, a facility in sinning, and the practice of an evil life are the road and, as it were, so many steps towards infidelity. For men are so fashioned by nature that they easily and readily believe what they desire, what pleases and delights them. It is not hard to convince voluptuous and carnal-living persons that priests should be married, that chastity is impossible, that fasting is superfluous, that selection in the matter of food is a superstition. It is not difficult to excuse usury before the avaricious, or simony among the ambitious, or fornication with the sensuous… It is no wonder, then, that so many should so easily have joined themselves first to Mohammed and, in our times, to Luther, when they came preaching license of the flesh and removing the restraints of the passions. For in both times, as can be seen from history, the morals of Christian peoples were in large part corrupted: the Sacraments, religion, ecclesiastical discipline were despised and attached, while all manner of vices were given free rein; so that men who were thus affected…were not made into heretics, because no one (originally) preached heresy to them. Rather they prepared themselves to embrace heresy (when it came along). They were like dry wood that is perfectly suited for burning, and needs only to have a spark applied to it to make it burst into flame. The devil was ready at hand to inspire his ministers to set fire (to the combustible mass) by their preaching and activity."[73] Consequently, granting that the majority of these "simple heretics" were not sinning against the light by their profession of Protestantism, Bellarmine would consider them at least guilty in *causa* for their loss of faith.

Membership in the Catholic Church

Whatever concession St. Robert gave to heretics for being in good faith, it was more theoretical than practical. So the corresponding question of whether he would consider material heretics as members of the Church is also more hypothetical than real. However, as will be seen, his principles on Church membership have been applied by Catholic theologians to exactly such people. So it will pay to examine how, at least theoretically, Bellarmine would explain the membership of material heretics, if he considered them in good faith.

Regarding their possible belonging to the soul of the Church, in the sense of possessing one or more gifts of the Holy Spirit, there is no difficulty. If they have at least the habit of supernatural faith in their souls, even though they are not in the grace of God, they belong to the soul of the Church.

However, since it is only membership in the visible Church of Christ, which Bellarmine properly considers membership in the Catholic Church, would he consider material heretics members of this organism, granting the possibility that their heresy is not formal? Yes, because, consistent with his interpretation of the doctrine *Extra Ecclesiam nulla salus,* he would have to allow them some kind of incorporation in the Church if they are to be saved. The term he would use would be *voto* membership, in will and desire. But what does *voto* mean here? What sort of desire must a heretic have to be at least *voto* in the Catholic Church? Certainly not the desire for Baptism, because he is already baptized. It could only be a desire to be incorporated in the Church by the removal of whatever obstacle separates him from actual membership. In practice, this would mean the repudiation of his heresy and re-instatement by the authorities of the Church. But here again, as with unbaptized persons, two possibilities arise: the repudiation of heresy may be explicit when a person actually recognizes his errors and desires to be reconciled with the Church; or the repudiation may be merely implicit, when a person would abandon his errors if he recognize them, which, however, he does not, so that he never seeks to be reconciled.

Bellarmine considers only the first of these possibilities, and then only in the case of a person who was excommunicated, whether for heresy or for some other reason, and now seeks to be reconciled. It occurs as an answer to the objection that excommunicated persons should be considered members of the Church. "A man who was excommunicated justly," say the objectors, "can repent... before being absolved. So he will be in the Church even while he is excommunicated." Bellarmine distinguishes, "I answer that such a person is in the Church by intention or desire *(animo sive desiderio)*, which is enough for salvation, but he is not (in the Church) bodily or by external communication, which properly makes a man belong to that visible Church which is on earth."[74]

To indicate how adamant Bellarmine was in requiring external absolution for reconciliation with the Church, he will not even allow a person who was unjustly excommunicated to be called an actual member of the Church before being absolved. In holding this position, he follows the lead of St. Augustine, whom he quotes as saying that "Divine Providence often allows even good men to be expelled from the assembly of Christians. If they suffer this contumely and disgrace patiently for the sake of the Church's peace and make no attempt at starting a new heresy or schism, they will teach (other) men how faithfully and with what sincerity of heart God should be served. The Father who sees in secret, will also reward in secret such as these."[75]

PART TWO

COMPARATIVE ANALYSIS

CHAPTER I

PIUS IX 1846-1878

I. DOCTRINE OF PIUS IX ON NON-CATHOLICS IN BONA FIDE

When declaring St. Robert a Doctor of the Universal Church in 1931, Pius XI said of him that "He has merited the remembrance of all those who truly love the Church, as Prince of Apologists and strong Defender of Catholic dogma, not only for his own, but for future times ... Like a brilliant lamp set in a house and seen by everyone, in word and in work he was a light to the faithful and to those who had drifted away from the unity of the Church."[76] His principal task in the seventeenth century was to oppose the vagaries of Luther and Calvin who appealed to an invisible Church, composed of all the believers, and independent of any external authority. His repetition and clarification of the doctrine that membership in the corporate, visible body of the Catholic Church is necessary for salvation, is one of the great contributions to orthodox theology. He was not interested in defending the condition of those who had broken away from Catholic unity, except to show them how they were in error and appeal to their better judgment to return to the one true Church, outside of which no one can be saved.

By the middle of the nineteenth century, however, it was seen that, while Bellarmine's principles on Church membership were immutable in so far as they represented traditional doctrine, they needed to be re-examined. If possible, new conclusions had to be drawn from the ancient truths to meet the current problems, notably the delicate question of the salvation of apparently sincere non-Catholics who never intended to enter the Church. Fundamentally it was a question of how to include these people as members of the Catholic Church. The supposition was that they were born and educated outside the true faith and, although living among Catholics, never entered the Church and, perhaps, were never baptized. How are they saved? According to traditional theology, there is no salvation outside the Church. According to Bellarmine, this means that membership in the Catholic Church, *re* or *voto*, is necessary for sal-

31

vation. To what extent can Bellarmine's doctrine on Church membership be applied to such people?

During the next two hundred years, following Bellarmine, this problem was widely discussed among theologians, and opinions were expressed which ranged from extreme laxism to extreme rigorism. According to the rigorist school[77], which found its support in certain statements of the Fathers and in the relative silence of the Church: since the promulgation of the Gospel had become world-wide shortly after the death of Christ, explicit faith in Christ, including actual baptism or at least the explicit desire to be baptized, was necessary for all to be saved. According to the laxist school[78], even a natural act of faith in the existence of God, implicitly containing everything else, including the desire for Baptism and entrance into the Church, was enough for salvation.

Not until Pius IX do we have what appears to be the first *ex-officio* pronouncement of the Holy See on the condition of non-Catholics, in *bona fide*, living not only among pagans but also in countries where the Church is established. Pius IX has been properly called one of the greatest defenders of the rights of the Church since Gregory the Great.[79] At least nine of his official documents, quoted in the *Fontes Codicis Iuris Canonici,* specifically repeat and defend the necessity of belonging to the Catholic Church. However, in two of these, and both before the meeting of the Vatican Council, the Pope explicitly deals with the complementary doctrine, namely, that it is possible for a person to be saved without actually professing the true religion.

The day after his solemn definition of the Immaculate Conception, Pius IX gave an allocution to the several hundred bishops who had assembled in Rome for the occasion. After exhorting them to oppose the error of those who claim that human reason can even penetrate the mysteries of God, he said, "Not without sorrow have we seen that another error, and one not less ruinous, has taken possession of certain portions of the Catholic world, and has entered into the souls of the many Catholics who think that they can well hope for the eternal salvation of all those who have in no way entered into the true Church of Christ. For that reason, they are wont to inquire time and time again as to what is going to be the fate and the condition after death of those who have never yielded themselves to the Catholic faith and, convinced by completely inadequate arguments, they expect a response that will favor this evil teaching. Far be it from us, Venerable Brethren, to presume to establish limits to the Divine mercy, which is infinite. Far be it from us to wish to scrutinize the hidden counsels and the judgments of God, which are "a great deep," and which human thought can never penetrate. In accordance with our Apostolic duty, we desire to stir up your Episcopal solicitude and vigilance to drive out of the mind of men, to the extent to which you are able to use all of your energies, that equally impious and deadly opinion that the way of eternal salvation can certainly be found in any religion. With all the skill and learning at your command, you should prove to the people committed to your care that this dogma of Catholic faith is in no way opposed to the Divine mercy and justice. Certainly we must hold as of faith that no one can be saved outside of the apostolic Roman Church, that this is the only Ark of Salvation, that the one who does not enter this is going to perish in the deluge. But nevertheless we must likewise hold it as certain that those who labor in ignorance of the true religion, if that (ignorance) be invincible, will never be charged with any guilt on this account before the eyes of the Lord. Now who is there who would arrogate to himself the power to point out the extent of such ignorance according to the nature and variety of peoples, regions, talents, and so many other things? For really, when loosed from these bodily bonds, we see God as He is, we shall certainly understand with what intimate and beautiful a bond the Divine mercy and justice are joined together. But, while we live on earth, let us hold most firmly out of Catholic doctrine, that there is one God, one faith, one baptism. It is wicked to go on inquiring beyond this."[80]

Nine years later, during the wars of unification, Pius IX issued an urgent appeal to the bishops of Italy for a more concerted effort to stem the tide of immorality and indifference to religion that was sweeping over the peninsula. He continued, "And here I must mention and reprove a most serious error into which some Catholics have fallen, imagining that men living in errors and apart from the true faith and from the Catholic unity, can attain to eternal life. It is known to us and to you that those who labor in invincible ignorance of our most holy religion, and who, carefully observing the natural law and its precepts, which God has inscribed in the hearts of all, and being ready to obey God, live an honest and upright life can, through the working of the Divine light and grace, attain eternal life, since God, who clearly sees, inspects and knows the minds, the intentions, the thoughts, and the habits of all, will, by reason of His supreme goodness and kindness, never allow anyone who has not the guilt of willful sin to be punished by eternal sufferings. But it is also a perfectly well known Catholic dogma that no one can be saved outside of the Catholic Church, and that those who are contumacious against the authority of that same Church, and who are pertinaciously divided from the unity of that Church and from Peter's successor, the Roman Pontiff, to whom the custody of the vineyard has been committed by the Savior, cannot obtain eternal salvation."[81]

II. COMPARISON OF BELLARMINE'S DOCTRINE WITH THAT OF PIUS IX

Beyond giving the full documentation just quoted, it is not our intention to make a comparative study of all the possible points of contact between Bellarmine and Pius IX. In accordance with our purpose to investigate only the membership in the Church of non-Catholics in *bona fide*, we limit ourselves to what is most pertinent, namely, that Pius IX confirmed certain elements in Bellarmine's doctrine and also expanded on his teaching.

Confirmation of Bellarmine on *Voto* Members in the Visible Catholic Church

On first inspection, it looks more like an *obiter dicta* than a significant clause when Pius IX declared that those "who have *in no way* entered the true Church of Christ" cannot hope for salvation. But on examination it is seen to be a confirmation of Bellarmine's basic doctrine that at least *voto* membership in the one visible Church is necessary for salvation.

In context, the Pope is refuting the errors of those who pleaded for a species of indifference in matters of religion. Lamennais, for example, appealed to what he called a universal revelation, and found that, "the knowledge of one eternal God, Father of everything that exists, has always been preserved in the world."[82] The existence of the Divine Law,[83] the immortality of the soul,[84] the eternity of future punishment and reward,[85] the existence of good and bad angels, the fall and corruption of human nature, the necessity of expiation and the expectation of a Mediator,[86] all these truths come from a primitive revelation and have been guarded by tradition in all nations. From which he draws the conclusion that, "Every true faith is a part of the Christian faith; every pure cult is a part of the Christian cult."[87] Consequently, anyone (even an unbaptized) can be saved, not by any relation to the Church founded by Christ but in virtue of whatever amount, small or large, of primitive revelation he possesses and which he follows as best he can. Incorporation in the true Church, therefore, is only a spiritual luxury; it is in no sense a necessity. To which the Pope replies, "not without sorrow have we seen that another error (besides Rationalism)… has entered into the souls of the many Catholics who think that they can well hope for the eternal salvation of all those who have in no way entered the true Church of Christ."[88]

It might be argued that the Pope is here speaking of belonging to the soul of the Church, in the sense of possessing the gifts of the Holy

Spirit. But the whole history and background of the 1854 Allocution is against such an interpretation. No one, not even the most ardent promoters of religious indifference, for example, the Calvinist, Jurie,[89] denied that possession of the grace of God was necessary for salvation. What they called into question was the absolute necessity of being in communion with the Roman Catholic Church by external profession of faith in its visible body.

Moreover, in the same context, when the Pope comes to declare what is the true doctrine, he says, "It must be held as of faith, that outside the Apostolic Roman Church no one can be saved, that this is the only Ark of Salvation, that the one who does not enter this is going to perish in the deluge."[90] Clearly, there is no question of possible salvation without infusion of grace, but of salvation outside the visible organization of the Catholic Church, which, in Bellarmine's terminology is the sensibly perceptible society founded by Christ.

Granting, therefore, that the Pope is speaking of the necessity of belonging to the one visible Church, does he approve Bellarmine's doctrine on *voto* membership as the alternate requisite for salvation. Yes, at least implicitly, because although again he does not use Bellarmine's terminology, he espouses his fundamental doctrine.

Both in the Allocution and in the Encyclical Letter of 1863, the Pope not only re-emphasizes as of faith, that "Extra Ecclesiam nulla salus," but he also describes the prospect of sincere non-Catholics attaining to heaven. Consequently, his basic principle which we are analyzing, that "There is no salvation for anyone who in no way enters the Church," should be interpreted in the fuller light of what he also says of those non-Catholics who *de facto* are not, and presumably will not ever be, actual members of the Church and yet, who can be saved. Clearly they cannot be included among those who have *in no way* entered the Ark of Salvation. They must have entered *some way*, otherwise they could not hope for salvation. What is this "some way" to which the Pope alludes? It is by their readiness to do the whole will of God, which implicitly at least, includes the willingness to be baptized and submit to Catholic authority, if this were known to them as part of the Divine will.

The Pope first presumes

- that there is objective ignorance of the true religion among all peoples and nations;

- secondly, that this ignorance may be inculpable regarding the past and invincible regarding the future;

- thirdly, that if, besides this negative exculpating element, a non-Catholic, through the help of Divine grace, also observes the natural law, is ready to obey God and lives an upright and honest life, he can attain to eternal salvation.

Only the last element is pertinent here, namely, that willingness to obey God is necessary to be saved. The will of God, objectively, is that salvation should be attained through Baptism and membership in the Church of Christ. Subjectively, the Pope allows, not all of God's will may be known to any one person. But if this individual is willing to do whatever God wants, and would be willing to enter the Church if he knew this to be Divine will, God will take his willingness as equal to the fact. Provided other conditions are satisfied, such a person will not be lost for not having been an actual member of the Visible Church. And if he is saved, it will be in virtue of his volitional, *voto*, membership in the true Church, which, although unknown to himself, is objectively recognized by Almighty God.

Expansion on Bellarmine, on the Limits of *Voto* Membership

According to Bellarmine, it is possible for certain people to be saved although they do not actually belong to the Church, if they have an earnest wish to become Catholics. This wish, he says, the Lord takes as equivalent to the fact. They are, therefore, saved through the Church because they are members of its Visible Body *in voto*, i.e. by volition or desire.

Now the difference between Bellarmine's concept and Pius IX's is that Bellarmine is more limited in the classes of people to whom he applies *voto* membership, and more restricted in the kind of desire which qualifies for it. The first restriction follows naturally from the second. For when Bellarmine directly treats the question of *voto* members in the Church, the only people to whom he credits this kind of membership are those who explicitly desire to be in the Church, namely, catechumens, excommunicates who wish to be reconciled, and those who mistakenly think they have been baptized and yet openly profess the Catholic faith.

Pius IX, on the other hand, makes no such limitations. He does not require an explicit desire to enter the Church or the explicit profession of the Catholic religion in order to qualify for sanctifying grace, which, however, presupposes some kind of membership in the body of the Church. Bellarmine requires knowledge of the Church which inspires an explicit wish to be in the Church, for voto membership in its body; the Pope is satisfied with ignorance of the Church which is invincible, coupled with that perfect readiness to do the will of God, which God sees as implicitly containing the willingness to profess Catholicism, if the necessity of this profession were recognized.

It might be argued, again, that when the Pope spoke of invincible ignorance of the Church, he had in mind only certain remote tribes of savages who had never heard the Gospel of Christ and, consequently, should not be held responsible for not knowing that membership in the Church is necessary for salvation. Since this is a crucial point in the whole argument, it deserves special attention. It can be shown from the circumstances, context, and an analysis of the Pope's statements that, to his mind, invincible ignorance of the Church can exist even among people living in places where the Gospel has been preached and the Catholic Church is fully established:

- Of the two documents in question, the Allocution of 1854 was addressed to the bishops who were assembled from all parts of the world, but especially from Christian countries in Europe and America. The Encyclical of 1863 was directly addressed to Catholic Italy.

- When describing the invincible ignorance which may excuse a person from actual membership in the Church, the Pope does not limit the scope or territory within which this ignorance is possible. In fact, he expressly widens it to embrace all countries, East and West, Christian and pagan, for he asks, "Who is there who would arrogate to himself the power to point out the extent of such ignorance according to the nature and variety of peoples, regions, talents and so many other things?"

- Finally, the Pope's apologia for God's mercy in favor of non-Catholics in good faith would be misplaced if he were not talking expressly or, at least especially, of those who live in regions where the Church is well established. Of course, we say, God will be merciful to those who labor in "physical ignorance" of the true faith, because no one has yet preached the Gospel to them. But what about those who ostensibly know the Gospel and the work of the Church because they have lived among Catholics all their lives? Is there such a thing as *moral ignorance* for them, to exculpate them, at least theoretically, from having explicitly to profess the true faith in order to be saved? Pius IX must be interpreted as saying so. Otherwise, the error of rigorism against which he was speaking, which presumed "to set limits to the Divine mercy," would not have been refuted. Otherwise, also, he would have been evading, instead of answering, as he did, those "who are wont to inquire time and time again as to what is going to be the fate and condition after death of those who have never yielded themselves to the Catholic faith," who physically, indeed, know the Catholic Church and its claims, but morally seem to be ignorant of its message.

John A. Hardon, S.J.

Is the Pope, then, saying something different than Bellarmine? Not at all. He, no more than St. Robert, presumes to say that people who are not actual members of the Church may be easily saved. But he saw conditions existing in the 19th century which Bellarmine did not see in the 16th, where people were not lapsed Catholics who had abandoned the true faith, but persons whose whole background was one of prejudice against the Church and who, therefore, could be living physically among Catholics, but morally were in a different world which knew nothing or very little about the true Church of Christ, of her doctrines and, least of all, of the necessity of belonging to her to be saved. Pius IX does not even suggest how common this invincible ignorance might be and, therefore, how frequently non-Catholics, even non-baptized, are in good faith, in the grace of God and *voto implicito*, in the visible Church of Christ. But he does recognize the possibility of such ignorance which Bellarmine, for his pre-occupation with other matters, did not consider.

CHAPTER II

VATICAN COUNCIL 1869-1870

I. PROGRESS OF THE THEORY OF AN INVISIBLE CHURCH, UP TO THE VATICAN COUNCIL

As we saw in the previous chapter, one of Bellarmine's principal tasks was to defend the visible character of the true Church against the Protestant Reformers who wished to reduce it to an invisible society, composed of all the believers, or all the just, or all the predestined, who are bound together only spiritually, and where external bonds also exist, these should be considered purely adventitious. It was a subtle temptation even for Catholics, to "spiritualize" their concept of the Church along Protestant lines, to include also those non-Catholics who were obviously not members of the Catholic body, but who were apparently in good faith and therefore would be saved in virtue of their connection with the Church of Christ. For, it was argued, if the Church is an invisible organization, there is no contradiction in saying that she also embraces persons who externally may be separated from her ranks but internally and really should be classed among her members.

In 1713, Clement XI condemned a series of propositions of Paschasius Quesnel, who postulated such an invisible Church bound together only by interior ties. Thus, according to Quesnel:

1. "The note of the Christian Church is that it is Catholic, comprehending all the angels of heaven, and all the elect, and all the just people on earth of all ages."[91]
2. "What is the Church except the assembly of the children of God, abiding in His bosom, of the adopted children of Christ, subsisting in His person, redeemed by His blood, living by His Spirit, acting by His grace, and awaiting the gift of a world to come."[92]
3. "The Church, or the integral Christ, has the Incarnate Word as its Head, and all the saints as its members."[93] What he understood by "saints" may be gathered from the next proposition.
4. "There is nothing more extensive than the Church of Christ; because all the elect and the just people of all ages compose it."[94]

In 1794, Pius VI passed judgment on the following proposition of the Synod of Pistoia:

"The doctrine which proposes that the Church should be considered as one Mystical Body, fashioned together from Christ the Head and the faithful …understood in this sense that no others belong to the body of the Church except the faithful who are perfect adorers in spirit and in truth, (is) heretical."[95]

During the pontificate of Pius IX, this tendency to spiritualize the Church took the form of religious indifferentism. It was used, for example, by those who wished to introduce Protestantism into Italy, as a ruse to deceive Catholics into joining the ranks of the sectaries. Their argument, in the words of Pius IX, was that, "the doctrines and practices of Protestantism…are only another form of the same true religion, in which one can as well please God as in the Catholic Church."[96]

At least eight of the official statements of Pius IX, prior to the Vatican Council and excluding the Syllabus of 1854, specifically condemn the prevalent error of indifferentism. Moreover, as a basis for what follows, it will pay to analyze this heresy briefly, to see that at bottom it is a throwback to the Protestant doctrine which Bellarmine opposed in the 16th century, which defined the Church of Christ as a purely mystical and hidden society. For what does indifferentism mean? It means that externally one Church may differ a great deal from another, say the Lutheran from the Catholic, even to the point of contradiction. But no matter. Internally they are quite the same. The *external* doctrines and ritual are man-made, limited, and therefore variable as between one religious creed and another. But the *internal* bonds of union which unite the members of different religious bodies are

- their common faith in Christ, or
- their common destiny as the chosen people of God, or
- their common possession of the grace of God.

In any case, it is by reason of this *internal* and *spiritual* bond that the Church of Christ is *really* formed; the *external* bonds of any one religion are merely social conveniences which do not affect the substantial, invisible source of unity that transcends the visible differences which distinguish various religious groups.

II.   THEOLOGIANS OF THE VATICAN COUNCIL ON MEMBERSHIP IN THE VISIBLE CHURCH.

Membership Constituted by External Profession of the Catholic Faith

On December 8, 1869, Pius IX opened the first session of the Vatican Council, the twentieth Ecumenical Council of the Catholic Church.

Actually, however, since March, 1865, a special congregation of cardinals had been erected to gather together and synthesize all the doctrinal and moral questions on which the forthcoming assembly was to decide. The opinions of eminent bishops and theologians throughout the world were solicited, collated, and condensed into a series of *Schemata* that were presented to the Vatican Fathers for decision. Unfortunately, the occupation of Rome in 1870 suspended the meetings of the Council, so that most of the work which had been planned (including the problem of membership in the Church and specifically the relation of non-Catholics to the Church of Christ), was never carried through to completion.

However, in lieu of any formal definitions on the subject, we can still profit a great deal from examining the so-called, *Schema Constitutionis Dogmaticae De Ecclesia Christi,* which was presented to the Vatican assembly as a basis for its projected decree on the nature of the Church. This *Schema* has no official conciliar authority. Yet it is most significant because it fairly represents the common doctrine of theologians in the late 19th century on the subject of non-Catholics in their relation to the Church and to that extent, at least, it offers a suitable instrument of comparison with the corresponding doctrine of Robert Bellarmine.

Four of the fifteen chapters of the *Schema*, namely, the fourth to the seventh, are pertinent to our subject, each representing a specific problem touching on the nexus between the true Church and non-Catholics in other denominations.

By way of introduction, in Chapter III, which is entitled *The Church is a True, Perfect, Spiritual and Supernatural Society*, the *Schema* reads:

> "We teach and declare that the Church possesses all the qualities of a true Society. This Society has not been left by Christ indefinite or unformed … Having proceeded from the inexhaustible font of the mercy of God the Father, having been founded through the ministry and labor of the Incarnate Word Himself, it has been constituted in the Holy Spirit … Since, however, men are enriched in the Church with the benefits (of Divine grace) through the Holy Spirit, since they are joined together in unity by the bonds of this same Holy Spirit, (therefore) the Church herself is a spiritual Society, and entirely of the supernatural order."[97]

But immediately this poses a problem. If the Church is a spiritual society, it is therefore invisible, bound together by spiritual ties of grace and virtue, and, consequently, not unlike the invisible church of the Reformers, or the mystical Church of modern Indifferentists.

The next, Chapter IV, entitled *The Church is a Visible Society*, promptly recognizes the problem and answers it by qualifying the spiritual character of the Church just described. It states:

> "God forbid that anyone should believe that the members of the Church are joined together only by unseen and internal bonds, so that the Church becomes an entirely hidden and invisible society. For the eternal wisdom and power of God willed that, to the spiritual and invisible bonds by which the faithful adhere through the Holy Spirit to the Supreme and invisible Head of the Church, there should correspond (such as are) also external and visible, so that this spiritual and supernatural Society might be seen externally and become openly conspicuous. Hence the visible magisterium, by which the faith that must be interiorly believed and exteriorly professed, is proposed; also the visible ministry which cares for and directs as a public duty, the visible mysteries of God by which interior sanctification is given to men and due honor to God; the visible government, which orders the communion of the members among themselves and disposes and directs the whole external and public life of the faithful in the Church; finally, the whole visible body of the Church, to which not only the just or the predestined belong, but also sinners, yet joined together with it (the body of the Church) by the profession and communion of faith. From which it follows that the Church of Christ is neither invisible nor concealed, but conspicuously erected, like a high and illustrious city on a mountain top, which cannot be hidden, and like a lamp on a lampstand which is illuminated by the Sun of Justice, it enlightens the whole world with its rays."[98]

Corresponding to this Chapter is the proposed Canon III, which says: "if anyone should say that the Church of the Divine Promises is not an external and conspicuous society, but wholly internal and invisible let him be anathema."[99]

Confirmation of Bellarmine on the Conditions Necessary for Actual Membership

The foregoing chapter of the *Schema* and its corresponding canon were implemented with a lengthy annotation, in which the only authority quoted besides the Popes and the Councils was Robert Bellarmine. The main argument of the Vatican theologians was that since the Church is a Society, it must have power and authority which, to be exercised, must be recognized and seen. But this is impossible if the Church itself is invisible. "Wherefore it is declared that in the Church there is a visible magisterium, a visible ministry and a visible government, instituted by Christ the Lord, through which three-fold, external and conspicuous power, the Church coheres together in a triple, external bond, which external bonds correspond to those which are internal and exist as their partial cause, and make the whole body of the Church visible and conspicuous so that, whosoever coheres with the body of the Church by this triple visible nexus, is to be regarded as a member of the true Church of Christ. 'For this,' says Bellarmine in *De Ecclesia Militante*, lib. 3, cap. 2, 'is the difference between our definition (of the Church) and all others, that all the rest require only internal virtues to constitute a person in the Church, and, therefore, they make the true Church something invisible. Whereas, we also believe that in the Church are found all the virtues: faith, hope and charity, and all the rest. However, for anyone to be called in some sense a part of the true Church, of which the Scriptures speak, we do not think that any internal virtue is required, but only an external profession of faith and communication of the Sacraments which can be perceived by the senses themselves. For the Church is an assembly of men, as visible and palpable as the assembly of the Roman people, or the Kingdom of France, or the Republic of the Venetians.'[100]

For our purpose, the immediate conclusion is that the Vatican authorities, no less than Bellarmine, would exclude from actual membership in and union with the true Church, everyone who professes any other religion except the Catholic. In terms of our thesis, this means that those who are not baptized, even catechumens within a moment of actual baptism, and heretics, even in the best of faith and in the grace of God, as long as they externally profess their heresy, are not actual members of the *Corpus Ecclesiae*, i.e., of the visible Church of Christ.

Further Confirmation of Bellarmine on the Necessity of External Profession to be United to the One True Church

By way of transition, the next chapter of the *Schema* treats of the unity of the visible Church. "We declare," it says, "that this visible and conspicuous Society is the same Church …which Christ wished to distinguish and adorn with so many prerogatives and privileges, that the same (Church) is so completely determined in its constitution that whatever societies are separated from the unity of faith and from the communion of this body, cannot in any way be called a part of it or a member; nor does (the true Church) show itself as dispersed and diffused throughout various associations bearing the Christian name, but as wholly conjoined and coherent in itself, (forming) in its manifest unity an undivided and indivisible body, which is the very Mystical Body of Christ. Of which the Apostle says, 'You have been called into one body and one Spirit, in the one hope of your vocation. One Lord, one faith, one Baptism. One God and Father of all, Who is above all, and throughout all, and in us all.' Eph.4:4-6."[101]

Corresponding to this chapter is Canon IV, which reads: "If anyone should say that the true Church is not in itself one body, but that it is formed from various and dissident societies bearing the Christian name, and through which it is diffused or that the various societies, differing among themselves in the profession of faith and separated in communion, constitute the one universal Church of Christ, as its members and parts, let him be anathema."[102]

The annotations to the above chapter and canon, where Bellarmine is again quoted with approval, are specially enlightening because they give us an insight into the development of Protestant theology from the 16th to the 19th century. In the annotation to the chapter, St. Robert is quoted in his refutation of the Reformers in his day who "conceive of two Churches: one true, and to which the privileges narrated in the Scriptures pertain, and this is the congregation of the saints who truly believe and obey God, and this is not visible except with the eyes of faith. Another (is) external, which is a Church only in name, and this is the assembly of men joined together in the doctrine of faith and use of the Sacraments, and in this (Church) the good and the wicked are found."[103]

In the annotation to the canon, it is said that, "Canon IV is directed against those who subvert the visible unity of the Church … Wherefore, the heresy which is condemned is:

1.   That of the Latitudinarians, so-called, according to whom all those belong to the Church of Christ who, although they are members of different communions bearing the Christian name, agree on certain articles (of faith), which they call fundamental. Consequently, they say that the true and universal Church of Christ is diffused among all the societies of the Christian name; that the Church of Christ's faithful does not depend on any external forms of a society, but that it is constituted by all the faithful who truly believe in Christ, existing in all the societies of the Christian name, although these may differ among themselves in certain external forms.

2.   That of the sect of the Anglicans who affirm that the one and universal Church of Christ is neither invisible, nor diffused everywhere, through Christian sects, nor even lacking in some form of constitution, but that it is composed of three definite societies, corresponding to as many members or parts, namely, the Anglican Society, the Greco-schismatic

Society, and the Roman Catholic Society, although the said societies may be separated from one another in the profession of faith or communion of body; so that they (the Anglicans) contend that the other societies (Anglican and Greco-schismatic) which are separated from the communion of the body of this, that is, the true Church, and which dissent from the full unity of its profession of faith, are (nevertheless) members and parts of the Church of Jesus Christ. But it is a dogma of faith that the visible unity of the universal Church is derived primarily from the unity, both in profession of faith and communion."[104]

It will be seen from the foregoing that while both the Reformers in Bellarmine's day and modern Latitudinarians postulate a purely invisible Church, there has been a considerable change in the purpose which this doctrine has been made to serve. With the original sectarians, notably Calvin, a completely invisible Church of Christ, to which alone pertain the promises of the Scriptures, was invented to justify the separation from the visible body of Roman Catholicism. In modern times, however, this concept of a "mystical church" is being used by non-Catholics to explain their fundamental "union" with the Roman Catholic Church, in spite of obvious differences in doctrine and cult which, it is claimed, are only external and accidental. In one sense, therefore, this indicates that in the three centuries since Bellarmine and Calvin, there has developed a growing sympathy towards Rome among certain non-Catholics, who wish to align themselves with the Catholic Church by making her a part of the larger spiritual organization to which they also belong. But, as will be seen in a later chapter, this has also been a temptation for a number of Catholics who, in their reciprocal sympathy towards Protestants, have tended to minimize the importance of *external* profession of the Catholic Faith as an indispensable condition for membership in the true Church of Christ.

III. THEOLOGIANS OF THE VATICAN COUNCIL ON THE RELATION OF NON-CATHOLICS TO THE CATHOLIC CHURCH

Necessity of Membership in the Catholic Church for Salvation

There follows Chapter VI of the *Schema*, entitled: *The Church is a Society Absolutely Necessary to Attain to Salvation*, which is a natural corollary to what preceeded. For if Christ is the unique Savior of mankind, and if He willed to accomplish the work of man's Redemption by establishing a Church, and if there is only one such organization which He founded — evidently membership in this Society is the Divinely appointed means for attaining to salvation. "Hence," the proposed Constitution reads, "let all understand what a necessary Society the Church is, in order to obtain salvation. Namely, this necessity is as great as that of being joined and united with Christ the Head and with His Mystical Body, outside of which He nourishes and favors no other communion as His Church, which alone He loves and for which He sacrificed Himself, that He might sanctify it, cleansing it by the laver of water in the word of life. …Therefore we teach that the Church is not a free Society, as though it is a matter of indifference to salvation to either know or not know, to enter or to leave it; but that it is absolutely necessary and, indeed, not only with the necessity of the Lord's precept by which the Savior prescribed that all men should enter into it; but also (with the necessity) of means, because in the established order of salutary providence, the communication of the Holy Spirit, the participation of truth and life is not obtained except in the Church and through the Church, whose Head is Christ."[105]

Again the chapter is followed by a canon, which states, "If anyone should say that the Church of Christ is not a Society absolutely necessary for attaining eternal salvation; or that men can be saved through worshiping in any religion whatsoever, let him be anathema."[106]

Relation of Non-Catholics to the True Church

But now arises the same dilemma that faced Bellarmine on a smaller scale. If there is only one true Church of Christ, and if membership in its visible body is necessary for salvation, what of those people, especially Christian non-Catholics, who do not belong to this Society by external profession? Can they be justified and eventually saved, after reaching the age of discretion, without giving their allegiance to the Catholic Faith? If so, how square this phenomenon with the doctrine that, *"extra Ecclesiam nulla salus"*?

Chapter VII of the *Schema* honestly faces the dilemma and answers it. Following the title, *Outside the Church, No One Can Be Saved*, the prospective constitution reads, "Moreover, it is a dogma of faith that no one can be saved outside the Church. However, those who labor in invincible ignorance of Christ and His Church, are not to be punished for this ignorance with eternal pains, since they are not burdened with guilt on this account in the eyes of God, Who wishes all men to be saved and to come to the knowledge of the truth, and Who does not deny His grace to the person who does what he can to enable him to attain to justification and to eternal life: but this (salvation) no one attains, who leaves this life culpably separated from the unity of faith and the communion of the Church."[107]

The canon which corresponds to this significant chapter, exonerates the Church from dogmatic injustice and reads, "If anyone should say that the intolerance by which the Catholic Church proscribes and condemns all religious sects separated from her communion, is not commanded by Divine right; or that it is possible to have only opinions but not certitude regarding the truth of religion; and that therefore all religious sects should be tolerated by the Church, let him be anathema." [108]

Following the chapter and canon, we have two annotations which explain in great detail the two complementary doctrines involved, namely: that membership in the Catholic Church is necessary for salvation, and that invincible ignorance of the Church excuses a person, under certain conditions, from actual membership in its body.

The first annotation, dealing with the necessity of the Church, says that, "This chapter was added on account of special difficulties, provoked by the previous dogmatic statement, and to explain the meaning of this statement *(Extra Ecclesiam nulla salus)*, more accurately. Relative to the first point… (the Calvinist) M. Jurieu writes: 'Papism is cruel in the highest degree, and entangles itself in a thousand absurdities when it claims, as a fact, that among all the societies which divide Christendom, there is only one which is the true Church, in whose number alone are found the elect and the truly faithful, who are the members of Jesus Christ, outside of which there is no salvation.'"[109]

Answering this charge of cruelty, the annotation quotes verbatim the two documents of Pius IX, analyzed in the previous chapter, in which the Pope first confirms the traditional doctrine on the necessity of the Church, and then adds a caution against condemning, prematurely, those non-Catholics who may be in good faith, and therefore eligible for salvation although separated from the visible unity of the Church.

The second annotation enlarges on the doctrine of Pius IX. "By the words, 'those who labor in invincible ignorance….'" is indicated the possibility that a person may not belong to the visible and external communion of the Church, and yet may attain to justification and eternal life… However, to forestall the possible conclusion that someone *can* be saved outside the Church, it was stated in another formula of the *Schema*, 'This (justification and eternal life) if attained (by non-Catholics, yet) they are not for that reason saved outside the Church; for all who are justified pertain to the Church either *re* or *voto*.' But since this formula, 'either *re* or *voto*, did not please some of the consultors, it seemed to be enough to declare *explicitly* that no one is saved who through his own fault leaves this life separated from the Church, while *implicitly* it is understood to mean that whoever is saved cannot be completely or simply, so to say, outside the Church. Since some thought this should be expressed more definitely, they suggested this form for the chapter: "This (justification and eternal life), no one attains who does not pertain to the Church in any way, and who departs from this life culpably separated from the unity of faith and from the communion of the Church." … The phrase, 'who does not pertain to the Church in any way,' means, 'who does not belong either to the body of the Church or to the soul of the Church;' and therefore, in no way belongs to the Church, that is, neither *re* nor *voto*.' These (distinctions) are clearly explained by Bellarmine in *De Ecclesia Militante*, lib.3, cap. 3, in *De Non-Baptizatis,* who, after he explained, cap.2, that catechumens are of the soul but not of the body of the Church, understanding the body of the Church as the visible communion of the faithful, to which *actually* and *properly* only they pertain who 'profess the faith and communicate in the Sacraments under the rule of their pastors,' asks: 'How then are catechumens saved if they are outside the Church?' And answers: 'When it is said that no one is saved outside the Church, this should be understood of those who do not belong to the Church either in reality or in desire, as theologians commonly say about Baptism. But since catechumens are in the Church, if not really *(re)*, at least in desire *(voto)*, they can be saved. Nor is there any valid objection in the analogy of Noe's ark, outside of which no one was saved, since analogies are not perfect in all respects."

The annotation continues, "Suarez teaches the same thing in *De Fide,* Disp. XII, sect. 4, num. 22, writing: 'When it is said… that outside the Church there is no salvation, some, e.g., Cano in *De Loc. Rel. de Sacram.*, p. II, say that the proposition is to be understood of the Church in general, as it always was, and not of that one Church which was specially instituted by Christ. But this answer is not satisfactory, both because the Church is always one and because the Councils really speak of the Church of Christ, so that it is of this (Church) that somehow must be verified (the statement) that outside of it there is no salvation. It is better, therefore, to answer according to the distinction given for a necessity *in re* or *in voto*. So that no one can be saved unless he enters this Church of Christ either in reality *(in re)*, or at least in willingness *(in voto)* and desire *(desiderio)*. Thus Bellarmine answers in *De Ecclesia*, III, cap. 3. It is clear that no one is actually in this Church unless he has been baptized, and yet he can be saved because the desire for Baptism is enough for him. So also the desire to enter the Church. Therefore, we say the same about any believer who is truly repentant but not baptized, whether he attains to an explicit faith in Christ or only implicit. For in the latter (implicit faith), he can have at least an implicit desire (to enter the Church), which is sufficient in the case of Baptism, as St. Thomas teaches.'"[110]

Comparison with Bellarmine's Doctrine on the Membership of Non-Catholics in the True Church

Apparent disapproval of the formula, "*re or voto*"

On first inspection it might seem as though the Vatican theologians did not approve of Bellarmine's classic distinction between *re and voto* membership in the Church for non-Catholics in good faith. The original *Schema,* it is remembered, stated that, "Those who labor in invincible ignorance of Christ and His Church are not to be punished with eternal pains for this ignorance," so that only those will not attain to eternal life who "leave this life *culpably* separated from the unity of faith and the communion of the Church." But this was not considered clear enough. On the one hand it was stated that even those who are ostensibly separated from visible unity *can* be saved. On the other hand it was said that *only* if this separation were culpable would a person not reach eternal life. But the underlying question still remained untouched, namely, how reconcile actual separation from the Church at death — even when it is inculpable — with the unqualified doctrine of the faith that outside the Church there is no salvation? Three possibilities suggested themselves:

- Either to leave the matter stand unchanged, merely declaring the fact that actual membership in the Church is not necessary, and that only culpable separation from the Church deprives a person of salvation.

- Stating at least negatively that no salvation is possible for anyone who in *no way* is united to the Church at death.

- Explaining positively in what the connection with the Church consists for those who are ostensibly separated from its visible communion at death, and yet can be saved.

In their first *Schema* of the constitution, the theologians of the Council had already declared the first fact, namely, that invincible ignorance of the Church is reconcilable with justification and eventual salvation. But, recognizing that this should be made more explicit, they drew up a second *Schema*, in which the third explanation was given, namely, that membership in the Church, either *re* or *voto*, is necessary to be justified and saved. In this, they were simply adopting the distinction of Bellarmine. "However," the report continues, "the formula, 'either *re* or *voto*,' was not pleasing to some of the consultors," and so a change was made. But, we may ask, why was the formula disapproved? Was it because the doctrine it contained was unsatisfactory, or because the form in which it was proposed was unsuitable? Since, as will be seen shortly, the theologians later on adopted the formula which they had previously rejected, it could not have been the doctrine but its manner of proposal which they disapproved.

Actual Approval of Bellarmine's Distinctions Between the Body and Soul of the Church, and *Re* or *Voto* Membership in the Church

Formally, therefore, the Vatican theologians preferred to state the doctrine in more general terms, merely saying that *some kind* of nexus with the Church is necessary for justification and salvation. But immediately they explained themselves on what this really means, and in giving their explanation, they gave the fullest approval to Bellarmine's two classic distinctions, on the body and soul, and *re* or *voto* membership in the Church. No one, they said, attains to salvation who does not in any way, *nullatenus*, belong to the Church. What does this *nullatenus* mean? It means, they continued, that a person "does not belong either to the body of the Church or to the soul of the Church, and, therefore, *in no way* pertains to the Church, that is, neither *re* nor *voto*."[111]

Referring to the two sets of formulas, the consultors further declared that, "These things are clearly explained by Bellarmine in *De Ecclessia Militante*.... where he says that catechumens are in the *soul* but not in the *body* of the Church, understanding the body of the Church to mean the visible communion of the faithful, to which only those pertain *actu* and *proprie* who profess the faith and communicate in the Sacraments, under the rule of (their) pastors."[112] "But how then," the theologians quote Bellarmine's objection, "are catechumens saved, if they are outside the Church?" Then the answer: "When it is said that no one is saved outside the Church, this should be understood of those who neither in reality nor in desire are in the Church... But since catechumens are in the Church, if not *really*, at least *voto*, therefore they are saved."[113]

However, a number of questions pose themselves, which need to be answered to see whether the Vatican theologians merely adopted Bellarmine's formularies or also gave them something of an interpretation. Thus, in the light of the consultors' statements:

In what sense is body and in what sense is *soul* of the Church to be taken here?

> The theologians of the Council say that the body of the Church is understood as the visible communion of the faithful. The supposition is that if a person had no internal virtue whatever, and from purely and human motives "professed" the true faith, hypocritically, he would not be a member of the body of the Church.

> The soul of the Church is taken generically to include all those who possess the gifts of the Holy Ghost. No direct reference is made as to whether membership in the soul of the Church must be *actu* or may be *in voto* as a condition for justification.

Can we infer that actual membership in the soul of the Church is not necessary for salvation?

Yes, in fact, we must infer as much. For when the consultors say that a person can be saved by belonging to the body or soul of the Church, *or* by real or votive membership in the Church, the sincere non-Catholic is simultaneously excluded from the body of the Church and from actual membership. Therefore, he does not belong *actu* either to the Church's body or to its soul. This is significant in view of the fact that not a few modern writers have interpreted Bellarmine to mean that non-Catholics in good faith *do,* indeed, belong only *voto* to the Church's body, but that they are *actu* in the Church's soul.[114]

How reconcile the two statements, that all those are saved who belong: to the body or soul of the Church, or belong to the Church *re* or *voto*?

By saying that no one is saved unless he belongs *re* or *voto* to the Church, the Vatican authorities meant that a person had to pertain either *actually* or *in desire* to the true Church of Christ, i.e. to its visible body under the influx of its soul, which is the Holy Spirit, with His gifts.

By saying that no one is saved unless he belong either to the Church's body or soul, they meant to express concretely the two classes of persons who are saved:

- In the body, i.e., professed Catholics, by their actual profession of the true faith;

- In the soul, i.e., sincere non-Catholics, by their *voto* profession of the true faith.

Would this mean that the body and the soul of the Church are mutually exclusive ?

No, the theologians of the Council no more than Bellarmine thought it was possible for a person to be justified and saved if he belonged only to the body of the Church; nor that a person could, *de facto*, be in the soul of the Church without some degree of corresponding membership in the Church's body. Moreover, as noted before, the consultors considered a person to be in the body of the Church if he belonged to the visible community of the *faithful*; so that a professed Catholic is declared to belong *actu* to the Church's body and *actu* to the Church's soul. By the same token, a sincere non-Catholic, besides belonging *voto* to the Church's soul, also belongs *voto* to the Church's body.

Expansion on Bellarmine's Doctrine

On the Limits of Voto Membership

We have seen that Bellarmine arrived at his doctrine of *voto* membership in the Catholic Church from the consideration of three concrete cases, where the persons in question are certainly not actual members of the Church and yet are eligible for salvation, namely, a catechumen who actually desires to enter the Church, an excommunicate who wants to be reconciled, and a person who has been excommunicated unjustly. The theologians of the Vatican Council accepted this principle but extended its application to include *all* non-Catholics, baptized or not, who are invincibly ignorant of the Catholic Church and at the same time fulfill the other conditions requisite for obtaining the infused gifts of Divine grace.

In the previous chapter, it was pointed out that Pius IX had already made the same advancement over Bellarmine, by extending "some kind" of membership in the one visible Church, beyond the original limits set by St. Robert. But Pius IX was not as explicit in using Bellarmine's doctrine as were the Vatican theologians, who also adopted his terminology. Because where the Pope was satisfied with stating the fact that salvation is impossible only for those "who in *no way* belong to the true Church of Christ," the Vatican authorities went on to interpret this doctrine in terms of Bellarmine's distinctions between *re-voto* and body-soul membership in the Church. So that, in the mind of the theologians, when the Pope allows for invincible ignorance of the Church even among those who live in Christian countries, and gives them a title to salvation, this should be interpreted to mean that such people are *voto* members of the visible Church of Christ, and for that reason they can be saved.

On the Nexus between Voto Membership and Justification

When Bellarmine spoke of certain people being *voto* members of the Church and therefore having a claim to salvation, he equated this claim with membership in the soul of the Church. However, a possible misunderstanding has to be cleared up. It is true that when he treats concretely of those who are only in the soul of the Church and not actually in the body, as, for example, catechumens, he says that they possess faith *and* charity. Does he, therefore, also intend to equate, theoretically, the soul of the Church with the possession of sanctifying grace? No, because in the same paragraph he described people who are actually in the body of the Church, that is, baptized and professed Catholics, who also belong to the soul of the Church, although they have lost the state of grace and have only supernatural faith left within them. How explain the apparent contradiction once he says that people who have only faith are in the soul of the Church, then he says that those who have faith and charity are in the soul of the Church? The answer is that both statements are true. Belonging to the soul of the Church, for Bellarmine, means the possession of the gifts of the Holy Spirit, in varying degrees, starting with the minimum of infused faith and ending with the perfection of charity. Now, while it is certainly possible for a catechumen who was once in the state of grace to lose the gift of charity and have only faith left, Bellarmine does not consider this concrete situation. If he did, he would also include such a catechumen in the soul of the Church, as he included professed Catholics who have lost the gift of charity, but not the gift of faith. However, as noted above, where a Catholic, even in sin, has actual membership in the Church's soul, a catechumen who has not lost his faith, belongs only *voto* to the *anima Ecclesiae*.

The Vatican theologians substantially accepted Bellarmine's doctrine on *voto* membership as their own. With him, they recognized that a sincere desire *(votum)* to enter the Church may be so united with other requisite dispositions as to justify a person and make him eligible for salvation. But where Bellarmine expressly treats of only isolated cases of *voto* membership, the theologians made a universal application: "All the justified," they said, "pertain to the Church either *re* or *voto*."[115] The simple meaning of this statement, in terms of Bellarmine's formula, is certainly not that every person who belongs to the Church is justified and in the state of grace. What it means is that if anyone is ever justified, and therefore eligible for salvation, he could not have attained to this state without first, by a priority of cause over effect, belonging to the visible Church of Christ by profession of the true faith, either actually or in desire, and the latter at least implicitly in a perfect readiness to do the entire will of God.

However, it was noted that the theologians of the Council expanded on Bellarmine to include, without restriction, those people who have only an implicit desire to enter the Church. The theological basis for this expansion was due to the teaching of Francis Suarez on *votum implicitum*, which the Vatican authorities quote with approval.

Suarez began by accepting Bellarmine's distinction between *re* and *voto* membership in the Church, as the logical explanation for the salvation of sincere non-Catholics who are not baptized. Then he went on to add what Bellarmine did not expressly teach. "It is manifest," he says, "that no one is really within this Church unless he is baptized, and yet he can be saved because a desire of Baptism is sufficient for him; so also the desire to enter the Church. We therefore say the same for any believer who is repentant and who is not baptized, whether he arrives at an explicit faith in Christ or only at one that is implicit, since through the latter he can have at least an implicit desire (to enter the Church), which is sufficient in the case of Baptism."[116]

CHAPTER III

LEO XIII 1878-1903

I. DOCTRINE OF LEO XIII ON HERETICS IN GOOD FAITH

Among the official writing of Leo XIII is the well-known Apostolic Letter, *Apostolicae Curae*, of 1896, in which he formally declared that, "Ordinations (to the priesthood) carried out according to the Anglican rite have been and are absolutely null and utterly void."[117] What is less familiar about the document is the concluding exhortation which the Pope addressed to the Anglicans themselves and in which he earnestly invited them to re-enter the Catholic Church. The importance of this exhortation lies especially in its being directed to the Anglicans as non-Catholics, and therefore represents the mind of the Holy See in the late 19th century, on the relation of heretics in *bona fide* and the Roman Catholic Church.

Immediately following on the solemn pronouncement that Anglican Orders are invalid, the Pope continued: "It remains for Us to say that even as we have entered upon the elucidation of this grave question in the name and in the love of the Great Shepherd, in the same we appeal to those who desire and seek with a sincere heart the possession of a hierarchy and of Orders. Perhaps until now, aiming at the greater perfection of Christian virtue, and searching more devoutly the Divine Scriptures, and redoubling the fervor of their prayers, they have, nevertheless, hesitated in doubt and anxiety to follow the voice of Christ, which so long has interiorly admonished them. Now they see clearly whether He in His goodness invites them and wills them to come. In returning to His one only fold, they will obtain the blessings which they seek, and the consequent helps to salvation of which He has made the Church the dispenser, and, as it were, the constant guardian and promoter of His Redemption amongst the nations. Then, indeed, 'they shall draw waters in joy from the fountains of the Savior.'[118] His wondrous Sacraments, whereby His faithful souls have their sins truly remitted, and are restored to the friendship of God, are nourished and strengthened by the heavenly Bread, and abound with the most powerful aids for their

eternal salvation. May the God of peace, the God of all consolation, in
His infinite tenderness enrich and fill them with all these blessings, who
truly yearn for them. We wish to direct Our exhortation and Our desires
in a special way to those who are ministers of religion in their respective
communities. They are men who from their very office take precedence
in learning and authority, and who have at heart the glory of God and
the salvation of souls. Let them be the first in joyfully submitting to the
Divine call, and obey it, and furnish a glorious example to others. Assuredly with an exceeding great joy, their Mother the Church, will welcome
them and will cherish with all her love and care those whom the strength
of their generous souls has amidst many trials and difficulties led back to
her bosom. Nor could words express the recognition which this devoted
courage will win for them from the assemblies of the brethren throughout the Catholic world, or what hope or confidence it will merit for them
before Christ as their Judge, or what reward it will obtain from Him in
the heavenly Kingdom. And We Ourselves in every lawful way shall
continue to promote their reconciliation with the Church in which individuals and masses, as We ardently desire, may find so much for their
imitation. In the meantime, by the tender mercy of the Lord our God,
We ask and beseech all to strive faithfully to follow in the open path of
Divine grace and truth."[119]

On analyzing the foregoing statement, we find that it contains the
following significant declarations made by Leo XIII:

Although addressing himself to the Anglicans who, by definition,
deny the Roman supremacy and are therefore heretical,

- He yet considers at least some of them to be in good faith, for he says,
"We appeal to those who desire and seek with a *sincere heart* the possession of a hierarchy and of Orders."
- He even credits some of their ministers of religion with honest sincerity, saying, "We wish to direct Our exhortation and Our desires in a
special way to those who are ministers of religion in their respective
communities. They are men....who *have at heart* the glory of God and
the salvation of souls."

But more than being only sincere in their profession of error, the
Pope also credits them with the fruit of their sincerity, which is the grace
of the Holy Spirit. They are, or may be, supernaturally justified, for he
speaks of them as "aiming at the greater perfection of Christian virtue,"
which presupposes the state of sanctifying grace.

Besides being possibly in the state of grace, they are also receiving
actual and special helps from God, which the Pope describes as "the
voice of Christ, which so long has been interiorly admonishing them."

However, in spite of the fact that they are sincere and in good faith, in the grace of God, and subject to His special interior aid, the Anglicans are still not members of the Catholic Church. Significantly, the Pope does not say that they are merely outside the Roman Catholic Church, which the Anglicans themselves would have been willing to admit, but they are outside the one, true Church founded by Christ. Thus he says:

- "In *returning* to His one true fold, they will obtain the blessings which they seek…"
- "Assuredly, with an exceeding great joy, their Mother, the Church, will *welcome* them and will cherish with all her love and care those whom the strength of their generous souls has, amidst so many trials and difficulties, *led back* to her bosom."
- "We Ourselves in every lawful way shall continue to promote their *reconciliation* with the Church."

Obviously, they cannot be considered members of the true Church if the sovereign Pontiff describes them as *returning*, as being *welcome*, as being *led back* and as being *reconciled* with the one Church of Christ.

In fact, when the Pope says that the Anglicans are receiving supernatural help from God, without denying that this Divine aid has other objects besides, he emphasizes its special function as a monitor and stimulus to lead them back to visible communion with the Roman Catholic Church.

II. COMPARISON OF BELLARMINE'S DOCTRINE WITH LEO XIII

All of this is a remarkable application and extension of Bellarmine's principles on Church membership, which we have been investigating.

> Thus, where Bellarmine only grudgingly credits the Protestants of his day with "sincerity," and then only the uneducated masses whose ignorance and wicked morals made them easy victims of heresy, Leo XIII makes a large concession in this regard in favor of many Anglicans in modern times.

> Corresponding with this concession of possible sincerity, the Pope also credits the Anglicans with the possession of sanctifying grace.

> However, in close correspondence with Bellarmine's principle that "The form of the Church is not internal faith …. but external, that is, the confession of the faith,"[120] Leo XIII clearly declares that Anglicans are severed from corporate ecclesiastical unity, not because they lack internal faith — which they may well have, even to being animated

by charity — but because they do not externally profess the true faith, which is that of the Roman Catholic Church. Such persons, therefore, in Bellarmine's terms, would belong to the soul of the Church because they possess one or more of the infused gifts of the Holy Spirit; but they do not belong to the Church as such which is entered only by the visible profession of the Catholic religion.

Here also, in Leo XIII, a new light is thrown on the operations of the Holy Spirit as the soul of the Church, for those people who are still separated from Catholic unity. Again, without disclaiming His other operations, the Spirit of Christ, more or less intimately united to the soul of a sincere non-Catholic, urges and inspires and stimulates him to find his way back into the Catholic body. Even though he is clearly speaking to those who never personally left the true faith, the Pope is explicit on this point. "The voice of Christ," he says, "which has so long interiorly admonished them," and which "invites them and wills them to come." Whither ? Into the Catholic Church. So that, "in returning to His one only fold they will obtain the blessings which they seek." The ministers of religion are especially admonished to "be the first in submitting to the Divine call and obey it and furnish a glorious example to others."

This represents a notable development on Bellarmine. For the closest that St. Robert comes to the same thesis is when he deals with a catechumen who receives the Holy Spirit and is justified before actual Baptism, in virtue of his sincere desire to be baptized and to enter the Church. Analyzing the idea of "*votum Baptismi*," and therefore, "*votum ingrediendi Ecclesiam*," he declares that, "true charity cannot exist without the Sacrament (of Baptism) either in *re* or in *voto*; nor can it happen that someone should love God above all things and yet not desire those remedies which God has instituted for the reconciliation of the sinner."[121] Here we have an instance of the Holy Spirit operating on the soul of a non-Catholic, leading him even to justification and the infusion of charity, through the indispensable medium of a sincere desire for Baptism which is at least an implicit desire to enter the Church. Bellarmine insists that this *votum Baptismi* is part of the working of the Holy Spirit and so essential that if the desire should be deliberately excluded, justification would not be attained. "For true charity and a real desire for Baptism do not permit a man to be (culpably) negligent or contemptuous of Baptism."[122]

Leo XIII amplified on this concept by describing the action of the Holy Ghost, now not in a catechumen but in a heretic, urging him through the impulse of interior grace to desire, now not to enter the Church through Baptism, but to "re-enter" it through submission to its Divinely established authority.

Elsewhere, in his Encyclical on the Holy Spirit, Leo XIII clearly distinguished between the operations of the Holy Ghost in the Church
as the Body of Christ, and His operation in individual souls. "By the
conspicuous apparition," he says, "of the Holy Ghost over Christ, and
by His invisible power in His soul, the two-fold mission of the Spirit is
foreshadowed, namely, the outward and visible mission in the Church,
and His secret indwelling in the souls of the just."[123] Moreover, this
outward and visible mission can be further distinguished, the Pope allows, into the mission by which the Church is animated and preserved
as an already existing unit, and that by which it is made to increase
in the number of its members by aggregation to its body, through the
Baptism of the unbaptized and the reconciliation of heretics and the
unreconciled.

Based on the premise that, "as Christ is the Head of the Church, so
is the Holy Ghost her soul," Leo XIII further declares that it is this same
Holy Spirit, as the soul of the Church, Who not only "perpetually supplies life and strength to preserve," but Who also operates to "*increase
the Church.*" Moreover, by the Holy Ghost, not only "are the bishops
constituted," but by their ministry are also "multiplied the children" of
the Church, who are aggregated to its body from the outside.[124]

Comparing the two cases, therefore, Bellarmine's and Leo XIII's,
in both instances the Holy Spirit is seen to operate not only interiorly to
sanctify individual persons, but also "exteriorly", or better "socially", as
the Soul of the visible *Corpus Ecclesiae.* And in the latter operation, He
functions not only intensively, to preserve the order and unity among the
members already united, but also *extensively*, to increase and multiply
the number of these members — by Baptism where this has been wanting, and by submission to Catholic authority where this is still lacking.

The difference between Bellarmine and Leo XIII in their teaching
on the action of the Holy Spirit as the soul of the Church, is that the Pope
is less restricted and more explicit in his statement of the doctrine. Thus,
in treating of non-Catholics, where Bellarmine limited the application of
his doctrine on the soul of the Church to catechumens with an explicit
desire for Baptism, and to excommunicates, who *actually* desire to be
reconciled, the Pope would extend the activity of the Holy Ghost as the
soul of the Church also to non-Catholics who are in material heresy, inspiring them to unite themselves to the body of the true Church.

Moreover, the Pope recognizes that people who were born and
reared in heresy, who are in good faith and perhaps in the grace of God,
may still have to wait a while before a sufficient grace is given to them
to make the difficult change from the religion of their childhood to that

from which their ancestors had withdrawn. For after multiplying motives for the Anglicans to return to the Church and declaring now "ardently We desire …. their reconciliation," the Pope is forced to conclude that, "In the meantime, by the tender mercy of the Lord our God, We ask and beseech all to strive faithfully to follow in the open path of Divine grace and truth."[125] True, they are not actual members of the Church of Christ, but they are members *in voto*, if, as is supposed, they sincerely wish to carry out the entire will of God. Eventually, however, in the Lord's own time, and if they are faithful to the graces which they presently receive, they may come to understand that the will of God also includes the necessity of open profession of the Roman Catholic Faith.

CHAPTER IV

BENEDICT XV, 1914 — 1922

I. DOCTRINE OF BENEDICT XV, REGARDING NON-CATHOLICS IN THEIR RELATION TO THE CHURCH, AS EMBODIED IN THE CODE OF CANON LAW

Statement of Canon Law:

The Code of Canon Law, which formally took effect on Pentecost Sunday, 1918, is the most important document of the Holy See, issued during the Pontificate of Benedict XV, which touches directly on the question of non-Catholics in their relation to the true Church. In order to appreciate how truly the Code of Canon Law represents the mind of the Holy See and of Benedict XV as the Vicar of Christ, we quote from the Apostolic Constitution which he published in 1917, in which the Codex was first presented to the Catholic world. "Having called upon the help of God," he declares, "resting on the authority of the Holy Apostles Peter and Paul, We, of Our own initiative, in the sure knowledge and in the fullness of the Apostolic power which We possess, do, by this Our Constitution, promulgate the present Code, which We desire to be perpetually valued even as it has been composed, We decree that after this it should have the force of law for the universal Church, We command and transmit (the same) to be preserved by your vigilance and care."[126]

Specifically, four Canons of the Codex deal directly with the subject under investigation: Canon 87, which introduces Section II, *De Personis*, and Canons 1322 and 1325, which introduce Section IV, *De Magisterio Ecclesiastico*.

Canon 87 reads: "Through Baptism, a human being is constituted a person in the Church of Christ, with all the rights and duties of Christians, unless, as regards rights, an obstacle stands in the way, which impairs the bond of ecclesiastical communion, or a censure imposed by the Church."[127]

Canons 1322 to 1325, in the paragraphs which pertain to our subject, read:

1322, #1: "Christ the Lord entrusted the deposit of faith to the Church, that she, with the assistance of the Holy Ghost, might preserve the revealed doctrine in holiness and declare it with fidelity."

#2: "To the Church, independently of any civil power, belongs the right and the duty to teach the doctrine of the Gospel to all nations; all are obliged by Divine Law duly to learn this (doctrine) and to embrace the true Church of God."[128]

1323, #1: "All those things are to be believed with Divine and Catholic faith which are contained in the word of God, written or handed down, and which the Church, either by a solemn judgment, or by her ordinary and universal magisterium, proposes for belief as having been divinely revealed."[129]

1325, #1: "The faithful are obliged openly to profess the faith of Christ as often as their silence, evasion, or manner of acting would implicitly amount to a denial of the faith, contempt of religion, an offense to God, or scandal to the neighbor."

#2: "Anyone who, after receiving Baptism, while remaining nominally a Christian, pertinaciously denies or doubts any of the truths which must be believed with Divine and Catholic faith, is a heretic; if he falls away entirely from the Christian faith, he is an apostate; finally, if he rejects the authority of the Supreme Pontiff, or refuses communion with the members of the Church who are subject to him, he is a schismatic."[130]

Doctrine of the Canon Law Explained:

CANON 87

On examining Canon 87, we first notice that the term "Baptism" is used without qualification, which means that Baptism, simply, that is, Baptism of water or the Sacrament of Baptism, is meant. For, as Canon 18 declares, "Ecclesiastical laws are to be understood according to the proper meaning of the words" in which they are expressed.[131] Consequently, it is only by valid, sacramental Baptism of water, or *in re*, that a human being is constituted a person in the Church of Christ.

"Human being", *homo* is used generically for men and women.

"is constituted," may be equated with, *"becoming that which he previously was not."*

"person" is a technical term which bears some explanation because nowhere in these Canons does the word *"member"* appear. Now although the two may be identified still, where *"member"* is properly the correlative to a living organism, as *part* is correlative to *whole*, "*person*" is rather a juridical term which describes a human being as an individual unit in a larger society; here, the society founded by Christ which is His Church, of which He said, "Thou art Peter, and upon this rock I will build My Church." Mat. 16-18. But more than merely a unit is the society, "person" also means "the subject of duties and rights," and here, "of all the duties and rights of Christians." For it is of faith that all the obligations of a Christian are contracted by the reception of Baptism, as declared by the Council of Trent: "If anyone says that those who are baptized are freed from all the precepts of Holy Church, which are either written or handed down, so that they are not obliged to observe them unless they spontaneously wish to submit to them, let him be anathema."[132]

What should be specially pointed out is that Canon 87 makes no exception or limitation, *per se*, to the duties incumbent on those who have once entered the Church by Baptism. Consequently they are applicable also to those who have been baptized into a Protestant sect, unless, as in a few cases like the form of marriage, they are clearly exempt from the common obligations which are binding on all Christians."[133]

On the other hand, there can be a limitation in the *rights* which a baptized person may enjoy. Since, as rights, they are properly connected with a person as an individual, they can be either not all acquired in the first place, or, once acquired, they can be lost, depending on whether or not a person places any obstacles "which impede communion with the Church."

These obstacles may be placed either before or after Baptism. Before Baptism, such an obstacle would be the absence of the true faith, as happens in the case of adults who are knowingly and of set purpose baptized into a heretical sect. However, even in this instance, as long as the Baptism is valid, at least one of the rights of a Christian is acquired, namely, the right to receive the other Sacraments, "*sub debitis conditionibus*", which implies "*obice remoto.*"[134]

Also subsequent to Baptism, many, if not all, of the rights already received, may be lost. This may happen either because the baptized person has voluntarily withdrawn from Catholic unity through apostasy, heresy or schism; or because he has been removed from communion with the faithful by formal excommunication, or even because some minor censure, like suspension, has deprived him of some of the privileges which other Catholics in good standing may still enjoy.[135]

CANON 1322

Paragraph #1 is self explanatory, except to note that it is at least suggestive of one of the propositions of the Modernists, *condemned by Pius X* in the Decree *Lamentabili*, stating that: "Revelation, constituting the object of Catholic faith, was not completed with the Apostles."[136] Historically, it should be recalled that one of the efforts of Modernism was to incorporate every sect in Christianity into the Church of Christ, and, consequently, even so-called heretics are true members of the Church. For, said the Modernists, "the universal rule" of rectitude for a Christian is that he follows his own "religious conscience". If we may speak of a Church of Christ at all, its membership is composed of those who are faithful to this mysterious religious conscience which, according to the Modernists, is "to be perfectly equated with Revelation itself, and to which all must submit themselves, not excluding even the authority of the Church."[137]

Paragraph #2 inculcates the necessity of knowing and entering the one, true, visible Church of Christ. This again is a paraphrase on a chapter from the Dogmatic Constitution, *De Fide Catholica,* of the Vatican Council, which reads: "Since without faith it is impossible to please God, Heb. 11-6, and to attain to the fellowship of His children, therefore, without faith no one has ever attained justification, nor will anyone attain eternal life, unless he shall have persevered in faith unto the end. Mat. 10-22, 24-13. And that we may be able to satisfy the obligation of embracing the true faith and of constantly persevering in it, God instituted the Church through His only-begotten Son, and has bestowed on it manifest notes of that institution that it may be recognized by all as the guardian and teacher of the revealed Word."[138]

Evidently, the Church to which the Vatican Council and Canon Law refer is the visible, corporate body of the Roman Catholic communion so that membership in *this* body is declared to be necessary for salvation.

CANON 1323

Paragraph #1 gives us the norm for determining who are members of the Catholic Church and who are not, on the score of what they believe. Two elements are declared to make up the content of "those things which are to be believed with Divine and Catholic faith", namely:

1. What is contained in the word of God, written or handed down, and
2. Which the Church, either by a solemn definition, or by her ordinary and universal magisterium, proposes for belief as having been Divinely revealed.

CANON 1325

Paragraph #1 states that all the faithful are obliged by Divine Law not only to believe in the true faith interiorly, but also to profess the same exteriorly. The obligation may arise from any one or all of four different sources, that is, whenever *mere* internal faith without its external expression would be:

- An implicit denial of the faith because, under the circumstances, no other interpretation could be taken from the person's refusal to make an external profession.
- Contempt of religion, as though the faith were not objectively true.
- An offense to God, for, as St. Thomas says, "The end of faith, as of the other virtues, should be referred to the end of charity, which is the love of God and of neighbor; and therefore, when the honor of God or the benefit of the neighbor requires, a man cannot be satisfied with being (personally) united by faith to the Divine Truth, but he must confess his faith externally."[139]
- The scandal of the neighbor, as, for example, when others would be turned away from the faith by witnessing the silence of someone who is supposed to be a believer.

Paragraph #2 is the most pertinent to our problem because on its basis are separated from membership in the Church three classes of people, according to three kinds of defection of which they may be guilty. Assuming that a person has been baptized and even retains the Christian name, he is nevertheless not a Catholic, but:

1. A heretic, if he pertinaciously despises or doubts any of the truths which must be believed with Divine Catholic faith.
2. An apostate, if he completely gives up the Christian religion.
3. A schismatic, if he refuses to submit to the Supreme Pontiff, or if he refuses to associate with the members of the Church who are subject to the Vicar of Christ.

Only the first part of this program interests us here, namely, that a heretic is declared to be a baptized person who pertinaciously denies or doubts one or another article of the Catholic faith. Two questions are in order:

• Does *baptized* person here mean only one who received the Sacrament in the Catholic Church and subsequently lost his faith through heresy, or does it mean that anyone who has been validly baptized, whether in or outside the true Church? The latter is the accepted and common interpretation of canonists.[140]

• Does the term *pertinaciously* also imply, *in mala fide*, so that, according to the Canon, a heretic is only one who *culpably* denies or doubts a revealed doctrine of the true faith ? No, not necessarily, because while it is true that a Catholic, for example, who, in bad faith denies even one of the truths proposed by the Church as revealed, automatically falls into a formal heresy and is excommunicated from the Church; yet, also a non-Catholic who pertinaciously, albeit in good faith, refuses to submit to the Church's magisterium because he denies its objective validity — such a person also comes under the scope of this canon and is therefore cut off from actual membership in the Church of Christ.[141]

II.   COMPARISON BETWEEN BELLARMINE AND CANON LAW, ON THE MEMBERSHIP OF NON-CATHOLICS IN THE CATHOLIC CHURCH

Regarding Baptism as a Condition For Membership

Canon Law perfectly vindicates Bellarmine's doctrine, which is traditional, that although three kinds of Baptism are possible (of water, blood and martyrdom), and all three confer Sanctifying Grace, only Baptism of water can incorporate a person as a real member of the visible body of the Catholic Church.[142]

However, there is one aspect of this doctrine in which Canon Law seems to differ from St. Robert, notably, his reputed teaching on invalid and putative Baptism.[143] When dealing with the subject of occult infidels and heretics as possible members of the Church, which he defends, the objection is raised that, "The strongest argument for including occult heretics as members of the Church seems to be in order to tell us infallibly which assembly of men constitutes the Church. But this certainty cannot be had even if occult heretics are said to pertain to the Church." One reason is that, "Those who are not baptized are not members of the Church. But no one knows for certain what persons are truly baptized, because "The baptismal character is invisible", and because, "When the exterior Baptism is performed, very few people are present, so that everyone else must be satisfied with only human testimony" that the Baptism actually took place.

To which Bellarmine answers: For anyone to belong to the body of the Church, the (baptismal) character is not necessary, but only external Baptism. In fact, not even external Baptism but only admission into the Church is required for anyone to be considered as belonging to and to be in the Church. For if a person asks to be admitted to the Church, this will not happen without Baptism. However, if someone should say that he is baptized and there is no evidence to the contrary, he may be admitted

to the other Sacraments and by this token he will be in the body of the Church. The reason is that if later on it should be discovered that he was not baptized, and that through his own fault, he will be expelled from the assembly (of the faithful), and will not be taken back until, after doing penance, he has been baptized. But if it was not his own fault, he will not be expelled, but will receive what he still needs, nor will he be considered as not having (previously) been in the Church, but only that he entered it by another than by the ordinary door. Thus Innocent III (II), in his letter, *Apostolicam Sedem*, on the unbaptized priest, decided that ....
he was truly in the Church, and ordered the Sacrifice to be offered for his soul as for the other faithful.[144] Also, Dionysius of Alexandria concluded that a certain individual was truly in the Church when it was clear that he had never been really baptized, but only that he had been receiving the other Sacraments as though he were baptized."[145]

Apparently, what Bellarmine seems to favor here as a possible exception to the general law that Baptism is absolutely necessary to enter the Church, is that, either:

- Invalid Baptism, where merely the external rite has been performed but no character was received, or
- Even putative Baptism, without the external rite, may suffice under certain circumstances for incorporation into the body of the true Church.

However, on examination, we find that Bellarmine definitely did *not* favor this doctrine. For he says, after stating what was quoted above, "This seems to have been the opinion of John Driedo in *De Scripturis et Dogmatibus Ecclesiasticis*, where he speaks as follows: 'All those who have somehow lived peaceably among the body of the Christian people are said to be in the Church, having been visibly inscribed in the Church through the sacrament of faith, until they are either judicially separated from the Church, or leave of their own accord by their contempt and persecution of the Church.'[146] So *he* says very clearly according to *him*, not only all the baptized are in the Church but also all those who are considered to have been baptized. However, we can also answer (to the original objection), and *more correctly*, that those who are not but who are regarded as having been baptized, are in the Church only in *external appearance*, that is, *putatively* and *not truly*. Nor does it follow as a consequence that the Church becomes invisible. For even though one or the other person cannot prove that he has been baptized, the majority can do so, and Baptism by its very nature is something visible."[147]

To conclude therefore, while Bellarmine at least speculates — although unfavorably — on the opinion that non-baptized persons who ostensibly live as Catholics are members of the true Church, Canon Law does not make even this concession. Baptism, which, as was noted, means real, valid, sacramental Baptism, is absolutely necessary for entrance into the visible Church of Christ. Invalid and putative Baptism would only give what Bellarmine properly calls a putative membership which, in the presence of good faith, would be identified with *voto* membership in the Catholic Church.

Regarding the Definition of Heresy

In the light of Canon 1325, which gives us the Church's official definition of heresy, the following comparison between Bellarmine's doctrine and that of Canon Law on the nature of heresy, will help to explain why St. Robert would exclude even material heretics from membership in the Catholic Church.

As often as he treats the subject of heretics, Bellarmine never considers them as belonging to the visible Church.[148] However, this by itself would not prove very much unless we also knew the reason why they are excluded. The reason, ultimately, is because they do not profess the true faith, but confess instead some other kind of Christian belief. Thus:

> "Alphonsus de Castro….teaches that heretics are members and parts of the Church, even though they *openly profess a false doctrine*. This opinion is evidently false."[149]

> "Since the Church is a united multitude…and this union consists especially in the *profession of one faith*, and in the observance of the same laws and rites, it is impossible, rationally, to say that people (that is, heretics and apostates of whom he is treating) who have no association with the body of the Church, nevertheless belong to it."[150]

"There are three parts to this definition of the Church:
- profession of the true faith,
- communion of the Sacraments and
- subjection to the legitimate pastor, the Roman Pontiff.

By reason of the first part are excluded….heretics and apostates."[151]

Against George Cassander, who defended the thesis that "To belong to the true Church it is necessary only to have faith in Christ and to live peaceably among men," Bellarmine argued that this was another version of the invisible church of the Protestants. For Cassander deduced from his principles that "Those who are hostile to Catholics

and Lutherans do not belong to the Church. Consequently, those who
are in the Church can only be invisible members, who in the company
of Catholics pretend to be enemies of the Lutherans and with Lutherans pretend to be opposed to the Catholics. For Catholics do not allow
anyone to remain in their fold, who by any *external sign* shows himself
to be favorable to the Lutherans. And among Lutherans, too, although
many different sects are permitted in one province, yet no single sect
allows anyone to remain in its company who is friendly with other religious groups. These good and peaceable men, therefore, must needs
all be hypocrites and liars, professing one thing with their lips and
concealing another conviction in their heart, followers of Herod who,
with the pagans was a pagan and with the Jews a Jew, for, as Josephus
relates, he erected temples to honor Caesar and at the same time to
honor the true God."[152]

Against the objection that "The foundation and, as it were, the form
of the Church is faith, since we read: 'As a wise builder, I laid the foundation... For other foundation no one can lay, but that which has been
laid, which is Christ Jesus.' I Cor. 3-10-11. And again: 'You are built
upon the foundation of the Apostles and prophets with Christ Jesus Himself as the chief corner stone.' Eph. 2-20. And: 'One God, one faith, one
Baptism.'" Eph. 4-6. --- Bellarmine answered: "The form of the Church
is not internal faith, unless we wish to have an invisible Church, but
external, that is, the confession of faith. Augustine very clearly teaches
this in his 19th book, *Contra Faustum*, Chapter 11, and the same is confirmed by experience. For those are admitted to the Church who *profess*
the faith. In the texts cited, faith is not said to be the form or foundation
of the Church, but rather the foundation of the justice or doctrine which
is in the Church. Moreover, the Scriptures speak in the same way about
charity and all the gifts of the Holy Spirit in the Church, as they do about
faith, and yet no Catholic teaches that those who lack charity or the gifts
of the Holy Ghost do not belong to the true Church."[153]

Coming back to the original question of how Bellarmine would define heresy, we see that, according to him, no matter what other quali-
fications a baptized person may have, as long as he professes any other
religion than the Catholic, he is a heretic, and, as such, is actually outside the communion of the one true Church.

This is confirmed by the first paragraph of Canon 1325, where the
necessity of professing the true faith externally is laid down as an in-
junction on all Catholics. Thus, "the faithful," who canonically are Catholics, "are obliged to make an open profession of the faith of Christ,"
at least at certain times. The supposition is that a Catholic will have oc-

casion to make such a profession. But, then, what about the non-Catholic who, although sincerely, yet quite openly, not only does not profess the Catholic religion but who consistently professes what is objectively heresy, especially refusing to acknowledge the Church's official magisterium ? Evidently, he does not meet even the minimum requirement of the "fideles," which is at least occasional, formal profession of the true faith. Consequently, he cannot be considered an actual member of the visible Church, whether dogmatically, on Bellarmine's principles, or juridically, according to Canon Law.

CHAPTER V

PIUS XII, 1939 TO THE PRESENT [Editor's Note: 1950]

I. DEFINITION OF THE CHURCH AND CONDITIONS FOR MEMBERSHIP

Doctrine of Pius XII

The ecclesiological doctrine of Pius XII is practically synthesized in his great Encyclical, *Mystici Corporis Christi*, issued in 1943. On analysis, we shall see that it represents a most comprehensive approval, from the highest authority in the Church, of Bellarmine's teaching on the relation of sincere non-Catholics to the visible Church of Christ.

Recalling Bellarmine's three-fold condition for membership in the true Church, we read in the *Mystici Corporis*, that "Only those are *really* to be included as members of the Church:

- Who have been baptized and profess the true faith, and
- Who have not unhappily withdrawn from Body-unity, or
- (Who) for grave faults have been excluded by legitimate authority.

" 'For in one spirit,' says the Apostle, 'were we all baptized into one Body, whether Jews or Gentiles, whether bond or free.' I Cor. 12/13. As, therefore, in the true Christian community there is only one Body, one Spirit, one Lord, and one Baptism, so there can be only one Faith. And so, if a man refuse to hear the Church, let him be considered — so the Lord commands — as a heathen and a publican. It follows that those who are divided in faith or government cannot be living in one Body such as this, and cannot be living the life of its one Divine Spirit."[154]

Doctrine of Pius XII Compared With Bellarmine

If there is any difference between Pius XII and St. Robert in defining membership in the Church, it consists in Bellarmine's going on to explain the various types of people who are outside the Church, where the Pope is satisfied with describing the status of those who are in the Church. Thus:

- If a person has not yet received Baptism, Bellarmine calls him an infidel or a catechumen.
- If he does not *"profess the true faith,"* he is either a heretic or an apostate, supposing that he has been baptized.
- If he has *"unhappily withdrawn from body-unity,"* and is *"divided from the Church in government,"* he is a schismatic.
- If for *"grave faults"* he has been *"excluded by legitimate authority,"* he is, in Bellarmine's vocabulary, an excommunicate.

What is most significant, however, is that Pius XII, like Bellarmine, describes a person who meets all the requirements previously quoted, as being really (*reapse*) a member of the true Church. Later in the Encyclical, the Holy Father will dwell more at length on the meaning of *reapse* in contradistinction to *voto*. Here it is enough to point out that Bellarmine's classic distinction, *re* or *voto*, has received in the *Mystici Corporis* the formal approval of the Holy See. Relative to the subject we are investigating, it is seen that Pius XII, practically using Bellarmine's terminology, would exclude from *real* membership in the Church, *all* the unbaptized, even though they are in good faith and possibly in the grace of God, and *all* who are divided from the Church in faith, as are heretics, even though again they are only in material heresy, and are not personally responsible for the condition which they are in.

II. IDENTIFICATION OF THE CATHOLIC CHURCH WITH THE MYSTICAL BODY OF CHRIST

Doctrine of Pius XII

While the Church of Christ has been identified with His Mystical Body already in St. Paul, and the doctrine of their identity is the common tradition of the Catholic faith, Pius XII emphasized and clarified this identification in a way that had not been done before. Thus he says: In the opening sentence of the Encyclical, "We first learned of the Mystical Body, which is the Church, from the lips of the Redeemer Himself."[155]

"If we would define and describe this true Church of Jesus Christ — which is the One, Holy, Catholic, Apostolic, Roman Church — we shall find no expression more noble, more sublime or more divine than the phrase which calls it 'the Mystical Body of Jesus Christ.' This title is derived from and is, as it were, the fair flower of the repeated teaching of Sacred Scripture and the Holy Fathers."[156]

"It was on the tree of the Cross....that He (Christ) entered into possession of His Church, that is, all the members of His Mystical Body; for they would not have been united to this Mystical Body through the waters of Baptism except by the salutary virtue of the

Cross, by which they had been already brought under the complete sway of Christ."[157]

And in the closing prayer of the Encyclical, speaking of the Mother of God, "She who corporally was the Mother of our Head, through the added title of pain and glory, because spiritually the Mother of all His members... Bearing with courage and confidence the tremendous burden of her sorrows and desolation, truly the Queen of Martyrs, she more than all the faithful "filled up those things that are wanting of the sufferings of Christ ... for His Body, which is the Church"; Col. 1-24, and she continued to show for the Mystical Body of Christ, born from the pierced Heart of the Savior, the same mother's care and ardent love with which she clasped the infant Jesus to her warm and nourishing breast."[158]

Doctrine of Pius XII Compared with Bellarmine

Bellarmine, no less than Pius XII, defines the Catholic Church as the Mystical Body of Christ. "The Church," he says, "is a certain integral and most beautiful Body, of which Christ, the God-Man, is the Head."[159]

Again, in commenting on the text of St. Paul, "For we, being many, are one bread, one Body," I Cor. 10-17, says that, "The similarity between the bread and the Church consists in this...that just as out of many grains (of wheat) through the use of water, there is one bread, so out of many men, through the waters of Baptism, or the Holy Spirit .... there is one people; because no one is in the Church who is not baptized, and does not participate in some gift of the Holy Spirit, internal or external."[160]

In arguing against Wyclif and the Calvinists, who said that, "The Mystical Body (of Christ) is like to a physical body. But the entire physical body of Christ with all its parts was saved and glorified. Therefore also the Mystical Body should be saved in all its parts and members"; Bellarmine answered that, "it can be proved from the parables of the Gospel that not only the predestined but also the reprobate belong to the Church." After disposing of the proofs from Scripture, he answers the objection: "The physical body of Christ was saved in all its formal constituents, but not in all its material parts... Even so, the Mystical Body will be saved in all its constituent elements — apostles, prophets, teachers, confessors — will be represented among the saved. It is not true, however, that all its material elements, that is, every numerical member of the Mystical Body, will finally attain to salvation."[161]

In defending the doctrine of the Real Presence, St. Robert has occasion to refute one of the Protestant theories which identified the Holy

Eucharist with the Mystical Body of Christ. "The adversaries," he writes, "explain the word *Body* (in the formula of institution), in three different ways. Some say that by this word is meant the Mystical Body of Christ … But this first explanation is impossible, there is no basis whatever for defending it, and it clearly contradicts the words which follow, namely, 'Which is given for you.' For it was not the Mystical but the true Body (of Christ) that was sacrificed for us. Even more directly does it contradict the words which are spoken in the consecration of the chalice; in as much as the Church, that is, the Mystical Body of Christ, cannot be called the chalice of blood, or of the Covenant; nor is it poured out for us unto the remission of sins."[162]

So clearly and consistently does Bellarmine identify the Roman Catholic Church with the Mystical Body of Christ, that even the Encyclical *Mystici Corporis* takes cognizance of the fact.[163] "As Bellarmine notes with acumen and accuracy," the Pope says, "this naming of the Body of Christ is not to be explained solely by the fact that Christ must be called the Head of His Mystical Body, but also by the fact that He so sustains the Church, and so in a certain sense lives in the Church that it is, as it were, another Christ." The context in Bellarmine occurs in his defense of the Roman Primacy, in answer to the objection of the Sectarians call that, "Nowhere (in Scripture) is the Church ever called the body of Peter, or of the Pope, but of Christ." St. Robert explains that, "The reason for this is that only Christ is the principal and perpetual Head of the Church. For just as a kingdom is not said to belong to the vice-regent, but to the king, and a home is not called the overseer's but the owner's, so the Church is not the body of Peter, or of the Pope, who governs only for a time and in someone else's place, but of Christ, Who rules it perpetually and by His own authority."

"Moreover, when the Church is called the Body of Christ, the word 'of Christ' can be properly referred not so much to Christ as the Head, as to the same Christ understood as the 'Hypostasis of His Body'; just as when we say, for example, that, 'There lies the body of Peter, there the body of Paul', we do not mean that Peter or Paul are the bodies but that they are the persons whose bodies these are. For Christ is not only the Head of the Church, but is Himself, as it were, a kind of great Body, composed of many and various members. St. Augustine makes reference to this[164] … when he points out that the Apostle, when he says, 'For as the body is one, and hath many members, and all the members of the body, whereas they are many, yet are one body,' does not add, 'so also is the Body of Christ,' but says, 'so also is Christ.' I Cor. 12-12. The Church is, therefore, the Body of Christ, and not of Peter, because

Christ, like as it were the *hypostasis* of this Body, sustains all the members, and operates all things in all."[165]

The importance of emphasizing this identification between the Catholic Church and the Mystical Body, as made by Bellarmine and Pius XII, consists in the danger of extending the Mystical Body not merely out of this world to include the saints in heaven and the souls in purgatory — which is perfectly legitimate — but of extending its membership on earth beyond the visible limitations of the Roman Catholic Church — which is contrary to Christian tradition.[166]

III. THE BODY AND SOUL OF THE CHURCH

Doctrine of Pius XII

Ultimately and logically, those who would extend the Mystical Body on earth beyond the visible limits of Roman Catholicism, must define the Mystical Body — or the Church — otherwise than as something visible. Against this heresy, which echoes the invisible Church of Luther and Calvin, Pius XII clearly distinguishes *within* the Mystical Body two elements, one visible and external, which he calls its *body*; the other invisible and internal, which he calls the *soul*.

The Body of the Church

"That the Church is a body," says the Holy Father, "is frequently asserted in Sacred Scripture. 'Christ,' says the Apostle, 'is the Head of the Body of the Church.'' Col. 1-18. If the Church is a body, it must be an unbroken unity according to those words of Paul, 'Though many, we are one body in Christ.' Rom. 12-5. But it is not enough that the Body of the Church be an unbroken unity; it must also be something definite and perceptible to the senses, as Our Predecessor of happy memory, Leo XIII, in his Encyclical *Satis Cognitum* asserts: 'The Church is visible because she is a Body.'[167] Hence they err in a matter of Divine truth, who imagine the Church to be invisible, intangible, a something merely 'pneumatological,' as they say, by which many Christian communities, though they differ from each other in their profession of faith, are united by a bond that eludes the senses."[168]

"Again, as in nature a body is not formed by any haphazard grouping of members but must be constituted of organs, that is, members that have not the same function and are arranged in due order; so for this reason above all the Church is called a body, that it is constituted by the coalescence of structurally united parts, and that it has a variety of members reciprocally dependent. It is thus the Apostle describes the Church when he writes: 'As in one body we have many members, but all the members have not the same office; so we being many are one body in Christ, and everyone members one of another.'" Rom. 12-4[169]

"Our union in and with Christ is first evident from the fact that, since Christ wishes His Christian community to be a Body which is a perfect society, its members must be united because they all work together towards a single end…. Now since this social Body of Christ has been designed by its Founder to be visible, this cooperation of all its members must also be externally manifest through their profession of the same faith, and their sharing the same sacred rites, through participation in the same sacrifice and practical observance of the same laws. Above all, every one must be able to see the Supreme Head, who gives effective direction to what all are doing in a mutually helpful way towards attaining the desired end, that is, the Vicar on earth of Jesus Christ."[170]

The Soul of the Church

But Pius XII acknowledges that the Catholic Church, like Christ Himself, is not only visible and external, but also and primarily invisible. Indeed, its invisible element, or soul, is what especially distinguishes the Body of Christ from all other human institutions. The very name, *Mystical*, "gives us to understand that the Church, a perfect society of its kind, is not made up of merely moral and juridical elements and principles," such as are implied in defining the body of the Church. "It is far superior to all other human societies… The juridical principles, on which also the Church rests and is established, derive from the Divine constitution given to it by Christ, and contribute to attaining its supernatural end; but what lifts the society of Christians far, far above the whole natural order is the Spirit of the Redeemer, Who until the end of time penetrates every part of the Church's being and is active within it. He is the source of every grace and every gift and every miraculous power. Just as our composite mortal body, for all its being a marvelous work of the Creator, falls far short of the eminent dignity of our soul, so the social structure of the Christian community, though eloquent of its Divine Architect's wisdom, remains still something inferior, when compared to the spiritual gifts which give it beauty and life, and to their Divine source."[171]

The Spirit of the Redeemer, the Paraclete Himself, therefore, is the soul of the Church. Previously the Pope had said that the body of the Church is the organic unity of the members of the Church, united in the profession of a common faith. But whence comes this unity? From the Holy Spirit Who dwells within the Body and the Soul. "To this Holy

Spirit," we are told, "as to an invisible principle, is to be ascribed the fact that all the parts of the Body are joined one with the other and with their exalted Head; for He is entire in the Head, entire in the Body and entire in each of the members. To the members He is present and assists them in proportion to their various tasks and offices and the greater or lesser grade of spiritual health which they enjoy. It is He who through His heavenly grace is the principle of every supernatural act in all parts of the Body. It is He who, while He is personally present and divinely active in all the members, also acts in the inferior members through the ministry of the higher members. Finally, while with His grace He provides for the constant growth of the Church, He yet refuses to dwell with sanctifying grace in members that are wholly severed from the Body. This presence and activity of the Spirit of Jesus Christ is tersely and vigorously described by Our Predecessor of immortal memory, Leo XIII, in his Encyclical Letter, *Divinum Illud*, in these words: 'Let it suffice to say, that, as Christ is the Head of the Church, so is the Holy Spirit her soul."[172]

Moreover, "if that vital principle by which the whole community of Christians is sustained by its Founder be considered now not in itself, but in its created effects, it consists in those heavenly gifts which our Redeemer together with His Spirit bestows on the Church and which He and His Spirit, from whom come supernatural light and holiness, make operative in the Church."[173]

Comparison Between Bellarmine and Pius XII

Bellarmine Vindicated in His Concept of the Body of the Church

According to Bellarmine, the body of the Church which, reduplicatively, would be the body of the Mystical Body of Christ, is the common external profession of the true faith by all those who belong to the Church of Christ. This, on inspection, is seen to be also the teaching of Pius XII.

The concept of the body of the Church is described by Pius XII under two aspects or forms, the one physical and concrete, the other metaphysical and abstract. Conceived under its concrete aspect, the Holy Father declares that the Roman Catholic Church, which is the Mystical Body of Christ on earth, is a body, because of:
1. its unbroken and organic *unity,* and
2. its perceptible and definite *visibility.*

In other words, in answer to the question: What is the body of the Church, concretely considered? — the Encyclical says: The body of the

Church are its human members, visibly and hierarchically united in the prosecution of a common supernatural end.

Metaphysically, however, it is not enough to say that the body of the Church are its visible members, joined together in an organic unity. We must further inquire: What precisely causes the members of the Church to be thus visibly and hierarchically united? Which is the same as asking: What is the element or essence which formally constitutes the body of the Church? And then the answer is seen to square perfectly with the doctrine of Robert Bellarmine, according to whom, "The form of the Church...is not internal but external faith, that is, the confession of faith."[174]

"That the Church is a body," says Pius XII, "is frequently asserted in Sacred Scripture... If the Church is a body, it must be an unbroken unity; it must also be something definite and perceptible to the senses." So far, describing the *physical* essence of the body of the Church; then he continues: "Hence they err in a matter of Divine truth who imagine the Church to be invisible, intangible, a something merely 'pneumato-logical', as they say, by which many Christian communities, though they differ from each other *in their profession of faith*, are united by a bond that eludes the senses."[175]

However, we remember that Bellarmine does not restrict the concept of profession of faith as the form of the Church's body, to mere expression of belief in the doctrines of the Creed. It is really a combination of three kinds of external profession namely, of belief in the true faith, communication in the same Sacraments, and submission to the Roman Pontiff. This again is also the doctrine of Pius XII. "Since this social Body of Christ has been designed by its Founder to be visible, this cooperation of all its members must also be externally manifest through their profession of the same faith, and their sharing the same sacred rites, through participation in the same sacrifice and practical observance of the same laws. Above all, everyone must be able to see the Supreme Head, who gives effective direction to what all are doing in a mutually helpful way towards attaining the desired end, that is, the Vicar on Earth of Jesus Christ."[176]

Bellarmine Vindicated in His Concept of the Soul of the Church

According to St. Robert, the soul of the Church is at once the Holy Spirit and the gifts of the Spirit; that is, the Spirit of Christ as infusing the created gifts of His grace. This is substantially the doctrine of the *Mystici Corporis*. However, there are several points in which, while Pius XII confirms Bellarmine, the confirmation is not immediately

clear. Moreover, they are exactly the points which are specially pertinent to our problem: the *membership* of non-Catholics in the Roman
Catholic Church. Hence the following analysis:

1. According to Pius XII, "To this Spirit of Christ... as to an invisible prin-
    ciple, is to be ascribed the fact that all the parts of the Body are joined
    one with the other and with their exalted Head."[177] But if, as Bellarmine
    admits, catechumens and other non-Catholics in good faith, belong to the
    soul of the Church, do they not also belong to the body — taking body
    here as the correlative of the soul of the Church? Yes, they must: other-
    wise how explain the statement of the Pope that the Spirit of Christ unites
    the various parts of the body? For the present, we are not interested in
    examining in what sense these people belong to the body of the Church.
    But we do ask: in what sense are they in the soul of the Church. Are we
    to say, as some have defended,[178] that non-Catholics *in bona fide* belong
    to the soul of the Church, Who is the Holy Ghost with His gifts, and yet
    not to the Holy Ghost as the soul of the Church? In other words, are we
    to conceive the Holy Spirit as operating separately and independently
    of the *body* of the Church on certain people, as non-Catholics, but on
    other people within and in virtue of their membership in the body of the
    Church, as on all professed Catholics ? Such bifurcation of the functions
    of the Spirit of Christ cannot be squared either with Bellarmine's prin-
    ciples or with the doctrine of Pius XII.

2. This conclusion is confirmed by a further statement of the Holy Father.
    Speaking of the Holy Ghost as the soul of the Church, he says that, "While
    with His grace He provides for the constant growth of the Church, He yet
    refuses to dwell with sanctifying grace in members that are *wholly* severed
    from the body."[179]

    Two items here are specially to be noted:

    •   The Pope declares that the Holy Spirit provides, with His grace,
        for the constant growth of the Church. In context, this can only
        mean the outpouring of actual graces into the hearts of men, with
        a view to either increasing sanctifying grace in their souls, or
        leading them to receive the state of grace, if they never had it, or
        lost it through sin.

    •   Then by way of a qualifying adversative, the Pope adds, "*However*,"
        that is, granting that actual graces are given to *all* men, "He (the Spirit
        of Christ) refuses to dwell with sanctifying grace in members that are
        wholly severed from the body." Which means that, given a person
        who has *no* connection with the body of the Church, while he will be
        receiving actual graces, he will never obtain sanctifying grace. This
        latter gift is reserved for those who *somehow* at least belong to the
        visible communion of the Church of Christ, *by some kind* of external
        profession of the true faith.

3.   A point of clarification is in place regarding Bellarmine's position that even
     the gift of faith, minus charity, is enough to constitute a person in the soul
     of the Church — assuming that he has some sort of union with the body.
     There is no difficulty in reconciling this doctrine with that of the *Mys-
     tici Corporia*. For speaking of the Holy Ghost, the Pope says that, "To
     the members He is present and assists them in proportion to their various
     tasks and offices and the greater or less grade of spiritual health which
     they enjoy. It is He who through His heavenly grace is the principle of
     every supernatural act in all parts of the body."[180] Consequently, as long
     as some nexus is retained with the body, even though a person's "spiritual
     health" may be at its lowest, short of extinction, in having only the gift
     of faith, — still the Holy Ghost assists such a person in a special way, so
     that the individual should be considered as really belonging to the soul of
     the Church. One qualification on Bellarmine's minimum requirement for
     membership in the soul of the Church is suggested by the following words
     of the Holy Father: "Men may lose charity and divine grace through sin
     and so become incapable of supernatural merit, and yet not be deprived of
     all life, if they hold on to faith and Christian hope."[181] This means to square
     ill with the words of Bellarmine, that there are some members of the body
     of the Church whose membership is so tenuous that, as far as their life in
     the Church is concerned, "they have only faith, without charity."[182] Both
     Bellarmine and the Pope are speaking of minimum membership in the soul
     of the Church. Yet, where Bellarmine conceives it as consisting in the pos-
     session of only faith, the Holy Father seems to say it includes not only faith
     but also hope. Two possible ways of reconciling the apparent contradiction
     suggest themselves:

     •   When the Pope says that a person is not deprived of all life in the Mys-
         tical Body, as long as he retains faith *and* Christian hope, he is speak-
         ing of the *normal* situation, where a person is in the state of sin, and
         therefore deprived of charity, but who has not formally sinned against
         the virtue of hope, and consequently still retains this gift along with
         faith, as an infused supernatural habit in the soul.

     •   When Bellarmine says that some people are so tenuously united to the
         soul of the Church that they have nothing left but faith, he does not
         mean to exclude the virtue of hope, which again, *normally*, is present
         along with faith even when charity has been lost. But in the last analy-
         sis, given a person who has *only* faith left in him as an infused habit,
         still even this is sufficient to qualify him for membership in the soul of
         the Church.[183]

4.   Bellarmine has been criticized[184] for the two aspects under which he
     views the soul of the Church: once as the uncreated Spirit of Christ Him-
     self, and again as His created gifts. But that is precisely what the *Mystici
     Corporis* has done. First, the Pope says, quoting Leo XIII, "Let it suffice
     to say that as Christ is the Head of the Church, so is the Holy Spirit her

soul."[185] Then he says, "If that vital principle by which the whole community of Christians is sustained by its Founder be considered now not in *itself*, but in it's *created effects*, it consists in those *heavenly gifts* which our Redeemer together with His Spirit bestows on the Church and which He and His Spirit, from whom come supernatural light and holiness, make operative in the Church. The Church, then, no less than each of her holy members, can make this thought of the Apostle her own: 'And I live now, now not I; but Christ liveth in me.'" Gal. 2-20.[186] Which means that:

- If the Holy Spirit is considered in Himself as "the vital principle by which the whole community of Christians is sustained" supernaturally, then *He personally* is the soul of the Church.[187]

- But if we consider the same vital principle "now not in itself, but in its created effects," then, not the Holy Spirit Himself, but the "heavenly gifts" of *His grace* are properly the soul of the Church.

5. We recall that Bellarmine considered at least the possibility of a person belonging *only* to the body of the Church, without also belonging to the soul.[188] Such would be a man who had no internal virtue at all, even no supernatural faith, but only externally professed the true faith. Does Pius XII vindicate such a possibility? Yes, at least negatively; and this for two reasons:

- When, in the Encyclical, the Pope describes the condition of sinners in the Catholic Church, he says that, "not every sin...is such as to sever a man automatically from the body of the Church, as does schism or heresy or apostasy. Men may lose charity and Divine grace through sin and so become incapable of supernatural merit, and yet not be deprived of all life, if they hold on to faith and Christian hope."[189] Consequently, as long as a person has faith and hope he is still an actual member of the Church. But, in context, this presupposes that he *also* externally professes the true faith, which, if he refuses to do, he falls into heresy, schism or apostasy, which automatically cuts him off from the true Church.

- Moreover, the sinner who has only faith and hope is, according to the principles of Pius XII, not only in the body but also in the soul of the Church. In the soul because he has at least the habit of faith; in the body because he professes the true faith. The Pope is silent on the further possibility, which is more theoretical than practical, of a person who has even lost his faith internally, but for some human motive or other, externally still professes to be a Catholic. Bellarmine allows that such a man may somehow belong to the Church, but only as a dead member, externally attached to the body of the Church. Pius XII prescinds from examining the case.

IV. RE AND VOTO MEMBERSHIP IN THE CHURCH OF CHRIST

"Re" Refers to the Visible Catholic Church

Doctrine of Pius XII

We have seen in a previous chapter that Bellarmine's distinction between *re* and *voto* membership in the visible Church was on the agenda
of the Vatican Council, but was never formally approved. Consequently,
the use of this distinction by Pius XII, specifically touching on non-
Catholics in good faith, is of capital importance in the "development of
Catholic ecclesiology."

Early in the Encyclical, the Holy Father declares that, "Only those
are *really* to be included as members of the Church who have been baptized and profess the true faith and who have not unhappily withdrawn
from body-unity, or for grave faults, have been excluded by legitimate
authority."[190]

Comparison of Bellarmine with Pius XII

Against the background of Bellarmine's principles, this definition of
a *real* member of the Catholic Church substantially approves and somewhat qualifies St. Robert's doctrine.

The reality in question refers to the one true Church of Christ. So
that, when the Pope, as Bellarmine, speaks of a *real* member of the Catholic Church, he means a real member of the corporate, visible Roman
Catholic communion, and nothing else. Four terms which the Holy Father uses show that this is what he meant:

- He says that a real member must be baptized, which means that he
  must have received the Sacrament of Initiation into the visible communion of the Church, or, as the Council of Florence expresses it:
  "Holy Baptism holds the first place among all the Sacraments, which
  is the door of the spiritual life; through it we are made members of
  Christ and of the body of the Church."[191]

- A real member of the Church must profess the true faith. Now it is
  precisely this profession of the true faith which, in Bellarmine's terminology, constitutes the essence of membership in the visible Church of
  Christ.

- A person who has been baptized remains a real member of the Church,
  until he withdraws from bodily-unity, obviously through heresy,
  schism or apostasy.

- Also, a person who has been baptized may be excluded from the
  Church by legitimate authority for certain grave faults.

However, the Pope would not allow, as Bellarmine does, that a person may be excluded from the community of the faithful by excommunication, even though he is innocent of the crime attributed to him. We remember how St. Robert explains the possible salvation of a man who was unjustly excommunicated, saying that, although he is not a real member of the Church, yet Divine grace will not be wanting to him, provided he does not rebel against ecclesiastical authority.[192] But here the Pope, following Canon Law,[193] makes it clear that there must have been a grave fault committed before real excommunication from the Church can take objective effect.

Non-Catholics as *Voto* Members of the Catholic Church

Doctrine of Pius XII

The substance of the teaching of Pius XII on the relation of non-Catholics to the true Church is summarized in his eloquent appeal to these "straying sheep… to return to their Father's house."

"How earnestly," he says, "We desire that the immense charity of those common prayers embrace those also who, not yet perceiving the light of the Gospel's truth, are still without the Church's safe fold, or for the regrettable conflict of faith and unity, are separated from Us who, though unworthy, bear the person of Jesus Christ on earth."[194]

"From the very beginning of Our Pontificate We have committed to the protection and guidance of heaven, those who do not belong to the visible organization of the Good Shepherd; We desire nothing more ardently than that they may have life and have it more abundantly. Calling on the prayers of the whole Church, We wish to repeat this solemn declaration in this Encyclical Letter in which we have retold the praises of the "great and glorious Body of Christ." From a heart overflowing with love We ask each and every one of them to be quick and ready to follow the interior movements of grace, and to look to withdrawing from that state in which they cannot be sure of their salvation. For even though unsuspecting they are related to the Mystical Body of the Redeemer in desire and resolution, they still remain deprived of so many precious gifts and helps from heaven, which one can only enjoy in the Catholic Church. May they then enter into Catholic unity, and united with us in the organic oneness of the Body of Jesus Christ, may they hasten to the one Head in the society of glorious love. With persevering prayer to the Spirit of love and truth, we wait for them with open arms to return not to a stranger's house, but to their own, their Father's house."[195]

"While We want this unceasing prayer to rise to God from the whole Mystical Body in common, that all the straying sheep may hasten to enter the one fold of Jesus Christ, yet We recognize that this step must come of their own free will; for no one believes unless he wills to believe. Hence they are most certainly not genuine Christians who, against their belief, are forced to go into a church to approach the altar and to receive the Sacraments. The 'faith without which it is impossible to please God', Heb. 11-6, is a wholly free 'submission of intellect and will.'"[196]

Analysis of the Doctrine Of Pius XII, and Comparison With Bellarmine

The above quotations represent, summarily, the official teaching of Pius XII, and therefore of the Holy See, on the relation of non-Catholics to the true Church of Christ. In some ways Pius XII is more explicit than Bellarmine; in others he is more detailed. But substantially, what he says is a perfect vindication of the doctrine of St. Robert, as will be seen from the following considerations:

Non-Catholics in bona fide are not actual members of the true church

> Pius XII uses practically all the expressions possible in a short passage to indicate that non-Catholics, even when they are certainly in good faith, are, nevertheless, actually and really outside the visible Church of Christ.

• "How earnestly We desire," he says, "that the immense charity of these common prayers embrace those also who, not yet perceiving the light of the Gospel's truth, are still *outside the Church's safe fold*." This would exclude all the unbaptized people *in bona fide*, as well as those who "for the regrettable conflict of faith and unity are *separated* from Us who, though unworthy, bear the person of Jesus Christ on earth."[197]

• Still speaking of those who presumably are in invincible ignorance for "not yet perceiving the light of the Gospel's truth," the Pope continues: "From the very beginning of Our Pontificate We have committed to the protection and guidance of heaven those who do *not belong to the visible organization* of the Good Shepherd."[198]

• Inviting them to enter the visible Church, he says, "With persevering prayer to the Spirit of love and truth, We wait for them with open arms to *return*, not to a stranger's house, but to their own, their Father's house."[199]

Bellarmine, we recall, did not expressly treat of material heretics and unbaptized persons who were not catechumens, on their possible membership in the Church. But, consistent with his principles that only actual Baptism and actual profession of the true faith constitutes a person an actual member of the visible Church, he would say what Pius XII says: that good faith, or good will, or even the grace of God do not, *per se*, constitute actual membership in the corporate body of the Church.

Non-Catholics in *bona fide* are not actual members of the mystical body

We recall how clearly the Holy Father identifies the Church with the Mystical Body. "If we would define," he says, "this true Church of Jesus Christ — which is the One, Holy, Catholic, Apostolic, Roman Church — we shall find no expression more noble, more sublime or more Divine than the phrase which calls it 'the Mystical Body of Jesus Christ.'"[200] It follows as a natural corollary, therefore, that if the two are identical, then the conditions for actual membership in the one, are the same as the conditions for actual membership in the other. In fact, the Holy Father uses the two terms interchangeably, once saying that non-Catholics are outside the Catholic Church, and again that they are outside the Mystical Body. Thus, the same persons who "are still without the Church's safe fold," are also invited to "enter into Catholic unity," that they may be "united with us in the organic oneness of the Body of Jesus Christ."[201]

Non-Catholics Are *Voto* Members of the Church

But if unbaptized persons and heretics are not actual members of the visible Church, can they still be saved? Yes, in spite of the fact that incorporation in the true Church is necessary, *simpliciter*, for salvation. Pius XII recognized the same dilemma that faced Bellarmine, and he answers it in the same way. "From a heart overflowing with love," the Pope writes, "we ask each and everyone to be quick and ready to follow the interior movements of grace, and to look to withdrawing from that state in which they cannot be sure of their salvation."[202] Note the Holy Father does not say: "cannot attain to salvation" but, "cannot be sure of their salvation;" which obviously presupposes the possibility, but beset with great difficulties. But now the problem. Why credit non-Catholics in good faith with even the *possibility* of salvation, when the orthodox doctrine is that, "Outside the Church no one can be saved"? Are non-Catholics inside or outside the visible, corporate Church of Christ? If inside, why invite them to enter? If outside, why say they can be saved? The Pope answers, as Bellarmine declared for catechumens, that such people are *inside* the Church, but not actually. "For even though unsuspectingly *(inscio)* they are related to the Mystical Body of the Redeemer in desire and resolution *(desiderio et voto)*, they still remain deprived of so many precious gifts and helps from heaven, which one can only enjoy in the Catholic Church."[203]

In order to do full justice to these words of the Encyclical, they have to be explained, especially the following terms:

> "Unsuspectingly… in desire and resolution," *(inscio quodam desiderio et voto)*. Here is a clear application of Bellarmine's distinction between *re* and *voto* membership in the Church. But where St. Robert limited his application of *voto* membership to catechumens and excommunicates in good faith, the Pope extends this kind of membership to all non-Catholics who are "ready to follow the interior movements of grace," that is, who are *in bona fide*.[204]

> "… they are related to the Mystical Body of the Redeemer," *(ad mysticum Redemptoris Corpus ordinentur)*, is significant for several reasons:

> In context, the Pope indicates that such non-Catholics are related *(ordinentur)* in desire and resolution, to the Mystical Body of the Redeemer, i.e., to the visible organization of Roman Catholicism. Important to note here is that this desire to enter the Church means a resolution, even implicit, to become a member of the visible Church of Christ, and therein entering under the salutary influence of its Invisible Head.

> He says that they are *related to* the visible Church, not that they are in or belong to the Church. The choice of verb is important. *"Ordinare,"* in classic theology means the movement of an object towards a preconceived end, implying that the end is not yet attained but only in the process of attainment.[205] So when the Pope says that non-Catholics are related to *(ordinentur)* the Mystical Body, he implies two things:

> • that non-Catholics are not yet *actually* in the visible communion of the true Church.

> • That they are moving towards actual membership when, though unsuspectingly, they desire to enter the Catholic unity because they sincerely wish to accomplish the entire will of God.

In Bellarmine's terminology, persons who are *voto* members of the Church "are not *actually* and *properly* in the Church, but only in potency *(in potentia);* like a human being who is conceived but not yet completely formed and given birth, is not called a man except potentially."[206] What St. Robert, therefore, was satisfied with illustrating in the form of an analogy, Pius XII explained in the *Mystici Corporis* in clear, theological language. However, the basic concept underlying both explanations is the same.

> Against the background of the Pope's teaching on the soul of the Church, and in terms of Bellarmine's classification, sincere non-Catholics belong to the soul of the Church, in as much as the Holy Spirit moves and directs them, actively *"ordinat"* to correspond to the passive *"ordinentur,"* to the end which He has in view, namely, that these people should be eventually and actually incorporated in the body of the Catholic Church, by actual, external profession of the true faith. The terminus of *"ordinentur,"* according to the Holy Father is that "those who do not belong to the visible organization of the Good Shepherd... may enter into Catholic unity, and, united with us in the organic oneness of the Body of Jesus Christ, may... hasten to the one Head in the society of glorious love." The *agent* on Whom, finally, the attainment of this terminus depends, is the Holy Ghost, the Soul of the Mystical Body. That is why the Pope concludes, "With persevering prayer to the *Spirit of love and truth*, We wait for them to return not to a stranger's house, but to their own, their Father's house."[207]

> "... they still remain deprived of so many precious gifts and helps from heaven, which one can only enjoy in the Catholic Church," (*... tot tamen tantisque coelestibus muneribus adiumentisque carent, quibus in Catholicis solummodo Ecclesia frui licet)*. Here the Pope assigns the reason why, although salvation is possible with only *voto* membership in the visible Church, yet actual membership is immeasurably more desirable. Previously he said that such people "are still outside the Church's *safe* fold." Now he says they are deprived of so many precious gifts and helps from heaven, to be received only through actual profession of the Catholic Faith. Superficially, this may seem like a compromise on the basic dogma that: *Extra Ecclesiam nulla salus*, as though it were only *more difficult* to be saved outside the Catholic Church than within, instead of its being *impossible*. Really, it is only an explanation of the dogma, because the Pope had already declared that the Holy Ghost "refuses to dwell with sanctifying grace in members that are *wholly* severed from the body" of the Church, that is, who have not at least an unsuspecting desire *(inscio desiderio)* to become Catholics. But now, even granting this *inscio desiderio*, with its concomitant *voto* membership, the further duty remains to correspond with

God's grace so as to actualize what so far exists only in resolution, namely, to actually enter the Church. And here two
great risks are encountered:

The danger that a present state of grace may be lost through
lack of correspondence with Divine inspiration, directing a non-
Catholic to enter the Catholic Church. For he retains the state
of grace only as long as he has at least an *inscio desiderio* to
become a Catholic. Objectively and theoretically, this implicit
resolution is destined, first to become explicit, and then to be
carried into execution. Subjectively and in practice, therefore,
the non-Catholic labors under a serious handicap, from which
the professed Catholic is happily freed. He must ever be so
faithful to the impulse of the Holy Spirit so as:

• To actualize this resolution by entering the Catholic Church,
given the grace of God.
• At least not to lose this resolution by sinning against the light
and refusing to become a Catholic, even after recognizing this
as the clear will of God.

The danger that *ex aliunde*, the state of grace may be lost through
lack of "so many precious gifts and helps from heaven, which
can only be had in the Catholic Church."[208] This is especially
true of the Sacramental system instituted by Christ, in which,
as the Pope says, "the Savior of mankind, out of His infinite
goodness, has provided in a marvelous manner for His Mystical
Body… so that by so many consecutive, graduated graces, as it
were, its members should be supported from the cradle to life's
last breath, and that the social needs of the Church might also be
generously provided for."[209]

In either case, however, the net result is the same, namely, that "those
who do not belong to the visible organization of the Good Shepherd" by
actual profession of the Catholic Faith, remain in "that state in which
they cannot be sure of their salvation."[210]

PART THREE

CRITICAL COMPARISON

CHAPTER I

INTRODUCTION

INSTRUCTION OF THE HOLY OFFICE ON "THE ECUMENICAL MOVEMENT"

The recent instructions of the Holy Office on "The Ecumenical Movement,"[211] while encouraging the efforts of zealous Catholics to bring non-Catholics into the true Church, lays special emphasis on the problems and dangers which this delicate work involves. Pertinent to our investigation are the following statements of the instruction:

• "The efforts of various people, whether of private persons or societies, to reconcile dissident Christians to the Catholic Church, as undertaken up to the present time, although inspired by the best of intentions, are not always founded on correct principles."[212]

• "Bishops should be on the watch, lest under false pretext of paying more attention to those things in which we are united (to non-Catholics) than to those in which we differ from them, a dangerous indifferentism be fostered, especially among those who are less instructed in matters theological and less faithful in the practice of their religion. For they must beware, lest, through what is called today the 'irenic spirit', Catholic teaching — whether in dogma or in things connected with dogma — should be entirely accommodated to the doctrine of the dissidents, doing positive injury to the purity of Catholic doctrine or obscuring its genuine and certain meaning."[213]

• "They (the bishops) will choose priests suitable (for ecumenical work) who are sedulously attentive to the doctrine and norms prescribed by the Holy See, for example, in the Encyclical Letters, *Satis cognitum, Mortalium animos*, and *Mystici Corporis Christi*."[214]

• "Catholic doctrine must, therefore, be proposed and explained in its fullness and integrity. There must not be passed over in silence or covered over with ambiguous words that which Catholic truth teaches on the true nature and means of justification, on the constitution of the Church, on the primacy of jurisdiction of the Roman Pontiff, on the one and only true union by which dissidents are to return to the one true Church of Christ."[215]

Although this instruction was addressed to the whole world, it has its most practical application in countries where non-Catholics are in the majority and where efforts have been most seriously made to bring these outsiders into the true fold. Wherever the ecumenical movement exists, the same problems and dangers arise. Consequently, in choosing the United States of America for special investigation, the reason was not that other countries have not made the same mistakes in their attitude and policy towards non-Catholics. The reason was simply that the writer is personally best acquainted with and naturally most interested in the American scene. Neither should the errors which have to be pointed out obscure the fact that the movement in the United States is based on the solid principles of Catholic orthodoxy, promoted and sanctioned by the hierarchy, and not infrequently commended by the Holy See.[216]

II. METHOD OF PROCEDURE

By way of introducing the critical study which follows, certain points should be clarified.

In accordance with the limits of our analysis, we shall investigate only one aspect of what might be called, "The American attitude towards the sincere non-Catholic," the *dogmatic* aspect, prescinding entirely from the practical methods of convert work.

In this dogmatic element, we shall be concerned with only one doctrine, namely, the possible membership of the non-Catholic, as a non-Catholic, in the true Church. In other words, is the sincere unbaptized person or heretic in any sense, and if so, in what sense, a member of the Catholic Church. Relative to the ecumenical movement this is of capital importance because much of the antipathy of outsiders to the Catholic faith arises from a misunderstanding of the doctrine that, *"Extra Ecclesiam, nulla salus."* For, it is argued, if salvation is possible only in the Catholic Church, then:

- The Catholic religion is unjust, because it teaches the monstrous doctrine which consigns all non-Catholics to eternal damnation.
- The Catholic religion is unreasonable, because *de facto* many obviously good people do not belong to the Catholic Church. Are they, nevertheless, in the state of sin and outside the friendship of God?[217]

In making the analysis, which will be at once comparative and critical, two norms will be followed:

1. Only recent American Catholic writers will be cited. And among these, only those whose doctrine or its expression on the point at issue seems open to criticism, will be quoted and analyzed.

2. In criticizing their statements, the basis of comparison will be the traditional doctrine of the Catholic Church, as formulated by St. Robert Bellarmine, and as clarified and developed by the Holy See.

The division of chapters will correspond to the different theories or explanations of Church membership for non-Catholics which are proposed. First will be given a complete statement of the doctrine, then a critical analysis. For obvious reasons, only the main theories suggested can be dealt with, and among their proponents, only a representative number, sometimes only one, can be treated in detail.

CHAPTER II

FIRST THEORY: NON-CATHOLICS ARE ENTIRELY OUTSIDE THE CATHOLIC CHURCH

I. COMPLETE EXCLUSION OF ALL NON-CATHOLICS FROM MEMBERSHIP IN THE CATHOLIC CHURCH

Statement of Doctrine

The following statement of doctrine appears in a current treatise on the Mystical Body, and originally formed the basis of lectures given to students beginning their theological training.[218]

> "Membership in the body of the Church, in the mystical organism whose head is Christ, is necessary by necessity of means. This necessity is not absolute but relative. It is *the* medium which God has chosen from all eternity. The church is the mystical organism, the body of Christ animated by the Holy Spirit, and those outside it are deprived of its supernatural life, hence also of the means of justification. Through Christ alone, the historical and mystical Christ, we come to the Father. He is *the* mediator between God and men. 'No man cometh to the Father,' said our Lord, 'but by me.' John 14-6. If those outside the church are to be saved (and we have no reason to doubt that many are saved), they are saved not *in* and *through* the church, but because God the Father has in his unbounded mercy provided some other means by which such men may come to him, yet come to him 'through Christ our Lord.' God wills the salvation of all men. Therefore He, the infinite Love, is pleased to accept some other means as equivalent to membership in the church if actual incorporation into Christ's mystical body is either physically or morally impossible. Christ died for all men without exception; hence all are offered the means, either ordinary or extraordinary, to attain salvation."[219]

Analysis of the Doctrine

The substance of the author's doctrine is contained in his declaration that, "Membership in the body of the Church, in the mystical organism

95

whose head is Christ, is necessary by necessity of means. This necessity is not absolute but relative. In other words, incorporation into the mystical Christ is the ordinary medium of salvation."

Previously he had defined the body of the Church as "the multiple, external, visible elements, clergy and laity, hierarchical structure, sacraments, sacramentals, etc."[220] Reductively this would mean the profession of the Catholic faith and therefore coincides with Bellarmine's and Pius XII's definition of the body of the Church. Now, according to the writer, membership in the visible organization of the Catholic Church is only the *ordinary* means of salvation. Consequently, salvation is possible even for those who do not belong to the Church of Christ.

On first inspection, this seems to be defensible. For if by ordinary means of salvation the author means actual membership in the body of the true Church, then any other kind of membership is extraordinary and we are faced with a variety of possible solutions, though not all satisfactory. Thus:

- even though a person does not belong to the body of the Church, he might be saved by belonging to the soul of the Church. Or,
- The necessity of belonging to the Church is only a necessity of precept but not of means. Or,
- belonging to the body of the Church is indeed necessary for salvation, but this membership need not be actual; it may be only in *voto* or desire.

However, all these explanations are explicitly ruled out by the author. After stating that, "It is beyond the scope of this book to explain fully how those outside the Catholic Church may be saved," he continues: "It is certain that they can be saved, although the manner or process of their justification may be difficult to understand. It is also certain that the theory which accounts for their salvation by making them belong to the soul of the Church is both psychologically and theologically inaccurate and therefore untenable."

"How, then, are we to explain the axiom: 'Outside the Catholic Church there is no salvation'"?

"Some have attempted to explain it, or rather to explain it away, by affirming that no reference need to be made to the soul of the Church. It suffices to say, according to this view, that those outside the Church who are invincibly ignorant of its divine mission are saved because they are in good faith. Or again, some suggest, the axiom simply means that it is not necessary to belong to the body of the Church by necessity of means but only by necessity of precept. Therefore, if anyone is inculpably ignorant of our Lord's precept to belong to the Church, as, for example, the pagan, the Jew, the Protestant, such a one can be saved. Another theory sets up the distinction between membership by desire (*in voto*) and membership in actuality (*in actu*) as a possible basis of correct interpretation."

"All these and similar interpretations of the axiom add to the already existing confusion. Lack of precision in theological terminology is indicative of lack of clearness in theological thought. The only correct interpretation of the axiom is that given by the Fathers of the Vatican Council who drew up the first draft on the Constitution of the Church. This interpretation alone is in harmony with the doctrine of the mystical body."[221]

Then follows the statement of his own doctrine, namely, that while "Membership in the body of the Church is necessary," yet, "This necessity is not absolute but relative. In other words, incorporation into the mystical Christ is the ordinary medium of salvation."[222]

Consequently, when speaking of the *ordinary* means of salvation, the author understands *actual* membership in the Church, which is correct enough. But when he says that non-Catholics may be saved otherwise than by actual membership, his term extra-ordinary is not to be equated with "extra-ordinary membership," that is, other than actual, but with "extra-ordinary means," that is, other than *any kind* of membership in the visible Church of Christ.

Thus, in terms of the Church's body and soul, both of which he admits, two possibilities offered themselves with reference to non-Catholics who are saved otherwise than by actual membership in the body of the Church:

- They are saved extra-ordinarily, that is,
  1. by a voto membership in the soul of the Church.
  2. by voto membership in the body of the Church.

- They are saved extra-ordinarily, that is
  1. by no kind of membership in the soul of the Church.
  2. by no kind of membership in the body of the Church.

Our author chose the second of these alternatives.

Or we can express his position otherwise. Of the two elements that could be distinguished in the axiom: *"Extra Ecclesiam, nulla salus"*

I.	Extra Ecclesiam =	Soul:	Re
			Voto
	=	Body:	Re
			Voto

II.   Nulla salus =   Ordinarily
                                                 Extra-ordinarily

the author chose the second and, therefore, equivalently says that the formula should read: *"Extra Ecclesiam nulla salus 'ordinarie'."*

In the first instance, *nulla salus* would remain undistinguished, and the formula would mean that universally and absolutely, no salvation is possible for anyone without some kind of membership in the Church.

In the second instance, which is the author's, *extra Ecclesiam* remains undistinguished, and the formula means that outside of actual membership in the one visible Church, there is no salvation ordinarily, i.e., where such membership is at least morally impossible. But even without any membership in the Church, body or soul, there can be salvation extra-ordinarily, i.e. for those for whom "actual incorporation into Christ's mystical body is either physically or morally impossible."[223]

It may be remarked in passing that no alternative is offered to actual membership in the Church, beyond saying that some sort of extraordinary means are involved. But that is not significant. What is significant is that the writer explicitly denies the need for any kind of membership in the Church as a requisite for salvation for non-Catholics. "If those outside the Church are to be saved," he says, "they are not saved in and through the Church, but because God the Father has in His mercy provided some other means by which men may come to Him."[224]

Criticism of the Doctrine

Denies the Universality of *Extra Ecclesiam Nulla Salus*

What the writer has done is denied that the axiom: *"Extra Ecclesiam nulla salus,"* has a universal application. For if we ask him why he says that no sort of membership in the Church is necessary for the salvation of non-Catholics, he will answer: because the formula, *"Extra Ecclesiam..."* does not pertain to all people. Specifically, it does not refer to those for whom "actual incorporation into the mystical Christ is either physically or morally impossible." For those chosen persons who have the physical and moral possibility of actual membership in the body of the Church, such membership is necessary for salvation. For everyone else, the doctrine has no more application than if it did not exist.

However, such restriction of the doctrine in question cannot be justified. It has a universal application to everyone, without exception, as may be seen from the following considerations:

1. The complete, contextual wording of the formula, as quoted by Bel-
    larmine and all the Popes, is proof in itself of its unrestricted applica-
    tion.
    •   In the Fourth Lateran Council, in which the definition first occurs,
        the axiom reads: "There is one universal Church of the faithful,
        outside of which no one at all (*nullus omnino*) is saved."[225]
    •   In the definitive Bull of Boniface VIII, *Unam Sanctam*, where
        membership in the body of the Church by profession of obedience
        to the Pope is required for salvation, the doctrine reads: "More-
        over, We declare, say, define and pronounce that to be subject to
        the Roman Pontiff is absolutely necessary for salvation for every
        human creature. *(omni humanae creaturae… omnino de neces-
        sitate salutis)."*[226]

It is hard to conceive how the universality of this dogma could have
been more clearly and explicitly stated, allowing of no exceptions, much
less saying that it describes only the ordinary providence of God, and
has no reference to the bulk of mankind which is actually outside the
visible Church of Christ.

2. All through the history of theology, but especially since the time of
    Bellarmine, theologians and the Church herself have wrestled with the
    problem that:
    •   While *no one* is saved outside the Church,
    •   Yet non-Catholics in good faith may be saved, although they are
        evidently not *actual* members of the Church of Christ.

But there would be no problem if we deny the universality of the
first proposition. Why be concerned with how non-Catholics can be
saved if the formula "*Extra Ecclesiam nulla salus*," does not apply to
them? Simply say that membership in the Church is the ordinary means
for those who can easily use them and that God provides, extra-ordinarily, means for everyone else, as for all non-Catholics. Of course, this is
no solution of the problem, but a denial that a problem exists.

Based on a Misconception of the Soul of the Church

What is the author's basis for his position that membership in the
Church is not necessary for salvation, and that the distinctions between
the body and soul, and between *re* and *voto* membership in the Church,
only add to the existing confusion? The basis is a logical development
of his doctrine on the soul of the Church. "The Holy Spirit," he says,
"is the quasi-substantial form, the soul of the Church, that is, the Holy
Spirit is its informing principle, elevating the church as a society and
giving unity and identity to Christ's mystical body." But then he deduces
a conclusion. "Because the Holy Spirit is the informing principle of this

body, he imparts supernatural life, the life of Christ, the life of God, to the organism as a whole. He imparts the same divine life to the individual because the individual is the unit of the organism. No person can belong to the soul of the Church, to the Holy Spirit as the soul, unless he belongs in some degree to the body also."

Ostensibly this looks like the traditional doctrine, until he continues. "A very important truth is involved here. We cannot dismiss the problem by saying that it is a question of words only. Rightly, therefore, does Hugh Pope stress this point when he writes: 'People often say that, though a certain person does not belong to the body of the Church, he yet belongs to its *soul*. The very expression is so consoling that we are apt to welcome it without reflection. ... In truth this expression is a most misleading one. For what can be the *soul* of the Church but the Holy Spirit? And while no one would question that people who are not actually members of the Church can have the Spirit of God, it is certain that they do not have the Holy Spirit as *quickening* the body of Christ which is the Church; hence it is not true that those outside belong to the soul of the Church, though they do belong to Him who is the soul of the Church.'"[227] To which the writer finally adds his own comment, that, "The bestowal of *created* grace, of that gift by which we become partakers of the divine nature, entails also the granting of the gift of the personal presence of the Holy Spirit, sometimes spoken of as *uncreated* grace... Those outside the body of the Church may receive grace and, therefore, also possess the Holy Spirit; they may be said to belong to the Holy Spirit. But being outside the mystical body of Christ, of which the Holy Spirit is the soul, or the informing principle, they do not belong to the soul of the Church."[228]

Incidentally, the author identifies membership in the soul of the Church with the possession of sanctifying grace which, as we saw, is not Bellarmine's doctrine.[229] Moreover, it is a very difficult thesis to sustain in view of the fact that professed Catholics in mortal sin certainly belong to the Mystical Body. But how explain their membership if you make a perfect identification between belonging to the soul of the Church, which is the Holy Ghost, and being in the state of grace? It is at least more reasonable to suppose that the Holy Spirit has some influence, as the soul of the Church, even on those *dead* members in the Church's body who have lost the gift of charity but not the gift of faith.

However, our immediate interest is to follow the main line of the argument proposed. And then we see that it reduces itself to a series of propositions:

- The Holy Spirit is the soul of the Church.
- No person can belong to the soul of the Church, to the Holy Spirit as the soul, unless he belongs in some degree to the body also, which means, 'some degree' of *actual* membership in the body.
- Therefore, since non-Catholics lack even the smallest degree of actual membership in the body of the Church, they cannot belong to the soul of the Church, that is, to the Holy Spirit *as animating* the Church and *as justifying* its individual members.

But then arises a difficulty. How are non-Catholics to be justified? Evidently through the Holy Spirit. Yet they do not belong to the body and, therefore, not to the soul. So the following solution is offered:

- Besides His function as the soul of the Church, the Holy Spirit also operates outside the body of the Church.
- He gives His grace, including the grace of justification, even outside the Church's body.
- Consequently, given the proper dispositions in a non-Catholic, he can receive sanctifying grace and therefore belong to the Holy Ghost, without any reference to the body of the Church.
- Such persons are said to belong to the Holy Spirit, indeed, but not in His capacity as the 'anima Ecclesiae," and therefore, they do not belong to the soul of the Church.

There is no need in answering these propositions in detail here, since the contrary doctrine has already been handled and proved.[230] It is enough to point out that fundamental to the author's position is his claim that the Holy Spirit operates in a double capacity in infusing the grace of justification; one inside and one outside the visible Catholic Church. How much concession can be granted to this theory? In other words, how can we square the universality of the doctrine *Extra Ecclesiam nulla salus*, with the claim that people can, *de facto*, receive the gifts of the Holy Spirit with no reference to the one true Church; the implication being that the Holy Spirit also operates wholly outside the visible Church of Christ.

Understanding the soul of the Church to be the Holy Spirit, we may conceive His activity on two types of human souls:

On those who are *actu* within the true Church, there is

- A visible supernatural activity, by which the members of the Church are united and cooperate in hierarchical unity, to the formation of the living, organic Mystical Body of Christ on earth.
- An invisible, interior supernatural activity, by which He sanctifies the actual members of the Church with the infusion of His graces and gifts.

On those who are not actually within the true Church, the Holy Spirit operates

- In His external mission, by leading and drawing such souls to join themselves in corporate unity with the visible Church of Christ.
- In His internal mission, by infusing His graces into these souls to purify them of sin and sanctify them in virtue. However, this infusion stops short of justification unless and until it meets in such souls that degree of responsiveness which the *Mystici Corporis* calls *voto* membership in the Mystical Body of Christ.[231]

Returning to the theory under consideration, we are told that non-Catholics, although in the state of grace, "May be said to belong to the Holy Spirit. But being outside the Mystical Body of Christ, of which the Holy Spirit is the soul, or the informing principle, they do not belong to the soul of the Church." This is acceptable only if we understand the writer to mean that these people do not belong *actually*; it is not correct if he means that they do not belong *in any way* to the *anima Ecclesiae*. For when we say, as Bellarmine and the *Mystici Corporis* allows us to say, that sincere non-Catholics belong *voto* to the Mystical Body of the Redeemer, and the Holy Ghost as its soul is essential to this Body, then the kind of membership we predicate of the whole Mystical Body, should likewise be predicated of its essential element. So that non-Catholics may not be said to belong *nullo modo* to the soul of the Church, but should be said to belong to it in the same way as they belong to the living Body which it animates, namely, by *voto* membership.

Claims that Membership in the true Church is only a Precept

There is another reason which led the theologian we are investigating to deny the universal necessity of belonging to the true Church as a condition for salvation. For he assumes that this necessity is only a matter of precept but not a necessity of means. Verbally, it is true, he says, "Membership in the body of the Church, in the mystical organism whose head is Christ, is necessary by necessity of means."[232] Yet, *de facto*, he denies the proposition. For he continues, "This necessity is not absolute but relative."[233] What does this mean? He answers, quoting another authority: "There are some means of salvation so necessary for the attainment of our last end that no substitute can take their place, which means that they are absolutely necessary. Certainly no one is saved who dies in enmity with God; no one is saved who dies in unrepented personal sin; no one is saved without faith (supernatural faith). Other requirements (for example, membership in the Church) are necessary by reason of the positive will of God. In themselves these latter requisites are not absolutely necessary. God, their author, reserves to Himself the right to substitute for them other means, or to be satisfied with equivalent acts in the case of those who, without any fault of their own, are unable to employ the divinely appointed means of salvation."[234]

Bellarmine's explanation of the difference between the two kinds of necessities is in order. He says: "There are two kinds of necessity. One is called the necessity of precept; the other a necessity of means. And although it sometimes happens that the two are joined together, since by the fact that something is a necessary means of salvation, it will also be a natural precept, if it is in our power to fulfill it; yet there is this difference, that when a person through invincible ignorance or through some other just cause does not fulfill a *precept*, he suffers no harm as a result. But if he does not use a necessary *means*, he suffers great harm, because he does not attain to the end, even though it was through invincible ignorance." Then he goes on to apply, by way of illustration, the difference between the two: "For example, the Sacrament of Confirmation is a precept but not a means which is absolutely necessary for salvation. And, therefore, if a person neglects to receive this Sacrament, he commits a sin, but if he fails to receive it for some legitimate reason, he does not sin, and is not deprived of salvation. But Baptism, *in re* or *in voto*, is both a precept and a means. So that, if a person is not baptized or certainly (culpably) does not desire Baptism, he is not saved, even though it was through ignorance or inability that this happened."[235]

Bellarmine does not directly apply this doctrine to membership in the Church, that is, in so many words; but only equivalently. For if we analyze the meaning behind necessity of precept and of means, we see that the distinction may be validly applied to the two kinds of membership in the true Church which, according to St. Robert, entitle a person to salvation:

- *Re* membership in the true Church is not absolutely necessary for salvation since, as we have seen, where invincible ignorance exists, coupled with other positive dispositions, actual non-membership is excusable. Thus we may say that actual membership in the Catholic Church is a matter of Divine precept, from which inculpable ignorance excuses.[236]

- At least *voto* membership in the true Church is absolutely necessary for salvation, from which invincible ignorance does not excuse. The reason is clear on analyzing that *voto* membership signifies, as Pius IX explains, that a non-Catholic, "… is in invincible ignorance of our most holy religion *and* carefully observes the natural law and its precepts, which God has inscribed in the hearts of all, and, being ready to

obey God, lives an honest and upright life, through the working of the
Divine light and grace."[237] From this minimum obligation no adult can
be excused. Therefore, at least *voto* membership for adults is necessary for salvation by a necessity of means.

It was in this sense that the Scheme of the Vatican Council, (Editor's
Note: First Vatican Council) in its Dogmatic Constitution, declared that:
"Let all understand what a necessary Society the Church is, in order to
obtain salvation. Namely, this necessity is as great as that of being joined
with Christ the Head and with His Mystical Body, outside of which He
nourishes and favors no other communion as His Church, which alone
He loves and for which He sacrificed Himself. ... Therefore we teach
that the Church is not a free Society, as though it is a matter of indifference to salvation to either know or not know, to enter or to leave it; but
that it is absolutely necessary and, indeed, not only with the necessity of
the Lord's precept by which the Savior prescribed that all men should
enter into it; but also (with the necessity) of means, because in the established order of salutary providence, the communication of the Holy
Spirit, the participation of truth and life, is not obtained except in the
Church and through the Church, whose Head is Christ."[238]

Implies That Infants Can Be Saved Without Baptism

Consistent with his principles, if the author holds that membership
in the true Church is only a matter of precept, he should excuse from its
observance not only non-Catholic adults, but also, and especially, non-
baptized infants for whom incorporation in the Church through Baptism
is both morally and physically impossible. However, we are not left to
deduce this conclusion from his promises, because he teaches it explicitly. In a long note to the paragraph in which he stated that non-Catholics
"are saved not in and through the Church," he writes: "The proposition declaring that Christ died for all men without exception, is *de fide*.
The doctrine teaching that all adults outside the Catholic Church, Jews,
Protestants and pagans, who follow the dictates of their conscience, will
receive graces sufficient for salvation, is *fidei proxima*. No entirely satisfactory solution has yet been offered concerning the fate of children
dying before Baptism. It is the common opinion of theologians that God
gives them graces sufficient for salvation.[239] However, theologians divide into two groups children dying before Baptism; first, those who die
in the maternal womb and, secondly, those who die after natural birth
before Baptism. The former, they maintain, are forever deprived of the
vision of God, but do enjoy a natural happiness in limbo; the latter may
be saved."[240]

Clearly our author would maintain that only infants who die in the womb are deprived of the Beatific Vision, and that those who die after natural birth may be saved even without actual Baptism. It is difficult to see what he means by the "common opinion of theologians" that children dying before Baptism receive sufficient graces for salvation, apart from and independent of Baptism. If anything, theological "opinion" is all to the opposite; in fact, it is not an opinion but common doctrine that no one, including infants, can be saved without Baptism in *re* or in *voto*. Writes a modern authority on the history of the Sacraments: "At the very outset it must be admitted that .... those infants who have not received Baptism in water, either in fact or in desire, will not attain to the Beatific Vision. This is the clear meaning of the words of the Lord to Nicodemus ... The mind of the Church, while it has never been expressed in an *ex cathedra* definition, has been so constant and so pronounced in its ordinary magisterium, as to exclude all reasonable doubt. The fluctuations which rise here and there only serve to show how strong the tradition is. To indicate the mind of the ancient Church, we may read, for example, the narrative of St. Augustine about an infant who died in the arms of his mother, who was called back to life through the invocation of the martyr, St. Stephen, and baptized. Then he died a second time and was carried to the grave by his mother, now consoled, as she had previously wept more over the fate of his soul than over the death of his body, having passed from tears to expressions of gratitude at seeing that her child was now assured of eternal life.[241] St. Thomas synthesizes on this point the mind of all the Christian centuries when he says that, in view of the necessity of Baptism, God has willed to make it accessible to everyone, both in the choice of its matter, which is most common, and in giving to everyone, in case of necessity, the power of conferring Baptism. Nor does St. Thomas forget that, 'God has in no sense limited His power to the Sacraments,' and therefore he allows for the possibility of a miracle.[242] But a miracle, it should be observed, does not pertain to the ordinary course of Providence... Not a few theologians have tried to find a common disposition of Providence to procure the salvation of these infants. In the fourteenth century, there was Durandus; in the fifteenth, Gerson and Biel; in the sixteenth, Cajetan. The latter believed he had discovered the secret in the prayer of a Christian mother for the fruit of her womb. But the Church never encouraged these efforts. Out of regard for the illustrious memory of Cajetan, the Council of Trent did not wish to condemn his opinion with an anathema. But the page on which his theory appeared was removed from his works by order of the Sovereign Pontiff, St. Pius V.[243] The following centuries also witnessed a goodly number of similar attempts. Thus, in the eighteenth century, Cardinal

Sfondrati, whose work, *Nodu Praedestinationis Dissolutus,* described as particularly enviable the lot of infants who die without Baptism, was put on the Index by Sossuet and four bishops of France; and although he was saved (from further condemnation) through the good graces of Pope Innocent XII, he was not excused. In the eighteenth century, Amort and Bianchi; in the nineteenth, Klee, Caron, Vosen and Schell more or less renewed the same efforts, which were condemned, but never praised, by the Church."[244]

Numerous documents of the Church confirm the fact that the constant Christian tradition is against conceiving any other means of salvation for infants, whether before or after birth, than the reception of the Sacrament of Baptism:

1. Thus, in the Council of Carthage (418), approved by Pope Zosimus, we read: "It has pleased all the bishops (to declare that), if anyone denies that children recently delivered from their mothers' wombs need not be baptized… let him be anathema."[245]

2. And in a letter of Pope Innocent I (417): "That which Your Fraternity declares that they (the Pelagians) are preaching, namely, that children can attain to the reward of eternal life even without the grace of Baptism, is most absurd."[246]

3. Also Pope Leo I (447): "Since the whole offspring of the human race has been vitiated by the prevarication of the first man, no one can be delivered from the lot of 'the old man', except through the Sacrament of the Baptism of Christ."[247]

4. And Innocent III, in recommending the baptism of infants: "God forbid that all the children, who die in such numbers each day, should perish without God in His mercy giving them a remedy to assure their salvation, since He desires no one to be lost."[248]

5. And the Council of Florence, in its Decree for the Jacobites: "Regarding children, because of the danger of death, as often happens, since no other remedy can be offered to them, by which they are snatched from the dominion of the devil and adopted into the sons of God, than the Sacrament of Baptism, (therefore the Council) admonishes that sacred Baptism is not to be deferred, but should be conferred as soon as can conveniently be done. But when there is imminent danger of death, they should be baptized immediately, without delay, even by a layperson or a woman."[249]

6. Also the Council of Trent: "This translation (from that state in which a man is born a child of the first Adam, to the state of grace and of the adoption of the sons of God through the second Adam, Jesus Christ), cannot, since the promulgation of the Gospel, be effected except

through the laver of regeneration or its desire, as it is written, 'Unless a man be born again of water and the Holy Ghost, he cannot enter into the Kingdom of God.'"[250]

7.   And more recently, Pope Benedict XIV, in the Profession of Faith prescribed for the Orientals, declared that: "Baptism is necessary for salvation, and, therefore, if the danger of death is imminent, it must be conferred immediately, without delay, and, no matter when or by whom conferred, with due matter and form and intention, it is valid."[251]

The fundamental reason, according to Bellarmine, why the actual Baptism of infants is necessary for salvation is the *universal* application of the doctrine that, *outside the Church there is no salvation.* Summarily, his argument appears in the form of two syllogisms, as given in the Controversies:

"It is possible for infants to be saved.
But outside the Church there is no salvation.
Therefore, they must enter the Church."

Then, after proving the premises from Scripture and Tradition, he continues:

"Infants must enter the Church.
But they cannot do this except through Baptism.
Therefore, they have to be baptized"[252]

Now, although St. Robert was arguing against the Anabaptists, who said that only adults should be baptized, and then only around the age of thirty after the example of Christ, yet his reasoning is equally effective against those, like the author of the *Mystical Christ*, who maintain that unbaptized infants, though not members of the Church through Baptism, can still enter heaven by some "extra-ordinary means."

Misinterprets Invincible Ignorance in Non-Catholics

Starting with the assumption that if non-Catholics are saved, "they are not saved in and through the Church, but because God the Father has in his unbounded mercy provided some other means," our author concludes that these extraordinary means will be granted by God to all "those who without any fault of their own are unable to employ the divinely appointed means of salvation."[253]

The difficulty with this argument is that it considers only one of the conditions on which non-Catholics may be saved; namely, invincible ignorance of the true faith, while it overlooks another condition which is far more important.

We recall that Pius IX on several occasions repeated in different words the statement that, "It is a perfectly well-known Catholic dogma that no one can be saved outside the Catholic Church."[254] Then he went on to explain that, in spite of this clear doctrine, "We must likewise hold it as certain that those who labor in ignorance of the true religion, if that ignorance be invincible, will never be charged with any guilt on this account before the eyes of the Lord."[255] This is a tempting statement and is also misleading if we stop here. Because then we have the Pope saying:

- No one can be saved outside the Catholic Church.
- But those who are in invincible ignorance of the Church can be saved.
- Therefore, membership in the Catholic Church is only a positive precept and not a necessity of means, since, by definition, invincible ignorance excuses a person from observing what is only a positive commandment of God.

The fact is that the Pope did not stop here. It is true he said: "Those who labor in invincible ignorance of our most holy religion…. can attain eternal life."[256] But that is only the negative side. Were this alone declared it would be, for example, a denial of the necessity of Baptism for infants who are obviously ignorant of the true religion. But, besides being ignorant of the true religion, these people must also, "carefully observe the natural law and its precepts, which God has inscribed in the hearts of all, and, being ready to obey God, live an honest and upright life."[257]

As we have seen in the previous chapters, this *positive* cooperation with Divine grace in obedience to the natural law and in the perfect readiness to obey the will of God, includes at least an implicit desire to enter the Church and gives such a person a title to *voto* membership in its society. But that is quite different than saying that God will provide some other means than Church membership for those who are in invincible ignorance of the true faith. Because, where in the one case, when Church membership is considered only a matter of precept, invincible ignorance *alone* excuses from further responsibility; in the other, when membership is regarded as also a means, ignorance alone is not enough. It must also, and especially, be coupled with a *positive* cooperation with the grace of God, and a *positive* fulfillment of His Divine will, even to including at least the implicit desire to enter the Catholic Church. True, this unconscious desire may never become explicit, much less be carried into effect. True also that, in the last analysis, only God is the judge when such a desire is really present. But present it must be, as something real and positive and beyond the mere invincible ignorance that membership in the Roman Catholic Church is necessary for salvation.

CONCLUSION

By way of transition to what follows, it should be pointed out that the theory just criticized is a fundamental one, based as it is on an arbitrary restriction of the axiom: *Extra Ecclesiam nulla salus*. Stated positively, the theory claims that, "Outside the Church there *is* salvation," arguing that the Holy Ghost not only gives actual graces but also justification, with no reference to the Visible Mystical Body of Christ, dismissing the anomaly with the statement that there are two roads to salvation, the ordinary, through the Church, and the extraordinary, outside the Church.

A variety of applications of this basic theme have been made. In a later chapter, we shall consider the most common of these, namely, that non-Catholics are saved by belonging to the "soul of the Church," where, whatever also it is, "the soul of the Church" as given by its theorists, is not the one visible Church of Christ.

CHAPTER III

SECOND THEORY:
"SINCERE HERETICS ARE FORMAL MEMBERS OF
THE CATHOLIC CHURCH, BUT LACK JURIDICAL
COMMUNION WITH THE FAITHFUL."

I. STATEMENT OF DOCTRINE

At the other extreme to considering sincere non-Catholics as completely outside the true Church, we have the theory which places at least some of them, namely, baptized heretics in good faith, *formally* within the visible Church of Christ. A clear statement of this opinion was given in answer to a question recently submitted to the *Homiletic and Pastoral Review,* published in New York City. The question read:

> "Please explain whether or not baptized non-Catholics are members of the Mystical Body of Christ. Is baptism of desire sufficient for membership in the Mystical Body?"

The answer was given by the director of the "Moral Cases" department of the *Review*, and reads as follows:

> "As to the first part of the question, if non-Catholics are validly baptized, they are incorporated into the Church, although by reason of being associated with an alien communion, they lack for the most part the rights of communion with the Church; and this lack is based largely on impediment rather than on censure. Canon 87 sums up in three or four lines the entire matter of personality in the Church of God, and makes a very clear distinction between *membership* in the Church and *communion with* the Church. Excommunicated Catholics lack the latter, but they don't lose membership in the Church; rather they lose their right to commune with her, to receive the Sacraments, to attend divine offices, and to exercise certain spiritual rights in the juridical order. On the other hand, non-Catholics, if they aren't validly baptized but wish to accomplish whatever God wants them to do, are members of the Church only by desire in the same way as are catechumens. These latter are given Christian burial, but they are in no strict sense members of the Church, any more than

111

a martyr is who was unbaptized, nor any more than the faithful were under the Old Dispensation. All true catechumens as well as those of the Old Law were none of them truly in the Church, being only virtual or prospective members, in desire. Were an unbaptized catechumen to die for the faith and were he to be raised to life again by a miracle-worker, he would be under precept to join the Church by receiving baptism."

I am just beginning to read for about the tenth time that priceless volume, *The Key to the Holy Eucharist,* by the late Abbot of Buckfast; and in a preliminary chapter this synthesizer of St. Thomas' Eucharistic doctrine brings out very well the two forms of union with God, and the only two forms of union with God: through the theological virtues alone or in the case of an adult who has been guilty of mortal sin after baptism, through the sacrament and the theological virtues, or through baptism alone in the formal or virtual infant. In past generations much ink was spilt through argumentation on being in the soul of the Church only, an ignorant expression for saying that a person has virtual membership in the Church if he is a sanctified catechumen; whereas, if he is a validly baptized non-Catholic, he has formal membership in the Church without possessing the rights of communion except in the hour of death for the necessary Sacraments if he possesses actual or presumptive good faith."[258]

II. ANALYSIS OF DOCTRINE

Broken down into essentials, the above statement contains the following points:

- Baptism is necessary for actual membership in the Mystical Body, which is the Catholic Church.
- Membership *only in the soul of the Church* is a wrong expression for saying that a person has virtual membership in the Church, if he is a catechumen in the state of grace.
- Catechumens, as all sincere non-baptized adults, are members of the Church only in desire.
- Canon 87 clearly distinguishes between *membership* in the Church and *communion with* the Church.
- Having communion with the Church, means to possess the right of communing with the Church, to receive the Sacraments, to attend divine offices, and to exercise certain other spiritual rights in the juridical order.
- Excommunicated Catholics lack communion with the Church, but they retain membership in the Church.
- Sincere baptized non-Catholics:

1. Lack only the right of communion with the Church, except in the hour of death when they have the right to receive the necessary Sacraments.
2. But otherwise, they belong formally to the Catholic Church.

- There are only two forms of union with God:
    For adults:
        through Baptism and the theological virtues;
        through the theological virtues alone.
    For infants:
        through Baptism alone.

III. CHRITICISM OF DOCTRINE

Eliminates the Term "Soul of the Church" Without Sufficient Reason:

Dr. Donovan is perfectly correct in saying that, "Non-Catholics, if they aren't validly baptized but wish to accomplish whatever God wants them to do, are members of the Church only by desire in the same way as are catechumens." But when he adds, "In past generations much ink was spilt through argumentation on being in the soul of the Church only, an ignorant expression for saying that a person has virtual membership in the Church if he is a sanctified catechumen," this is not entirely defensible, for the following reasons:

- The traditional use of "soul of the Church" was applied to non-Catholics, as in Bellarmine and the Acts of the Vatican Council, does not say that such people belong only to the soul of the Church.
- The term "soul of the Church" is hardly "an ignorant expression," if for no other reason, than at least because it emphasizes the fact that sincere non-Catholics *can* and *do* have the gifts of the Holy Spirit, expressed by the terms *anima Ecclesiae*, even though they do not actually profess the Catholic faith, expressed by the term *corpus Ecclesiae*.

Based on an Inadequate Distinction Between Membership and Communion in the Catholic Church:

According to Dr. Donovan, Canon 87 "makes a very clear distinction between membership in the Church and communion with the Church." This is only partially acceptable. First, we have the text of the Canon: "Through Baptism a human being is constituted a person in the Church of Christ with all the rights and duties of Christians, unless, as regards rights, an obstacle stands in the way which impairs the bond of ecclesiastical communion or a censure imposed by the Church."

The meaning of Canon 87 has already been explained[259] according to which we saw that the Canon says nothing directly about a difference between membership in and communion with the Church. The distinction which the Canon makes is rather between the rights (*jura*) and the duties (*officia*) which the Sacrament of Baptism imposes on a Christian. The duties, we are told, remain *per se* intact, while the rights are lost in greater or less degree, according to the nature of the obstacle that a person places which impairs the bond of ecclesiastical unity, and according to the gravity of the censure which the Church may impose upon him.

Accordingly, it is erroneous to say that a baptized person can retain *membership* in the Church, while lacking *communion* with the Church, except in the following isolated cases:

- here only a minor censure is imposed, like suspension, which, by definition, merely wants to restrict some of the privileges of a Catholic as a corrective or punitive measure, without intending to cut him off formally from the visible unity of the Church.
- where the penalty of excommunication is not imposed in its highest degree; though even here some authorities, like Bellarmine, do not distinguish, but simply say that excommunication, as such, severs the bond of Catholic unity.[260]

We see, therefore, that while the distinction between membership and communion is valid up to a point, its application is limited. It definitely does not extend to those who:

- Voluntarily and culpably withdraw from Catholic unity, through apostasy, heresy or schism.
- Voluntarily, though inculpably, after Baptism, openly profess a heretical or schismatic form of Christianity.
- Involuntarily are censured by the Church with formal excommunication, at least in its most solemn and rigorous form.

These three classes of persons do not retain actual membership in the visible Church of Christ, even though they have been validly baptized. Our concern here is not with the first class, i.e., with formal heretics, schismatics and apostates; nor with the third, i.e., excommunicated persons; but exclusively with the second, i.e., with baptized non-Catholics, and specifically, with heretics in good faith.

However, we should also note in passing that at least as regards major excommunication, the statement that, "Excommunicated Catholics…don't lose membership in the Church," is hardly consistent with Christian tradition.

Thus Bellarmine, summarizing the doctrine of the Church up to his time, says, "That excommunicated persons are not in the Church....is proved from Canon Law[261]... from the Fathers[262] ... and by reason."[263] According to the wording of Canon Law, he points out, "Following the canonical statutes and the example of the Holy Fathers, by the authority of God and the judgment of the Holy Ghost; *we eliminate from the bosom of Holy Mother Church and from association with all Christianity, the violators of the Churches of God.*"[264] Moreover, "When excommunicated persons are absolved," St. Robert adds, "it is said: 'I restore you to the *unity of the Church* and to participation with its members.' This is a clear sign that an excommunicated person is separated from the unity of the Church."[265]

And recently, Pius XII in the Encyclical *Mystici* Corporis, declared that, "Only those are really to be included as members of the Church who have been baptized and profess the true faith, and who have not unhappily withdrawn from body-unity, or for grave faults have been *excluded by legitimate authority*."[266] The last clause evidently refers to those who have been excommunicated, of whom the Pope explicitly says that they are not really to be included as members of the Church. No question here of mere deprivation of juridical rights, but of separation from the visible unity of the Catholic Church.

Reasoning from his distinction between membership and communion in the Church, Dr. Donovan concludes that baptized non-Catholics retain their formal membership acquired at Baptism, but lack only the juridical privilege of receiving the Church's Sacraments, communing with the Church, attending divine offices, etc. But this conclusion is not admissible, for the following reasons:

- When the term "communion with the Church" involves such essentials as participation in the same Sacraments and submission to the Church's common authority vested in the Pope, it is to be identified with "membership in the Church." So that, given a person who does not communicate with the Church in these essentials, he is, *by that very fact*, not a member of the body of the Church of Christ, which is constituted by the common profession of the same faith, participation in the same Sacraments, and obedience to the same supreme authority.
- In the case in point, the writer has confused "communion in *some* privileges enjoyed by Catholics in good standing" with "communion in the essential practices of the Catholic faith," such as participation in the same Sacraments and obedience to the Roman Pontiff. The first kind of communion, it is clear, may be lacking while formal membership is retained. Thus, for example, a recalcitrant priest may be suspended *"a*

divinis." He is, therefore, "lacking in communion with the Church," to the extent that, as a priest, he may not celebrate the Divine mysteries; yet, for all that, he is still a member of the Catholic Church.

But the second kind of "communion with the Church" may not be distinguished from "membership in the Church," as though the two concepts, *communion with* and *membership in,* were mutually exclusive. For, in the instance, communion with the Church *is* membership in the Church. Not that such communion exhausts all the qualities of formal membership. But in the sense that if *this kind* of communion is lacking, membership in the Church is also lacking.

The reason for this is evident from all that has been said of the essence of membership in the one visible Church, which is external profession of the true faith, manifested in the confession of the same Creed, participation in the same Sacraments, and obedience to the same visible Head. From which it follows that baptized non-Catholics:

- Are lacking in communion with the Church in those essentials which constitute actual membership in the Church's visible organism.
- Therefore, they are not to be considered formal members of the one true Church founded by Christ.

Based on the Concept of a Purely Invisible Church

What evidently led Dr. Donovan to reach the conclusions he did regarding both excommunicates and baptized heretics, was his concept of incorporation in the Mystical Body by something less than visible ties, given initial incorporation through Baptism. Quoting Vonier on the point, he explains that for adults there are only two ways of being united to God: through the theological virtues and Baptism, and through the theological virtues alone. Catholics, in common with baptized heretics, enjoy the first kind of union; catechumens the second. But in either case, profession of the Catholic faith is not considered necessary for membership in the Mystical Body, for we are told that these are "the *only* two forms of union with God," including mere Baptism for virtual or formal infants. Of course a professed Catholic enjoys obvious advantages over the heretic, in confessing the true faith and using the means for sanctification which the Church places at his disposal. But these benefits in no way make him any more truly a member of the Catholic Church because "if he is a validly baptized non-Catholic," in spite of his professing heresy, "he has *formal* membership in the Church," that is, in the one true Church of Christ.

If we look for a justification of this strange position, we may find it in the theologian, Vonier, whom Dr. Donovan quotes with approval. In

the same volume and chapter in which Vonier expresses himself on the
two forms of union with God, Baptism and/or the theological virtues, he
also says:

> "A man who has faith has laid his hand on the salvation of
> Christ. It is the most universal way of coming into touch with
> the redemption of the Cross; it is an approach which is pos-
> sible from every direction, from the past as well as from the
> present. … Adam, in his very fall, plunged into it headlong;
> and it will be present to the last human generation. … Any-
> one who has faith is in the supernatural state and therefore is
> directly in touch with Christ's life, though he be otherwise
> in a state of mortal sin… A man ceases to be Christ's solely
> through the sin of infidelity; he does not cease to be Christ's
> through any other sin, however heinous. As long as his faith is
> a true faith, he remains a member of Christ's Mystical Body,
> though there be grievous sores of mortal sins in him… Unless
> we grasp that function of faith as the psychic link between
> Christ and the soul, Catholicism becomes unintelligible…
> The Church is constituted primarily through faith, and her
> powers are for those who possess that responsiveness of
> soul called faith. …Actual incorporation with Christ … has
> a three-fold degree: the first is through faith, the second is
> through charity of life, the third is through the possession of
> heaven."[267]

Now, in context, Vonier is defending a position not unlike Melchior
Cano's, whom Bellarmine refuted, who explained the axiom: *Extra Ecclesiam nulla salus,* by invoking a universal Church of all the believers,
from Adam, to Abraham, to the end of the world. For it is not true to say
that "a man ceases to be Christ's solely through the sin of infidelity," in
the sense that, "As long as his faith is the true faith, he remains a member of Christ's Mystical Body, though there be grievous sores of mortal
sins in him." A heretic and schismatic may retain their faith and yet they
are not members of the Catholic Church. True, as Pius XII says, "Not
every sin, however grave and enormous it be, is such as to sever a man
automatically from the body of the Church," but the Pope is careful to
add, "as does schism or heresy," and not only infidelity or apostasy.[268]

Remembering that we are here dealing with the question of membership in the Church, if we say that infidelity alone severs the bond between a Christian and Christ's Mystical Body, then, logically, no matter
what external profession of faith a man makes, as long as he is not an
infidel, he remains an actual member of the Catholic Church which he
entered at Baptism.

We see, therefore, how Dr. Donovan, in following Vonier's lead, ended up with the conclusion that baptized non-Catholics are formally in the true Church of Christ. The process of reasoning may be summarized as follows:

1. Through Baptism a person actually enters the Catholic Church.
2. The essential bond of unity in the Church is interior faith.
    *   If this faith is coupled with charity, the person is an actual and living member of the true Church.
    *   If this faith is lacking in charity, the person is nonetheless an actual, but no longer a vital member of the Church.
3. If a Christian loses his faith by infidelity, only then does he cease to be a member of the Church, either actually or vitally.
4. But as long as he retains this interior faith, he remains actually incorporated in the Mystical Body of Christ, in spite of his external profession of heresy or schism.

Consistent with these principles, Dr. Donovan should also include formal heretics and schismatics, but for our purpose it is enough to see that he would certainly incorporate material heretics as actually in the body of the visible Church of Christ.

The simplest answer to this theory is that the basis on which it rests is inadmissible. To distinguish, as he does, between membership in the Church and communion with the Church is correct only to the extent that a Catholic may be deprived, as a penalty, of some of the privileges of communion with the rest of the faithful, while remaining an actual Catholic. It is false when applied, as here, to all who have been validly baptized, saying that, although they lack communion with the Church even in essentials, they are nevertheless formally incorporated in Catholic unity. To defend such a thesis, the only alternative is to fall back on an invisible unitive bond, like faith and charity, which unites all Christians in a cosmic Catholic Church, and which transcends the visible ties of participation in the same Sacraments and communion with the Roman Pontiff. But this is the doctrine of the latitudinarians and a contradiction to the teaching of Pius XII, who pointed out, "How grievously they err who arbitrarily picture the Church as something hidden and invisible.... who conjure up from their fancies an imaginary Church, a kind of Society which finds its origin and growth in charity."[269] For, invisible the Catholic Church must be, if every "validly baptized non-Catholic," short of an open apostate, "has formal membership in the Church," founded by Christ.

CHAPTER IV

THIRD THEORY:
"ACTUAL CATHOLICS ARE MEMBERS OF THE BODY OF THE CHURCH; NON-CATHOLICS ARE MEMBERS OF THE SOUL OF THE CHURCH."

I. STATEMENT OF DOCTRINE

It is significant how consistently those who write on the subject of non-Catholics in their relation to the Church, invoke the distinction between the body and soul of the Church; in the sense first enunciated by Robert Bellarmine. The following statement of doctrine attempts to solve the problem by declaring simply that professed Catholics belong to the body and sincere non-Catholics to the soul of the Church. It represents a section of one chapter in *Apologetics*, written by Dr. Paul J. Glenn, of St. Charles Seminary, Columbus Ohio. He says:

"The statement, 'Outside the true Church there is no salvation,' means… that there is no salvation outside the Catholic Church. Now, who are outside the Catholic Church? Those are outside the Catholic Church, and consequently outside the way of salvation, who know the Catholic Church to be the true Church, yet do not become true and faithful members of that Church. Further, those are outside the Catholic Church who refuse to interest themselves in the quest of the true Church and will not even consider the claims of the Catholic Church to be the true Church. Those who are *within* the Catholic Church are all her actual members, and also those who are not her members, but sincerely believe that the Church to which they belong is the true Church. The actual members of the Catholic Church constitute the *body* of the Church; non-Catholics who are honestly convinced that their own sect is the true Church are, provided they are in the state of grace, members of the *soul* of the Catholic Church.

"Membership in the true Church (whether of her body of faithful or of her spirit or soul) are not 'saved' by mere membership. Membership in the true Church, the Catholic Church, is prerequisite to salvation, but it is not *all* that is requisite. The members of the Catholic Church must lead lives in accordance with her teaching, they must avoid sin and keep in God's grace if they are to be saved. The actual members of the group or *body* of the faithful have here an obvious advantage over the members of the soul of the Church alone. For the actual members partake of the grace-giving Sacraments; they can have their sins definitely and unmistakably forgiven if they confess them in sincere contrition and with determination of avoiding them for the future, to Christ's authorized minister, the priest; they can be actually united in body and soul with Jesus Christ in Holy Communion. Those outside the body of the Church, but members of the soul, have not these advantages. Therefore, let no one say that sincere non-Catholics ought not to be disturbed about their belief, but ought to be left in their sincerity as members of the soul of Christ's Church. Christ wills all men to enter His visible society for salvation, the bodily group of the faithful; He wills all to confess His faith and His Church *before men*; He wants all to have the inestimable benefits of the Sacraments and of the graces that flow to the actual members of the Church through her ministry. Let not the Catholic apologist think that he may take his ease in the comforting thought that after all many non-Catholics, many who are actual and bitter enemies of what they think the Catholic Church is, are nevertheless less true members of her soul. Let him be alert for the spread and the defense of the truth."[270]

II.   ANALYSIS OF DOCTRINE

Dr. Glenn's theory may be summarized in a series of propositions. Thus:

1.   Outside the Church there is no salvation means: Outside the *Catholic* Church there is no salvation.

2.   The following persons are outside the Catholic Church:
     •   Those who know the Catholic Church to be the true Church, yet do not become true and faithful members of the Church.
     •   Those who refuse to interest themselves in the quest of the true Church, and will not even consider the claims of the Catholic Church to be the true Church.

3.   The following persons are within the Catholic Church:
     •   Those who are actual members of the Catholic Church.
     •   Those who are not her members but sincerely believe that the church to which they belong is the true Church.

4.   The Catholic Church is composed of a body and a soul, in which:
     •   The actual members constitute the body of the Church.
     •   Non-Catholics who are honestly convinced that their own sect is the true Church, provided they are in a state of grace, are members of the soul of the Church.

5.   Membership in the Catholic Church is prerequisite for salvation, but it is not all that is requisite. The members of the Church must also:
     •   Lead lives in accordance with Christ's teaching.
     •   Avoid sin and keep in God's grace.

6.   The advantages which the members of the body of the Church have over those who belong only to the soul are that:
     •   They can have their sins forgiven definitely in the Sacrament of Confession.
     •   They can receive Holy Communion.

7.   Sincere non-Catholics should not be left undisturbed in their sincerity as members of the soul of Church because:
     •   Christ wills all men to enter His visible society for salvation.
     •   Christ wills all to confess His faith and His Church before men.
     •   Christ wants all to have the benefits of the Sacraments of the graces that flow to the actual members of the Church through her ministry.

III.   CHRITICISM OF DOCTRINE

Background of the Theory
Statement of Problem

Dr. Glenn, unlike the author of the first theory examined, seriously faces the problem which Bellarmine intended to solve, namely, how to reconcile the doctrine *Extra Ecclesiam nulla salus*, with the fact that even those people who are not actual members of the true Church can be saved. Like Bellarmine, he realized that the necessity of belonging to the Church refers exclusively to the Catholic Church. However, when he comes to resolve the dilemma, while he goes back to one of Bellarmine's principles, the distinction between the body and soul of the Church, he overlooks another, and more basic, distinction, which is, *re* or *voto* membership in the Church. As a result, his solution is not clear and precise and is, in fact, partly erroneous, as will be seen in the subsequent analysis.

Solution of the Problem

According to Dr. Glenn, the problem of the salvation of non-Catholics is solved by interpreting the classic formula as follows:

> *No salvation outside the Catholic Church's Body*
> *No salvation outside the Catholic Church's Soul*

which means that no one will be saved unless he belongs *either* to the body of the Church *or* to its soul. Evidently sincere non-Catholics, whether baptized or not, do not belong to the Church's body which is constituted by the profession of the true faith. Yet, they can be saved, and, necessarily, by some kind of association with the Catholic Church. Therefore, we are told, it must be in virtue of their membership in the Church's spirit or soul.

What precisely does this mean? In context, the soul of the Church is declared to be:

1. Distinct from the body of the Church, that is, from the group or body of the faithful.
2. Something invisible, as distinct from the visible society which Christ founded.
3. Composed of those sincere non-Catholics who are in the state of grace.

Basis of the Theory

Presupposes That Membership in the Visible Catholic Church is Not Necessary for Salvation

If we go back to Bellarmine's statement of the same problem, we recall that he also distinguished membership in the Church in order to explain how non-Catholics can be saved. But his version was this:

No salvation outside the Catholic Church, *Re* or *Voto*

In other words, what Bellarmine recognized immediately was the necessity of belonging to the Catholic Church, as such, to be saved: and then he went on to explain that no one can be saved, including non-Catholics, unless he belongs either *re* or *voto* to the true Church of Christ. There was no question in his mind of explaining the dogma in terms of the body and soul of the Church. It was always membership in the *Church* which had to be vindicated, even in the case of those who do not belong to it by actual profession.

Dr. Glenn, on the contrary, does not consider belonging to the Church, as such, i.e., body *and* soul, as necessary for salvation. For, as he says, only actual Catholics belong to the Church's body, whereas non-Catholics *in bona fide* belong to the soul. For him, the dichotomy is simply either body or soul, with salvation equally possible, although not equally easy, in the one as in the other.

However, in interpreting the formula to mean:

	Corpus	
Extra Ecclesiae	*vel*	*Nulla Salus*
	Animam	

he has really stripped it of all intelligible meaning. For what value is there in first saying, "There is no salvation outside the Catholic Church," and then going on to admit that people who have no connection with the *visible* Catholic Church can nevertheless be saved ? To explain the salvation of non-Catholics by relegating them to the soul of the Church is really to avoid the problem at issue. For, as we have seen at length, it is membership in the visible Catholic Church, body *and* soul, which Christian tradition has always declared to be necessary for salvation.

Assumption That the Body and Soul of the Church are Distinct and Independent Entities

Dr. Glenn makes the unusual distinction here between being a *member* of the Church and being *within* the Church. The latter he considers more general and extensive, and also as including the former. So that, being within the Church includes:

- Membership in the body of the Church which, in the concrete, means all the faithful who actually profess the Catholic faith.
- Membership in the soul of the Church, which, concretely, means all sincere non-Catholics who are in the state of grace.

However, underlying this distinction is an untenable hypothesis, namely, that the body and soul of the Church are not only mutually exclusive but completely independent of each other; so that a person can belong to the body without also belonging to the soul, and vice versa. The complete disjunction between the body and soul of the Church, however, as proposed by Dr. Glenn, is not defensible. For if we say, as he does, that a person may be in the body of the Church and possess the grace of God, without belonging to the Church's soul; or that he may be in the soul of the Church and possess sanctifying grace, without belonging to the Church's body — we equivalently say that justification is possible in either the one or the other, which is not correct.

First, to say that actual Catholics belong to the body of the Church as distinct from being in the soul, is to misuse our terms. For while it is true that a person can, at least according to Bellarmine, "belong" to the Church as a dead member attached to the Church's body although he has no internal virtue but only externally professes the faith, yet this sort of truncated "membership" will never get him to heaven. To be justified and saved, he must also possess the gifts of the Holy Spirit, notably and indispensably the gift of charity, which puts him into the soul of the Church. Otherwise, for all his membership in the Mystical Body on earth, he will be cut off from the Mystical Body at death. Not membership in the body of the Church alone, therefore, but membership in the body and soul of the Church is necessary for salvation.

So also with regard to non-Catholics, if we say that they are justified by simply belonging to the soul of the Church, we are begging the question. Of course they are saved if they possess at death, sanctifying grace along with the other gifts of the Holy Spirit. But then we are not answering the question of how this is possible. The correct answer is that sincere non-Catholics may indeed belong *voto* to the soul of the Church, i.e. the Holy Spirit *ut informans Ecclesiam*, and can be saved in virtue of this membership. But their possession of grace is not explained but merely declared, unless we say that they also belong to the body of the Church by their desire, at least implicit, to enter into the visible unity of the Catholic Faith.

CHAPTER V

FOURTH THEORY: "NON-CATHOLICS ARE NOT MEMBERS OF THE CHURCH IN ANY SENSE. THEREFORE, WITH RARE EXCEPTIONS THEY CANNOT ATTAIN TO SALVATION."

I. STATEMENT OF DOCTRINE

A recent opinion in America, which has since been officially censured by the Holy See, holds that there is only one kind of membership in the Catholic Church, namely, an actual one. Consequently, since membership in the Church is necessary for salvation, non-Catholics, with a rare exception, cannot be saved if they die before becoming actual members of the Roman Catholic communion. Before quoting citations from this theory, it should be noted that its first approach was practical and concerned itself, originally, with a problem of fact. The question was whether, *de facto*, non-Catholic adults, notably those living in Christian countries, are sincere in their non-acceptance of the Catholic Faith. The unequivocal answer was: they are not. As a result, the approach to the dogma *Extra Ecclesiam nulla salus*, will also be different than what has been in the previous theories investigated. Very simply, there is not much need of theorizing about how to reconcile the salvation of non-Catholics with the necessity of membership in the true Church if one of the presupposite is denied; to wit, the possible salvation of anyone except an actually professing member of the Catholic Church.

For the sake of convenience, the main points of this theory will be summarized, from quotations, under the following heading:

Explicit Faith in the Catholic Church and in Her Teachings is Necessary For Salvation

"Explicit faith in the articles of the Creed is necessary for salvation. But is this enough? Saint Thomas teaches that it is enough only if the person is unable to know more truths explicitly, and does not deny any articles of the Faith (2/2/2/7). On the contrary, a man who professes to hold the truths of the Faith and at the same time explicitly denies even one truth, does not have the Faith at all, and therefore cannot be saved (2/2/3/3). This would be true in the case of a man who denied the supremacy and infallibility of the Catholic Church and the necessity of the Church for salvation.

"For further proof that explicit belief in the Catholic Church *is* necessary for salvation, let us quote St. Thomas… "Neither formed nor formless faith remains in a heretic who disbelieves one article of faith…. Consequently whoever does not adhere, as to an infallible and divine rule, to the teaching of the Church, which proceeds from the First Truth manifested in Holy Scriptures, has not the habit of faith, but holds the things which are of faith otherwise than by faith," (2/2/5/3).

"Proof of the necessity of explicit belief in the Catholic Church and the acceptance of all the revealed truths proposed by her for belief in order to be saved is found all through the writings of the Fathers, the Doctors, and in the Councils… (Thus) the Council of Constance condemned the 41st proposition of John Wycliff in which this heretic said that it was not necessary for salvation to believe in the supremacy of the Roman Church.[271]

"The Encyclical *Quanto Conficiamur* by Pius IX is universally quoted by liberals to support their doctrine that a man totally ignorant of the Catholic Faith can be saved. But what does Pius IX say ? *'It is known to Us and to you that those who labor under invincible ignorance of our holy religion, and who, zealously observing the natural law and its precepts… are able, by the powerful workings of God's light and grace, to attain eternal life.'*[272]

"This means that God, in His mercy, will find a way of enabling the man who is invincibly ignorant of the Church and who follows the natural law, to achieve his salvation. But Pius IX nowhere says that this can be done without the Catholic Faith. On the contrary, he explicitly says, a few lines later, that it is "a Catholic dogma that no one can be saved outside the Catholic Church.'[273] Thus, God will find the way to enable that man to save his soul, and this way will be the Catholic Faith and the Catholic Church."[274]

There is Only One Kind of Membership in the Catholic Church

"Let us examine whether there is any such thing as 'membership in the Church *in voto*.' A man cannot be more or less a member of the Church. He either is a Catholic, or he is not a Catholic, for the Catholic Church is the Mystical Body of Christ. This means that it is a body in the real sense of the word, and not in a metaphorical sense. Like any other real body, therefore, no member of it can be more or less a part of it. The same soul animates it all, and if a member is separated from the body, it is cut off from it, and is no longer animated by the soul, hence it has no life in it.[275]

"Let us ask, therefore, who can be called a member of the Church in any sense? No one can be called a member of the Church in any sense who does not confess the truths of the Faith, does not partake of the Sacraments, and does not submit to the infallible authority of the Supreme Pontiff.[276]

(Two theologians, Bainvel and Caperan, are charged with "liberalism" for teaching otherwise.) In the third chapter of his book, *Is There Salvation Outside of the Church?* Father Bainvel examines some solutions given by other liberals to what they call a 'contradiction' in Catholic dogmas. These solutions, 'good faith, the soul of the Church, the invisible Church, the necessity of precept,' he finds inadequate… But in the next chapter he proposes his own solution:

> 'The solution of the problem lies in the fact that we can be members of the Church in two ways, externally (visibly) and internally (invisibly).'[277]

Later in the same book, Father Bainvel says:

> 'This distinction between union with the Church *in act* and *in desire* dates far back into Christian antiquity.'[278]

"But this is not the worst. Not only does Bainvel say that affiliation with the Church can be in desire and invisible, but he goes as far as to say that it can even be unconscious, when there is no desire at all of joining the Church. He says:

'Souls affiliated with the Church unconsciously are united to her by invisible ties, for they are affiliated with her internally, by an implicit desire, which God is pleased to regard as equivalent to external membership.'[279]

"This is the end of all Christianity and all sanity… Caperan says the same thing in the following two quotations:

> 'When, by reason of invincible ignorance, incorporation into Catholic society is not realized in fact, even an implicit desire to be so incorporated takes the place of actual incorporation.'[280]

> 'Concerning the necessity of Baptism and the necessity of membership in the Church, an implicit desire which is included in the general will to do God's will is sufficient.'[281]

"This destroys one of the most central doctrines of the Church, for the Church has always taught that she is a visible society and the only kind of membership in her must necessarily be an external and visible one. St. Robert Bellarmine teaches that no one can be a member of the Church who is not *visibly* affiliated with the one visible society founded by Christ. To quote St. Robert Bellarmine:

'The Church is a society, not of Angels, nor of souls, but of men. But it cannot be called a society of men, unless it consist in external and visible signs.'[282]

"Let no one…misunderstand St. Robert's statement in another chapter of the same work when he says that catechumens are not in the Church *in fact*, but *in voto*. This in no way states that there are two ways of being members of the Church, in fact and *in voto*. It simply means that catechumens have the explicit intention of coming into the Church and of becoming members of the Church, which membership they do not at all have at the moment. St. Robert Bellarmine proves conclusively in various places that catechumens are *not* members of the Church in any sense.[283] For example, after giving his definition of the Church, St. Robert says that catechumens are excluded from this definition because they do not have the communion of the sacraments."[284]

Those Who Remain Separated From the Catholic Church Cannot Be Saved

"… that those who know the Catholic Church and the Catholic Faith can remain outside the Church either innocently and with a good excuse, or obstinately and without excuse, and that only the latter cannot attain eternal salvation… is against Catholic doctrine. No one can refuse to enter the Church and be saved. When Pope Pius IX mentions those who obstinately remain separated from the Church, he does not contrast them with those who remain innocently separated, but with those who never heard about the Catholic Faith. What he says is that those who are ignorant of the Church because they never heard of it, if they have faithfully kept the natural law implanted in their hearts by God, can, with His help, come to the knowledge of the Catholic Church, in which alone they can be saved. But, on the other hand, those who know about the Catholic Church and refuse to enter her, will perish. It is to emphasize the heinousness of their refusal that Pope Pius IX calls it contumacious and obstinate, not to distinguish between it and some other hypothetical kind of refusal which would not be obstinate."[285]

All Protestants Are Formal Heretics

"St. Augustine says: 'If any there are who defend their opinion, though it be false and perverse, without obstinate fervor, and who seek the truth with all solicitude, ready to correct their opinion when they have found the truth, they are not at all to be accused of heresy.'[286]

"Only a faithful Catholic who obeys the Church and is ready to correct his opinions according to her admonitions, can be in error in this sense without being a heretic. This we call material heresy. A man who is in material heresy does not intend to contradict the authority and teachings of the Church. On the other hand, a man who does not intend in the least to follow the teachings of the Catholic Church and to be corrected by her cannot be called a material heretic. It is clear, therefore, that Protestants are not material heretics. Are they, then, *formal* heretics? What is a formal heretic?

"St. Augustine says, 'A heretic is one who either devises or follows false and new opinions.'[287] (Since) the teachings and opinions of Protestants fall under this last designation… Protestants, therefore, hold heresy *formally*."[288]

Justification Before Baptism — Possible Only With an Explicit Desire to Enter the True Church

"It must be noted that the Holy Spirit cannot possibly effect sanctification in a man apart from any sacrament or visible sign. Thus, before the coming of Christ, sanctification came to men by means of circumcision, sacrifice and the other sacraments of the Old Law. Since the coming of the Messiah, sanctification comes by means of the sacraments of the Church, which are seven in number.

"The first of these sacraments … is Baptism. And Baptism is invalid for an adult if he does not have the explicit purpose of receiving it, and unprofitable if he does not explicitly confess Christ and His Church.[289]

"But there could be a case when a man, together with the explicit intention of receiving a sacrament, and with the profession of the Catholic Faith and of the Catholic Church, would make an act of perfect charity, even before the actual reception of the sacrament. In that case the man can receive sanctifying grace before the sacrament, *if* he firmly intends to receive the sacrament at the earliest possible opportunity. (Thus) in the case of Baptism…if the catechumen to be baptized can make an act of perfect charity, remission of his sins can precede the actual reception of Baptism, provided explicit faith and an explicit intent to receive Baptism are not lacking.[290]

"Justification, therefore, and sanctifying grace, can come to a person before the actual reception of the sacrament of Baptism, provided explicit faith in Christ, explicit purpose to receive the sacrament and to join the Catholic Church, and perfect charity, are not lacking."[291]

Sanctifying Grace Before Baptism Is Not Sufficient For Salvation

"Is, then, the reception of sanctifying grace through Baptism of the Spirit a real substitute for Baptism of water, so that a man like Cornelius did not need Baptism and could have been saved without it? Are there two ways of belonging to the Church, one through Baptism of water and the other Baptism *in voto*, so that the one would be sufficient without the other for salvation?

"St. Augustine says: 'Cornelius would have been guilty of contempt for so holy a sacrament if, even after he had received the Holy Ghost, he had refused to be baptized.'[292]

"To repeat then, sanctifying grace can be received ahead of the Sacrament of Baptism, and in that case it is sufficient for *justification*, but this does not mean that it is sufficient for *salvation* if the actual Sacrament of Baptism is not received. Cornelius and his friends received sanctifying grace and the Holy Spirit even before the actual reception of Baptism... The water of Baptism would have seemed totally superfluous for them, and yet they could not have been saved without it. That is why, as St. Augustine adds, 'they were baptized, and for this action we have the authority of an apostle as a warrant.'[293] Again, St. John the Baptist was born in the state of sanctifying grace, and yet he had to be baptized by the Baptism of Christ before he died, for as St. John Chrysostom says (Homily 4 on Matthew), 'Since, when John said: 'I ought to be baptized by Thee, Christ answered: Suffer it to be so *now*, it follows that afterwards Christ did baptize John.'[294]

"The catechumen who confesses the Catholic Faith and has perfect charity and the intention of joining the Church can therefore receive sanctifying grace before the actual reception of Baptism. It is in this sense that St. Augustine (as quoted by St. Robert Bellarmine) says that such a catechumen may be said to be of the soul of the Church (because the theological virtues and the Gifts of the Holy Ghost are the vivifying principle in the Church).[295]

"Membership in the Church is necessary for salvation... We also showed that sanctifying grace can be received before Baptism, but in that case it does not confer membership in the Church. Therefore, even though a man can be justified before the actual reception of Baptism, as the Council of Trent says, this does not mean ... that this justification is sufficient for the man's salvation."[296]

Single Exception When Baptism of Desire Is Sufficent For Salvation

"Is there any case when Baptism of the Holy Spirit without actual reception of Baptism can be sufficient for salvation? ... In answer to our question ... we shall say that according to the majority of the Fathers and the Doctors, baptism of the Holy Spirit, without actual reception of Baptism of water, can be sufficient for salvation if the following five conditions are fulfilled:

> First, that person must have the Catholic Faith. We have already proved that no one can be saved without the Catholic Faith, and that not even the Sacrament of Baptism can be profitable for salvation if the subject does not confess the Catholic Faith.

> Second, he must have an explicit will or desire to receive the Sacrament of Baptism

> Third, he must have perfect charity. For St. Robert Bellarmine says that only 'perfect conversion can be called baptism of the Spirit, and this includes true contrition and charity.'[297]

> Fourth, he must have an explicit will to join the Catholic Church — for, as we have shown, not even actual Baptism is profitable for salvation if it is received outside the Catholic Church (except for babies) and without an explicit will to join the Church. Much less, therefore does baptism *in voto* profit for salvation if it does not include an explicit will to join the Catholic Church.

> Fifth, he must be dying, and although yearning for the Baptism of Water is unable to receive it because of an absolute impossibility, not because of a contempt for it. Thus... St. Thomas says, 'It is necessary, in order that a man might enter into the Kingdom of God, that he approach the baptism of water actually (*in re*), as it is in all those who are baptized; or *in voto*, as it is in the martyrs and the catechumens who were hindered by death before they could fulfill their intent (votum); or in figure, as in the ancient Fathers,'[298] — that is, in those before Christ."[299]

All Non-Catholics Guilty if They Die Before Becoming Actual Members of the Catholic Church

"Not only is the Catholic Church the one means of salvation, and he who remains outside it cannot be saved, but ... the person remaining outside the Church is to be blamed for it.

"If faith is a gift, no man can have it who refuses it when it is offered to him, or who does not ardently desire it when far from it. The reason then, why so many men have not the 'gift of faith'... is because they will not take it. It is true to say that they 'cannot' believe, but this is only because they 'will not.' Consequently, according to His Sacred Covenant, God also 'will not' save them — unless before they die they become members of His Church.

"Although God bestows his graces freely, He has freely promised to give every human being all the graces necessary to lead him to the Catholic Church; and He has freely promised that whoever shall act according to these graces will certainly have the opportunity to become a Catholic before he dies. Faith is a free gift of God, since we have intrinsically and naturally no right to it. But because God has promised to bestow this gift on all men of good will, He *cannot* withhold it from any man, except if this man has wickedly resisted all the graces already given to him, and would also resist this grace.

"But this is not what liberal Catholics mean when they speak of faith as a 'gift.' What they mean is that God can and does keep in ignorance of the truth, some people who are extremely virtuous and good willed. This erroneous opinion is due to the *myth* of the virtuous native who dies in invincible ignorance. The dogmas of the Faith absolutely preclude the existence of such a man; and no amount of sociology or geography can prove the contrary."[300]

Criticism of Doctrine

There are at least two ways of analyzing and refuting the aforesaid statements of doctrine. One would be to take the eight listed headings and answer each one of these separately; the other is to break down the whole theory into its constituent elements and answer these in logical order. The second method will be followed. Accordingly, on examining the fundamental errors involved in the theory, we find that they may be reduced to four, namely:

1. There is only one kind of membership in the Catholic Church, and that is actual.
2. With a single exception, actual Baptism is necessary for the salvation of all men.

3. Sanctifying grace without actual Baptism is not sufficient for salvation.
4. Among baptized persons, only those who actually profess the Catholic Faith can be saved.

We shall examine each of these errors in sequence:

There is Only One Kind of Membership in the Catholic Church, and That is Actual.

Fortunately, for our purpose, the authors of this theory relied in great part on the doctrine of St. Robert Bellarmine. In the instance, they invoke his authority to support the claim that there is no other kind than actual membership in the Church of Christ.

After decrying the liberalism of men like Bainvel, Caperan and Karl Adam, which "destroys one of the most central doctrines of the Church," its visibility, by allowing people to belong *voto* to the Church, they continue: "St. Robert Bellarmine teaches that as one can be a member of the Church who is not visibly affiliated with the one visible society founded by Christ, subject to the authority of His Vicar, the Roman Pontiff." However, they recognize that Bellarmine, if anyone, clearly speaks of those who do not actually belong to the visible Church, and that he credits them with *voto* communion with the Catholic Church. How get around the difficulty? Is Bellarmine for or against their theory? According to them, "A man cannot be more or less a member of the Catholic Church." Consequently, to the question, "whether there is any such thing as 'membership' in the Church in *voto*," they answer with an emphatic *No!* But Bellarmine himself uses the term *voto* in reference to catechumens. What does he mean? And then we are told. "It simply means that catechumens have the explicit intention of becoming members of the Church, which membership they do *not at all* have at the moment."[301]

This is a blatant misrepresentation of Bellarmine's doctrine. He explicitly declares that catechumens belong *voto* to the Catholic Church. Thus, "Since Catechumens are, if not *re*, at least *voto* in the Church, therefore they can be saved."[302] What the rigorists have done is to admit that Bellarmine uses the term *voto* regarding catechumens, and then arbitrarily and against the plain statement of the saint to the contrary, attached a new meaning to the term used. Schematically, we have:

Votum:	Subjectively,	the desire or intention of a non-Catholic to enter the True Church.
	Objectively,	the result of this desire or resolution, which is *Voto* Membership in the visible Church of Christ.

So that *votum*, taken subjectively, is a psychological fact which no one can deny, namely, that some people, who are not actually in the true Church, nevertheless have the will (votum) or desire to be enrolled among its members. Both Bellarmine and the authors of the rigorist theory freely admit *votum* in this sense.

Votum taken objectively is a dogmatic fact which rests on the principles of Christian tradition. It is the logical conclusion to a series of premises lined up and followed by Bellarmine:

- Since the dogma, *Extra Ecclesiam nulla salus* has universal application,
- Since there are some people, like catechumens who die before entering the Catholic Church *actu,*
- Therefore, unless we are to deprive all non-Catholics of the chance of eternal salvation, we must credit them with some kind of membership in the Church. The name is indifferent.
- But conveniently, it may be called *voto* membership, inasmuch as this term best describes the basis of a sincere non-Catholic's connection with the true Church, namely, his will and resolution to die in the Catholic communion.

Our theorists will not follow Bellarmine through the whole syllogism, and therefore they deny his conclusion. Specifically, they are willing to deprive catechumens of eternal salvation on the grounds that:

- The dogma, Extra Ecclesiam nulla salus, not only has universal application, but
- Its proper meaning is: *Extra Ecclesiam, actu, nulla salus.*

But in so doing, they openly disavow Bellarmine's doctrine which they pretend to follow, but which says that:

	Re	
Extra Ecclesiam	vel . . . . Nulla Salus
	Voto . . . .

Significantly, they omit quoting those passages in which Bellarmine teaches the doctrine of *voto* membership in the Church, although they quote other statements of St. Robert from the same chapter where these explicit passages occur.[303] And with good reason, because it would be hard to find in Christian tradition anyone more explicit than St. Robert to contradict the theory that only actual members of the Catholic Church can be saved.

By way of transition, we should note that the fundamental thesis of the opinion we are investigating is the foregoing, i.e. "Outside of *actual* membership in the Catholic Church there is no salvation." Now the question arises: What is meant by actual membership as a condition for salvation? And the answer given is:

Actual Membership in the Catholic Church means—
- Actual Baptism of water, plus
- actual profession of the Catholic Faith.

Logically, therefore, we have two applications of the theory to investigate, claiming that:

Only actually baptized persons have a chance of salvation. And this Includes:

1. All infants everywhere,
2. All adults in pagan lands,
3. All adults in Christian lands.

Excludes:

1. Only those persons who are not baptized and
2. Who explicitly desire Catholic Baptism,
3. Explicitly desire reception into the Catholic Church, or
4. Who die before it is at all possible to baptize them.

Requires the logical denial that sanctifying grace alone is sufficient for salvation, because Trent teaches clearly that even *voto* Baptism can confer the gift of infused charity.

Only those who *actually* profess the Catholic Faith have a title to salvation. This means that besides actual Baptism for all people, they must also actually profess the Catholic religion. In other words, everyone, without exception, once he reaches the age of reason must actually profess the true faith to be saved — not excluding the rare catechumen who dies before Baptism can be given to him.

What follows is a continued analysis and criticism of the above divisions of the theory, in the order listed.

With a Single Exception, Actual Baptism Is Necessary For The Salvation of All Men.

According to the rigorist theory, the only case where "Baptism of the Holy Spirit without actual Baptism of water can be sufficient for salvation (is) if the following five conditions are fulfilled:
- That person must have the Catholic Faith.
- He must have an explicit will or desire to receive the Sacrament of Baptism.
- He must have perfect charity.
- He must have an explicit will to join the Catholic Church.
- He must be dying, and although yearning for the Baptism of water is unable to receive it because of an absolute impossibility."[304]

Among the conditions listed, only number three, i.e., perfect charity, is fully admissible. As for the rest, for purposes of refutation, it is
enough to show:

> *Negatively*, that the Holy See, by its silence, has never de-
> clared that all these requirements are necessary for the salva-
> tion of the unbaptized. Thus, if we examine the various docu-
> ments in which the Holy See deals officially with the problem
> of infidels, especially in pagan lands, nowhere is there a hint
> that an explicit desire to be baptized, with an explicit wish
> to become Catholic, with death alone preventing the fulfill-
> ment of this wish, are absolutely necessary to guarantee the
> possible salvation of unbaptized non-Catholics.[305] Nineteen
> hundred years of silence by the Church on as essential a point
> of Catholic doctrine as this, is, in itself, an eloquent argu-
> ment against the theory of opposition. However, it is not all,
> because we also see:

> *Positively*, that the classic document of the Council of Trent,
> treating of the necessity of Baptism, is interpreted by the
> most authoritative moralists in the Church against the rigorist
> theory under investigation.

First the statement of Trent, which reads: "… since the promulgation of the Gospel, justification …cannot be effected except through the
laver of regeneration or its desire, as it is written: 'Unless a man be born
again of water and the Holy Ghost, he cannot enter into the kingdom of
God.'"[306]

Trent, therefore, recognizes the desire for Baptism as sufficient, *per
se,* to justify a man. But the question arises: What does the desire (*votum*) of Baptism mean here? How much does it have to include to be
effective of sanctification before actual Baptism? The answer of the rigorists is that: "The Council of Trent … teaches unmistakably that this
justification comes from Jesus Christ and only to those who believe in
Him according to the true faith, as the Apostle says, (Rom. 3: 23-26)…
Justification, therefore, and sanctifying grace, can come to a person
before actual reception of the sacrament of Baptism, provided *explicit*
faith in Christ, *explicit* purpose to receive the Sacrament and to join the
Catholic Church, and perfect charity, are not lacking."[307] In other words,
three explicit requirements are laid down as necessary to make the *votum Baptismi* valid:

- An explicit desire to receive Baptism.
- An explicit faith in Christ.
- An explicit intention to join the Catholic Church … and all these three
  only a moment before imminent death.

Now we are not left with the bare words of Trent in this important matter. For *votum Baptismi* as an instrument of justification has been explained at great length by the Church's theologians, especially the moralists, but in a way, most authoritatively by St. Alphonsus Liguori. Only this year [April, 1950; Editor's note] St. Alphonsus received another title of approval from the Holy See when Pius XII declared him to be the patron of confessors and teachers of moral theology. Already before him, Pius X said that, "All may safely follow the doctrine of the Holy Doctor in his moral teachings."[308] And now Pius XII declares that his "moral and pastoral doctrine…has been often most rightly approved by the Sovereign Pontiffs as a safe and strongly recommended norm for those who administer the Sacrament of Penance and have the direction of souls."[309]

On inspection, we find that St. Alphonsus eliminates all three of the aforesaid conditions as being absolutely certainly necessary to justify a person before Baptism.

1. Thus, by way of eliminating the absolute necessity of an *explicit* desire for Baptism, Liguori says: "Baptism of desire is a perfect conversion to God by contrition or the love of God above all things, with an explicit or *implicit* desire for true Baptism of water."[310]

2. By way of eliminating the absolutely certain necessity of an explicit faith in Christ, St. Alphonsus says: "Of the things which the faithful are obliged to believe explicitly, some must be necessarily believed with the necessity of means or of end, without which the ultimate end cannot be attained even by those who are inculpably ignorant; others by a necessity of precept, without which, if inculpably omitted, the end can be attained." Then he gives several categories, as follows:

"By necessity of means, these two are necessary:
Explicitly to believe that God exists and that He is the Rewarder of the good, according to the Apostle, Heb. 11-16 and the *credere oportet* of Trent.

After a sufficient promulgation of the Gospel, explicitly to believe, as says Molina, or at least *implicitly,* as certain others teach (like Connick and Layman) with *probability*, in Christ and the Most Holy Trinity." In order to explain this last point, he further asks: "Whether the mysteries of the Most Holy Trinity and of the Incarnation, after the promulgation of the Gospel, must be believed with an explicit faith, by a necessity of means or of precept?" And he answers: "The first opinion, which is more common and seems more probable, teaches that they must be believed by a necessity of means … But the second opinion, *also quite probable,* says that all are needed to believe these mysteries by a necessity of precept; and that by necessity of means it suffices if they are believed implicitly."[311]

3. By way of eliminating the absolute necessity of an explicit desire to join the Catholic Church, St. Alphonsus makes a category of those things to be believed only by a necessity of precept. Concretely, they represent that body of truths which specifically belong to the Catholic Faith, the acceptance of which is equivalently a desire to enter the Catholic Church. He says: "By necessity of precept each of the faithful is held under grave obligation explicitly to believe, at least in a rude sort of way and as regards essentials, the following:
    *   The Creed
    *   The Lord's Prayer
    *   The Precepts of the Decalogue and of the Church
    *   The most necessary Sacraments, i.e., Baptism, Eucharist and Penance; the others when the person desires to receive them…All of which is to be understood to mean: unless inability or invincible ignorance excuses."[312]

Sanctifying Grace Without Actual Baptism Is Not Sufficient For Salvation

Up to this point, the rigorist position may be summarized thus:

1. Actual Baptism is necessary for justification, except where—
2. Baptism of desire is coupled with:
    *   An explicit desire for Baptism
    *   An explicit faith in Christ
    *   An explicit intension to enter the Catholic Church…death alone preventing the Baptism and actual entrance into Catholic communion.

Now, regarding the *votum Baptismi*, they conceive of two possibilities in the practical order:

1. For a person who is dying and it is absolutely impossible to give him Baptism of water, he is not only justified but may also be saved.
2. For a person who is not dying, though all the other conditions are fulfilled, including perfect charity, he is only justified but cannot be saved, unless and until he receives actual Baptism. Thus we are plainly told: "Sanctifying grace can be received ahead of the Sacrament of Baptism, and in that case it is sufficient for *justification,* but this does not mean that it is sufficient for salvation if the actual Sacrament of Baptism is not received." Even John the Baptist, although "he was born in the state of sanctifying grace…yet he had to be baptized by the Baptism of Christ before he died," otherwise he would not have been saved.[313]

We have here a distinction between justification and salvation that is not unfamiliar in the history of error. Various reasons have been given at different times for distinguishing between the two, and denying that a person who is justified is *ipso facto* entitled to salvation. But always the Church has vindicated an equality between the two, in the sense that a person who is justified is truly a friend of God, an heir to heaven, and nothing, *per se*, stands in the way of his salvation if he dies in the state of grace.

> Thus, the Council of Trent, in the very decree in which it allows Baptism *in re* or *in voto* as a means of justification, further identifies this justification with a title to salvation. "*Justification* of a sinner," it is said, "cannot, since the promulgation of the Gospel, be effected except through the laver of regeneration or its desire, as it is written: 'Unless a man be born again of water and the Holy Ghost, he cannot enter into the kingdom of God.'"[314]
>
> And shortly after, again, Trent says: "Justification (by whatever means achieved, even by *voto Baptismi*) is not only a remission of sins but also the sanctification and renewal of the inward man through the voluntary reception of the grace and whereby an unjust man becomes just, and from being an enemy becomes a friend, that he may be an heir according to the hope of *life everlasting*."[315]
>
> More recently, St. Pius V condemned the following proposition of Baius, that: "In men who are penitent before the Sacrament of Absolution, and in catechumens before Baptism, there is true justification, but separated from the remission of sins," and consequently not entitling them to eternal salvation.[316]

Moreover, when Bellarmine treats the subject of *voto* membership in the Church for catechumens, he explicitly declares that they are not only justified, but also have a title to salvation. Neither does he require a person to have an explicit desire to be baptized in order to qualify for *voto* membership.[317] There is not the slightest suggestion that he considered justification and the possession of sanctifying grace as inadequate for salvation, even when justification was received before Baptism and there was no imminent danger of death. For when Bellarmine speaks of *voto* membership in the Church, it is always as a means of salvation and not merely of justification. Indeed, the very reason why he concludes to such membership is to explain the *salvation* of those people who die before receiving actual Baptism. Catechumens, he says, "are *fideles* and can be *saved*."[318] And, "when it is said that outside the Church no one can be *saved*, it must be understood of those who are in the Church neither in reality nor in desire, as theologians commonly speak about Baptism. But since catechumens are in the Church, if not *re*, at least *voto*, therefore, they can be *saved*."[319]

It is worth special mention to see how the rigorists misrepresented Bellarmine on this issue in a way that is almost unbelievable. They claim that St. Robert is in favor of their position that sanctifying grace before Baptism does not entitle a person to salvation. To prove the point, they quote a Protestant objection from the *Controversies* and then give the objection itself as the doctrine of St. Robert. Parallel columns will illustrate the case:

Quite obviously, Bellarmine gives an answer to this objection which he quotes from the Sectarians. He says: "Cornelius had unquestionably received the forgiveness of his sins before Baptism, at least after he heard the faith from Blessed Peter and had a desire for Baptism. For, as it is said in Acts 10, he also had the Holy Spirit dwelling within him. But Augustine, in the passages quoted, is speaking of the time when

Bellarmine	Rigorist Theory
"Sixteenth objection: … Moreover Augustine (says) in Epist. 57 *Ad Dardanum*; in lib.1, cap. 7 *De Praedestinatione Sanctorum*; in lib.1, quaest.2 *Ad Simplicianum*; in lib.7, cap.8 *De Baptismo*; and in lib. IV, cap.21 of the same, that although Cornelius the Centurion was praised in the Scriptures, he was not yet such that he could have been saved, unless he became incorporated in the Church through the Sacrament of Baptism."[320] The objection is one of seventeen raised by the Protestants against the thesis that: Perfect Contrition can remit sin.	"It is clear that Cornelius, who was already in the state of sanctifying grace even before the actual reception of Baptism, would not have been saved if he had not sent for Peter to be baptized by him … St. Robert Bellarmine says … on the authority of St. Augustine: 'Further, Augustine, in his Epistle 57 to Dardanus, in Book 1 *On the Predestination of the Saints*, Chapter 7; in Book 1, Question 2, *To Simplician*; in Book 1, Chapter 8, *On Baptism;* and in Book IV, Chapter 21 of the same, says that Corelius the Centurion, although he was praised in the Scriptures, was not yet such that he could have been saved, unless he became incorporated in the Church through the Sacrament of Baptism."[321]

Cornelius had not yet heard of Christ and did not even have a desire for Baptism. For, speaking of the later time, Augustine himself says (quest. 35 in *Numbers*): 'Cornelius, hearing and believing what Peter preached, was so cleansed that even before visible Baptism, he, together with those who were with him, received the gift of the Holy Spirit.'"[322]

Among Baptized Persons, Only Those Who Actually Profess The Catholic Faith Can Be Saved:

Consistent with the principle that there is only one kind, i.e., actual, membership in the true Church, the rigorists consider every adult Christian who does not profess the Catholic religion as being in formal heresy and consequently outside the path of salvation. Thus, "Only a faithful Catholic who obeys the Church and is ready to correct his opinions according to her admonitions can be in error... without being a heretic. This we call material heresy... it is clear, therefore, that Protestants are not material heretics. Are they then formal heretics? St. Augustine says: 'A heretic is one who either devises or follows false and nex opinions.'[323] The teachings and opinions of Protestants fall under this last designation. ... Protestants, therefore, hold heresy *formally*." No exception is allowed. Quoting a "Liberal Catholic" who says: He (Pius IX) teaches...that only those who are *contumaniter* and *pertipaciter* divided from the Church cannot be saved as long as this condition exists," they answer, "In saying this he gives us the impression that those who know the Catholic Church and the Catholic Faith can remain outside the Church either innocently and with good excuse, or obstinately and without excuse, and that only the latter cannot attain eternal salvation. This is against Catholic doctrine. *No one* can refuse to enter the Church and be saved."[324]

Against this theory of the absolute necessity of actual profession of the Catholic Faith for salvation, we have the mind of the Church which has clearly recognized the subjective, albeit erroneous, sincerity of non-Catholics, including non-Catholic Christians, in professing another than the Catholic Faith, and the possible possession of sanctifying grace by such persons which, as we saw, is an equivalent title to eternal salvation.

Thus we have:

1. The statement of Pius IX who expressly allows the possibility of salvation for people who are not actual members of the Catholic Church. The pertinent passages occur in the two documents, already treated at length. Says the Pope:

"Certainly we must hold as of faith that no one can be saved outside of the apostolic Roman Church, that this is the only Ark of Salvation, that the one who does not enter this is going to perish in the deluge. But nevertheless, we must likewise hold it as certain that those who labor in ignorance of the true religion, if that (ignorance) be invincible, will never be charged with any guilt on this account before the eyes of the Lord. Now who is there who would arrogate to himself the power to

point out the extent of such ignorance according to the nature and variety of peoples, regions, talents, and so many other things?"[325]

"It is known to you and to us that those who labor in invincible ignorance of our most holy religion, and who, carefully observing the natural
law and its precepts, which God has inscribed in the hearts of all, and
being ready to obey God, live an honest and upright life can, through
the working of the Divine light and grace, attain eternal life, since God,
who clearly sees, inspects and knows the minds, the intentions, and the
habits of all, will, by reason of His supreme goodness and kindness,
never allow anyone who has not the guilt of willful sin, to be punished
by eternal sufferings."[326]

From which the argument is simply this:

An explicit profession of the Catholic Faith presupposes an explicit
knowledge of the Catholic religion.

But: Pius IX allows that people who are in ignorance of the Catholic religion can be saved through the workings of Divine grace, if their
ignorance is invincible.

Therefore, explicit profession of the Catholic Faith is not absolutely
necessary for salvation.

The minor is clear from the documents quoted. However, the objection is raised by the rigorists that the Pope did not say that such people
would *die* in their ignorance of the true faith. But if this were true, the
words of the Pope cannot be excused from duplicity. For on the one
hand, he says that, "those who labor in invincible ignorance of our most
holy religion…can attain eternal salvation." On the other hand, if he
means that they *cannot* attain eternal life unless or until their invincible
ignorance is dissipated and they explicitly embrace the Catholic faith,
he is talking deceptively. For then he is making conditional, mentally,
what is declared absolute, verbally. The condition is: If this invincible
ignorance is displaced by profession of the true faith before death. But
the condition is *not expressed*, it is purely mental, without a suggestion
to its existence to be found in the words of the Pope.

Moreover, besides intrinsic evidence, we have the authority of the
theologians of the Vatican Council that Pius IX is to be understood in
the sense explained and not as the rigorists pretend. As noted before,
the subject of the salvation of sincere non-Catholics was on the agenda
of the Council. And to this end, the two pertinent documents of Pius IX
on invincible ignorance among non-Catholics were quoted *in extenso*
in the Acta. Then, commenting on the essential terms, the councilior

authorities explained that: "By the words, 'those who labor in invincible ignorance...' is indicated the possibility that a person may not belong to the visible and external communion of the Church, and yet may attain to justification and eternal life."[327] Not only was the term "invincible ignorance" as used by Pius IX, explained, but it was also incorporated into the following proposed definition:

> "It is a dogma of faith that *no one can be saved outside the Church.* However, those who labor in invincible ignorance of Christ and His Church are not to be punished for this ignorance with eternal pains, since they are not burdened with guilt on this account in the eyes of God, Who wishes all men to be saved and to come to the knowledge of the truth, and Who does not deny His grace to the person who does what he can to enable him to attain to justification and to eternal life; but this (salvation) no one attains, who leaves this life culpably separated from the unity of faith and the communion of the Church."[328]

2. The official teaching of the Vatican Council, in the *Constitution Dogmatica de Fide Catholica*, is its third chapter, *De Fide*, where we read:

> "Since, without faith, it is impossible to please God, Heb. 11-6, and to attain to the fellowship of His children, therefore, without faith no one has ever attained justification, nor will anyone obtain eternal life, unless he shall have persevered in faith unto the end.[329]

The significant term in this passage is evidently "faith" (*fides*). But what kind of faith is meant? Is it an explicit Catholic Faith, or is it something less? If it means an explicit Catholic Faith, then the rigorists are right; if it means anything less, then the highest authority in the Church is against their position. Fortunately, we do not have to resort to conjecture because the history and proceedings of the Vatican Council settle the issue beyond a cavil.

In the original draft of the *Constitutio Dogmatica*, the pertinent passage reads as follows:

> "Moreover, by divine and Catholic Faith all those things must be believed which are contained in the word of God, written or handed down, and which are proposed by the Church, either by a solemn judgment or by her ordinary magisterium, as having to be believed.

"This is that faith without which it is impossible to please God and attain to the fellowship of His children. Therefore, just as without it justification never comes to anyone, so, no one, unless he shall have persevered in the same unto the end, will obtain eternal life."[330]

But, before the final and definitive form was drawn up and presented to the assembled Fathers for acceptance, an essential emendation was made and the reason for the change was explained in the following statement of Monsignor Conrad Martin, Bishop of Paderborn, speaking in the name of the Commission *De Fide*, which he was representing:

"We have made a substitution, in the fifth paragraph, which begins with the words, *Haec est illa fides*. Most Reverend Fathers, yesterday I proposed, in the name of the delegation, an emendation for the beginning of this paragraph, which we desired in order to remove all difficulties and ambiguities. The emendation of the beginning of this paragraph is the following: namely, that instead of the words: *Haec est illa fides*, etc., there be substituted the following words: *Quoniam vero sine fide impossibile est placere Deo (ut in textu) et ad filiorum eius consortium pervenire; ideo nomini unquam sine illa contigit justificatio, nec allus, nisi in ea perseveraverit usque in fidem, vitam aeternam assequetur.* Thus, for the words, *Haec est illa fides sine cua*, let there be substituted the words, *Quoniam vero sine fide,* etc.; and removing the punctuation mark before the word, *Quare,* instead of the words *Quare sicut nomini,* let there be substituted the words, *ideo nomini unquam.* Finally, for the words: *ita nemo,* let there be substituted the words, *nec ullus*; all the rest remains the same. I have explained to you yesterday, Most Reverend Fathers, the reason for this change. The reason, to repeat in brief, is this: to remove the close connection between this and the preceding paragraph, lest it appear that an act of the Catholic Faith is necessary for salvation, for all people. For this is false. I ask you, therefore, Most Reverend Fathers, to accept the formula modified by us."[331]

The change was accepted, as may be seen in the final wording of the *Constitutio.* And the reason for the change, we may conclude, was also accepted by the Vatican Council and by Pius IX, namely, that it is possible for a person to attain to salvation by professing that faith without which it is impossible to please God, but not necessarily, the explicit faith of the Roman Catholic Church, as the rigorist theory would have us suppose.

3.   In his Encyclical, *Mystici Corporis*, Pius XII addressed an urgent appeal to nonCatholics, bidding them to enter into Catholic communion. He said:

"How carefully We desire that the immense charity of these common prayers embrace those also who, not yet perceiving the light of the Gospel's truth, are still without the Church's safe fold, or, for the regrettable conflict of faith and unity, are separated from Us who, though unworthy, bear the person of Jesus Christ on earth.

"From a heart overflowing with love, We ask each and every one of them to be quick and ready to follow the interior movements of grace, and to look to withdrawing from that state in which they cannot be sure of their salvation. For even though unsuspectingly they are related to the Mystical Body of the Redeemer in desire and resolution, they still remain deprived of so many precious gifts and helps from Heaven, which one can only enjoy in the Catholic Church."[332]

And earlier in the same document, the Holy Father described the operations of the Spirit of Christ in the Mystical Body, saying:

"It is He Who, through His heavenly grace, is the principle of every supernatural act in all parts of the Body… Finally, while with His grace He provides for the constant growth of the Church, He yet refuses to dwell with sanctifying grace in members that are wholly severed from the Body."[333]

We have already examined these words in another connection. Here they may serve to show us that, whatever else Pius XII says about non-Catholics, including non-Catholic Christians, he does not teach that it is absolutely impossible for them to be saved unless they actually enter the Catholic Church. For, if this were true, he could not logically say:

- That such people are "still outside the Church's *safe* fold". The supposition is that if they profess the faith outside the true Church they may be saved, indeed, but their salvation is very unsafe and insecure.
- That they are "to look to withdrawing from that state in which they cannot be sure of their salvation." Again, if they cannot be saved *at all* unless they become actual members of the Church, there is no question of being only less certain of one's salvation, but of salvation being impossible for professed non-Catholics.
- That the Holy Ghost "refuses to dwell with sanctifying grace in members that are wholly severed from the Body." For we ask: whom is the Pope talking about and what kind of severance from the Mystical Body deprived a person of the chances of sanctifying grace? Is it the severence of sincere non-Catholics from the vis-

ible Catholic Church? It cannot be, for "they are, although unsus-pectingly, related to the Mystical Body of the Redeemer by desire and resolution." What such persons lack, therefore, if other condi-tions are fulfilled, is not sanctifying grace, but the security of their salvation and the reception "of so many precious gifts and helps from heaven, which one can only enjoy in the Catholic Church."

SUMMARY CONCLUSION

As stated in the introduction, the purpose of the foregoing study was to find out whether and to what extent, in the light of Bellarmine's principles, non-Catholics in good faith may be considered members of the Roman Catholic Church." To this end, the question was examined from three viewpoints:

1. Giving a statement and explanation of the pertinent passages in St. Robert's own writings.
2. Comparing Bellarmine's teaching with the corresponding doctrine of recent Popes and the theologians of the Vatican Council.
3. Critically analyzing some present-day misinterpretations of Bellar-mine's doctrine in the United States.

A brief summary of the conclusions reached in the course of our in-vestigation is specially necessary because not all the issues treated were equally important. Moreover, so many allied questions entered into the study that a final sifting of essentials from accidentals is called for.

• According to Bellarmine and confirmed by the teaching of sub-sequent Popes, the following proposition may be laid down as certain: "Sincere non-Catholics who die before actually entering the true Church may be saved in virtue of their *voto* membership in the visible Catholic Church founded by Christ."

• According to Bellarmine and also confirmed by the Roman Pon-tiffs, the Catholic Church is the Mystical Body of Christ. Conse-quently, non-Catholics, although sincere and even in the grace of God, are not actual members of the Mystical Body even as they are not actual members of the Roman Catholic Church.

• According to Bellarmine and consistent with papal teaching, the Catholic Church is composed of a body and a soul: the body com-posed of its visible elements; reductively, profession of the true faith, participation in the same Sacraments and subjection to the Roman Pontiff; the soul being the Holy Spirit, the Spirit of Christ, as inform-ing the Church and bearing the supernatural gifts of His grace.

Deducible from Bellarmine's principles, but not directly treated by him, we may further conclude that:

The two elements, *corpus et anima Ecclesiae*, are parallel entities, so that if a person belongs actually to the Church, he also belongs actually to the Church's body and soul; but if he is only *voto* in the Church, he is *voto* both in the Church's body and in the Church's soul.

On the vital question of belonging to the *anima Ecclesiae*, a sincere non-Catholic cannot be said to belong actually to the soul of the Church, which is the Holy Spirit, *prout informat Ecclesiam*. However, the Holy Spirit has two functions with regard to the Church:

- That by which He animates the Church; *informans Ecclesiam*. In this sense, sincere non-Catholics can belong to the soul of the Church only *voto*.

- That by which He directs persons from the outside towards the Church; *conducens in Ecclesiam*. In this sense, sincere non-Catholics may be said to belong actually to the soul of the Church. But the expression is not a happy one, and is liable to misinterpretation.

Endnotes

PART I
EXPOSITION OF BELLARMINE'S DOCTRINE
CHAPTER I
GENERAL PRINCIPLES ON CHURCH MEMBERSHIP

1   "Nostra autem sententia est. Ecclesiam unam tantum esse, non duas, et illam unam et veram esse coetum hominum eiusdem christianae fidei professione, at eorundem sacramentorum communione colligatum, sub regimine legitimorum pastorum, ac praecipue unius Christi in terris vicarii romani pontificis." *De Ecclesia Militante*, cap. 2. This work forms the third part or *Liber tertius*, in a series of four disputations on the nature and structure of the Church. The other three books, in order, are: *De Conciliis et Ecclesia, De Conciliorum Auctoritate*, and *De Notis Ecclesiae*. Together they give a conspectus of Bellarmine's ecclesiology. References to the *Controversies* will be only to the title and chapter, because the chapters are very short, sometimes less than a page, in folio. The edition used for the *Controversies* is that of Natale Battezzanti, Milan, 1857 dqq.

2   "Ex qua definitione facile colligi potest, qui homines ad Ecclesiam pertineant. Tres enim sunt partes huius definitionis. Professio verae fidei, sacramentorum communio, et subiectio ad legitimum pastorem romanum pontificem. Ratione primae parties excluduntur omnes infidels tam qui numquam fuerunt in Ecclesia, ut Judaei, Turcae, Pagani; tam qui fuerunt et recesserunt, ut haeretici et apostatae. Ratione secundae, excluduntur catechumeni et excommunicati, quoniam illi non sunt admissi ad sacramentorum communionem, isti sunt dimissi. Ratione tertiae, excluduntur schismatici, qui habent fidem et sacramenta, sed non subduntur legitimo pastori, et ideo foris profitentur fidem, et sacramenta percipient." Idem.

3   "Includuntur autem omnes alii, etiamsi reprobi, scelesti et impii sint." Idem.

4   "D. Dichiaratemi parola per parola tutto l'Articolo (nono). E prima, che vuol dire Chiesa? M. Vuol dire *Convocazione*, e *Congregazione* d'Uomini, i quail si battezzano, e fanno professione della Fede, e Legge di Cristo sotto l'obbedienza del sommo Pontefice Romano: si chiama *Convocazione*, perche` Noi non nasciamo Cristiani, siccome nasciamo Italiani, o Francesi, o d'altro Paese; ma siamo chiamati da Dio, ed entriamo in questa Congregazione per mezzo del Battesimo, il qual'e come la porta della Chiesa: ne basta esser battezzato per essere nella Chiesa; ma bisogna credere, e confessare la santa Fede, e Legge di Cristo, come o'insegnano i Pastori, e Predicatori di essa Chiesa; ne anche questo basta; ma bisogna stare all' obbedienza del Sommo Pontefice Romano, come Vicario di Cristo, cioe riconoscerlo, e tenerlo per Superiore supremo in luoge di Cristo." *Dichiarazione piu Copiosa della Dottrina Cristiana*, Roma, 1824, pg. 52. There are two versions of the *Dottrina Cristiana,* the smaller, published in 1597, and the larger, in the following year. For the original schema of these catechisms, Bellarmine used the notes of the instructions which he gave to the Coadjutor Brothers, years before. As of 1930, the *Dottrina Cristiana* had been translated into 56 different languages or dialects. Writes a recent biographer: "Probably no single book outside the Scriptures and the *Imitation of Christ* could boast of so many editions." Von Frentz, *Vita di S. Roberto Bellarmino*, Isola del Liri, 1930, pg. 112. The significance of this wide diffusion lies in the extent to which Bellarmine's doctrine of the Church may be said to have penetrated the modern Catholic mentality.

149

5   "Atque hoc interest inter sententiam nostram et alias omnes, quod omnes aliae requirunt internas virtutes ad constituendum aliquem in Ecclesia, et propterea Ecclesiam veram invisibilem faciunt: nos autem, et credimus in Ecclesia inveniri omnes virtutes, fidem, spem, charitatem, et caeteras; tamen ut aliquis aliquo modo dici possit pars verae Ecclesiae, de qua Scripturae loquuntur, non putamus requiri ullam internam virtutem, sed tantum externam professionem fidei, et sacramentorum communionem, quae sensu ipso percipitur. Ecclesia enim est coetus hominum ita visibilis et palpabilis, ut est coetus populi romani, vel regnum Galliae, aut respublica Venetorum." *De Ecclesia Miliante*, cap. 2.

6   "Ecclesia enim est societas quaedam, non angelorum, neque animarum, sed hominum. Non autem dici potest societas hominum, nisi in externis, et visibilibus signis consistat; nam non est societas, nisi se agnoscant ii, qui dicuntur socii, non autem se possunt homines agnoscere, nisi societatis vincula sint externa et visibilia. Et confirmatur ex more omnium humanarum societatum; nam in militiam, in civitatem, in regnum, et alia similia nom aliter homines adscribuntur, quam signis visibilibus. Unde Augustinus lib. 19 cont. Faustum, cap. 11: 'In nullum', inquit, 'nomen religionis, seu verum, seu falsum, coagulari homines possunt, nisi aliquo signaculorum, vel sacramentorum visibilium, consortio colligentur.'" Idem, cap. 12.

7   Ibidem.

8   *De Notis Ecclesiae*, cap 10. According to Bellermine, the seventh of the fifteen notes of the true Church, by which she can be recognized as divinely instituted by Christ, is the concord and unity which exists among her members, all united under the one visible head, the Roman Pontiff. But this unity would be impossible unless the Church were a visible society, visibly bound together by sensibly perceptible signs. Thus he writes: "Septima nota est Unio membrorum inter se, et cum capite; nam Ecclesiam esse unum corpus, unam spousam, unum ovile, passim Scripturae docent, ad Rom. 12, Cantic. 6, Joan. 10, et in symbolo constantinopolitano, dicimus unam Ecclesiam. Praecipua autem unitas Corporis consistit in coniunctione membrorum cum capite, et inter se… Certum est, concordiam esse signum regni Dei, quod stare debet in aeternum: Discordiam autem, regni diaboli, quod tandem ruere debet." So much *de iure*; but also *de facto*: "Omes catholici, toto orbe dispersi de omnibus dogmatibus fidei sentiunt idem. Nec possunt aliter sentire, cum omnes subjiciant sensum suum sensui unius, et ejusdem summi pastoris ex cathedra Petri cum consilio aliorum pastorum Ecclesiam dirigentis."

9   Among the edited letters of Bellarmine is one which Lessius wrote to him in Rome, in which he says: "Belliolanus has recently published a certain book on the Church in which the opinion of Your Reverence…that for a person to be a member of the Visible Church there is no necessity for internal faith…has been strongly opposed as erroneous. He also told certain bishops…that he argued with Your Reverence about the fact that, as long as errors are being attributed to the professors of the Society (as in the present case), they will lose all their authority. All the arguments which he brings forward to prove the necessity of requiring faith in every member of the Church are beside the point, and can be easily answered by anyone who reads, in your same treatise (*De Ecclesia Militante*), about the different ways in which a person can be a member of the Church." Letter of Lessius to Bellarmine, Louvain to Rome, March 19, 1588. In Le Bachelet, *Bellarmine avant son Cardinalat*, Paris, 1911, pg. 168.

10   *De Ecclesia Militante*, cap. 2. "Notandum autem est ex Augustino in breviculo collat. 3, Ecclesiam est corpus vivum, in quo est anima et corpus, et quidem anima

sunt interna Dona Spiritus Sancti, fides, spes, charitas, etc. Corpus sunt externa profession fidei, et communictio sacramentorum. Ex quo fit, ut quidam sint de anima et de corpore Ecclesiae, et proinde uniti Christo capiti interius et exterius; et tales sunt perfectissime de Ecclesia; sunt enim quasi membra viva in corpore, quamvis etiam inter istos aliqui magis minus vitam participeat, et aliqui etiam solum initium vitae habeant, et quasi sensum et non motum, ut qui habeat fidem sine charitate. Sursum aliqui sint de anima, et non de corpore, ut catechumeni, vel excommunicati, si fidem et charitatem habeant, quod fieri potest. Denique, aliqui sint de corpore, et non de anima, ut qui nullam habent internam virtutem, et tamen spe aut timore aliquot temporali profiteatur fidem, et in sacramentis communicant, sub regimine pastorum, et tales sunt sicut capilli, aut ungues, aut mali humores in corpore humano."

11   "Definitio igitur nostra solum comprehendit hunc ultimum modum existendi in Ecclesia, quia hic requiritur ut minimum; ut quis possit dici esse pars visibilis Eclesiae." Ibidem.

12   "Quod autem est anima corpori hominis, hoc est Spiritus Sanctus corpori Christi, quod est Ecclesia; hoc agit Spiritus Sanctus in tota Ecclesia, quod agit anima in omnibus membris unius Corporis." *Sermo 267 in die Pentecostes,* ML 38, 1231.

13   "Quod est spiritus noster, id est anima nostra, ad membra nostra; hoc Spiritus Sanctus ad membra Christi, ad Corpus Christi, quod est Ecclesia. Ideo Apostolus, cum corpus unum nominasset, ne intelligeremus mortuum corpus. 'Unum' inquit, 'corpus.' Sed rogo te vivit hoc corpus ? Vivit. Unde? De uno spiritu. 'Et unus spiritus.' " S*ermo 268 in die Pentecostes,* ML 38, 1232.

14   "Unum quippe corpus est tota sancta universalis Ecclesia, sub Christo Iesu, suo videlicet capite, constituta…Christus itaque cum tota sua Ecclesia, sive quae adhuc versatur in terris, sive quae cum eo iam regnat in coelis, una persona est. Et sicut est una anima quae diversa Corporis membra vivificat, ita totam simul Ecclesiam unus Spiritus Sanctus vegetat et illustrat. Sicut namque Christus, qui est caput Ecclesiae, de Spiritu sancto coceptus est, sic santa Ecclesia quae corpus eius, eodem Spiritu sancto repletur ut vivat: eius virtute firmatur, ut in unius fidei et charitatis compage subsistat. Unde dicit Apostolus: Ex quo totum corpus per nexus et coniunctiones subministratum et constructum in augmentum Dei (Col. II, 2). Istud est corpus, extra quod non vivificat spiritus. Unde dicit beatus Augustinus: Si vis vivere de spiritu Christo, esto in corpore Christi (Tract. 26 in Joan.). De hoc spiritu non vivit haereticus, non vivit schismaticus, non vivit excommunicatus; non enim sunt de corpore. Ecclesia autem spiritum vivificantem habet, quia capiti suo Christo inseparabiliter inhaeret. Scriptum est enim: Qui adhaeret Domino, unus spiritus est cum eo, (I Cor. 6, 17)." *In Septem Psalmos Poenitentiales, Expositio,* ML 79, 602.

15   "Ecclesia gubernatur a Christo, tamquam a capite sponso suo, et a Spiritu Sancto, tamquam ab anima, ut patet Ephes. 1. 'Ipsum dedit caput super omnem Ecclesiam quae est corpus ipsius.' Et Ephes. 4. 'Unum corpus, et unus Spiritus; 'Ephes. 5. 'Vir caput est mulieris, sicut Christus caput Ecclesiae.' Ergo si Ecclesia in dogmatibus fidei, vel morum erraret, Christo et Spiritui sancto error tribueretur. Quocirca Joan. 16. Dominus ait: 'Spiritus veritatis docebit vos omnem veritatem' ". *De Ecclesia Militante,* cap. 14.

16   "Dico igitur, episcopum malum, presbyterum malum, doctorem malum, esse membra mortua, et proinde non vera, Corporis Christi, quantum attinet ad rationem membri, ut est pars quaedam vivi Corporis: tamen esse verissima membra in ra-

tione instrumenti, idest, papam et episcopos esse vera capita, doctores veros oculos, seu veram linguam hujus Corporis etc. et ratio est, quia membra constituuntur viva per charitatem, qua impii carent: At instrumenta operativa constituuntur per potestatem sive ordinis, sive iurisdictionis, quae etiam sine gratia esse potest. Nam etsi in corpore naturali non possit membrum mortuum esse verum instrumentum operationis, tamen in corpore mystico potest. In corpore enim naturali opera pendent, ex bonitate instrumenti, quia anim non potest bene operari, nisi per bona instrumenta, nec opera vitae exercere, nisi per instrumenta viva: at in corpore mystico opera non pendent ex bonitate, aut vita instrumenti. Anima enim huius Corporis, idest, Spiritus Sanctus aeque bene operatur per instrumenta bona et mala, viva et mortua." Idem, cap. 9.

CHAPTER II
APPLICATION OF PRINCIPLES ON CHURCH MEMBERSHIP

17 "...qui non dederunt nomina sua Christo per baptismum, sed aliquas alias religiones sequuntur." Idem, cap. 3.

18 "Ratione primae parties (professio verae fidei) excluduntur omnes infideles tam qui nuquam fuerunt in Ecclesia, ut Judaei, Turcae, Pagani; tam qui fuerunt et recesserunt, ut haeretici et apostatae." Idem, cap. 2.

19 "D. Dunque gli S*comunicati* sono fuor della Chiesa, come i Giudei, e gli altri infedeli?

M. Cosi è: ma vi e questa differenza, che i Giudei, e Turchi sono fuori della Chiesa perche non ci sono entrati, non avendo il santo Battesimo. Gli Eretici, che sono battezzati, ma hanno perduta la Fede, son fuori, perchè sono usciti...gli Scommunicati...non escono da sè, ma sono scacciati perforza." *Dottrina Christiana*, pg. 57.

20 "De catechumenis est Paulo maior difficultas, quia sunt fideles, et salvari possunt, si moriantur in eo statu, et tamen extra Ecclesiam nemo salvatur, sicut neo extra aroam Noe, iuxta illud concilii lateranensis, cap. 1, 'Una est fidelium universalis Ecclesia, extra quam nullus omnino salvatur.' At nihilominus certum est, catechumenos non esse in Ecclesia actu et proprie sed tantum in potentia; quomodo homo conceptus, sed nondum formatus et natus, non dicitur homo, nisi in potential." *De Ecclesia Militante*, cap. 3.

21 *De Sacramento Baptismi*, cap. 8.

22 "...extra Ecclesiam non est salus...ideo in symbolo coniungimus cum Ecclesia, remissionem peccatorum: 'Credo sanctam Ecclesiam, sanctorum communionem, remissionem peccatorum.' Ideo etiam comparator Ecclesia cum arca Noe; quia sicut regnante diluvio periit, qui in arca non fuit; ita et numc pereunt, qui in Ecclesia non sunt, ut ait Heironymus in epist. ad Damasum de nominee hypostasis. Idem testatur celebre illud Cypriani dictum, lib. de Unitate Ecclesiae: 'Non habet Deum patrem, qui non habet Ecclesiam matrem.'" Ibidem.

23 "Ego nullum primum nisi Christum sequens beatitudini tuae, id est cathedrae Petri, communione consocior. Super illam petram aedificatam Ecclesiam scio. Quicumque extra hanc agnum domum comederit, profanus est. Si quis in Noe arca non fuerit, periet regnante dilubio." *Epistula I ad Damasum*, ML 22, 355.

24 "Adulterari non potest sponsa Christi, incorrputa est et pudica. Unam domum novit, unius cubiculi sanctitatem casto pudore custodit. Haec nos Deo servat, haec filios regno quos generavit assignat. Quisque ab Ecclesia segregatus adulterae iungitur, a promissis Ecclesiae separatur, nec pervenient ad Christi praemia qui reliquit Ecclesiam Christi. Alienus est, profanus est, hostis est. Habere non potest Deum

patrem qui Ecclesiam non habet matrem. Si potuit evadere quisque extra arcam Noe fuit, et qui extra Ecclesiam foris fuerit evadit." *De Catholicae Ecclesiae Unitate*, ML 4, 502.

25   *De Sacramento Baptismi*, cap. 8.

26   "Una vero est fidelium universalis Ecclesia, extra quam nullus omnino salvatur." Concilium Lateranense IV, cap. 1, "De Fide Catholica." Mansi XXII, 982 sqq., DB 430.

27   "…entriamo in questa Congregazione per mezzo del Battesimo, il qual 'e come la porta della Chiesa." *Dottrina Christiana*, pg. 52.

28   "Ubi (Actor. 2/41) videmus, baptizari nihil esse aliud, quam Ecclesiam intrare. Unde Patres communi consensu distinguunt catechumenos a fidelibus, ac docent illos, quod baptismo careant, nondum esse intra Ecclesiam, nec dici possunt fideles." *De Sacramento Baptismi*, cap. 8.

29   Ibidem.

30   "Primum omnium sacramentorum locuM tenet sanctum baptisma, quod vitae spiritualis ianua est; per ipsum enim membra Christi ac de corpore efficimur Ecclesiae." *Decretum pro Armenis*, Mansi XXXI, 1054 B sqq., DB 696.

31   "Non, igitur actuet proprie sunt catechumeni de Ecclesia. Quomodo igitur, inquies, salvantur si sunt extra Ecclesiam?" *De Ecclesia Militante*, cap. 3.

32   Ibidem.

33   Bellarmine makes two references to the *De Ecclesiasticis Dogmatibus*, in *De Ecclesia Militante*, cap. 3, and *De Sacramento Baptismi*, cap. 6. In the first he makes no mention of the spurious character of the work, beyond omitting St. Augustine's name, and saying instead: "Auctor libri *De Ecclesiasticis Dogmatibus*, cap. 74, aperte respondet, catechumenos non salvari." In the second reference he expressly says: "Liber qui inscribitur *De Ecclesiasticis Dogmatibus*, qui falso tribuitur Augustino, cap. 74, aperte dicit: Catechumenum non salvari, etiamsi in bonis operibus vixerit, nisi baptismo aqua, aut sanguinis purgatus fuerit." The following are some places in Peter Lombard's *Book of Sentences*, where *De Ecclesiasticis Dogmatibus* is directly attributed to St. Augustine: Lib. II, dist. 35, cap. "Quocirca"; Lib. II, dist. 35, cap. "Quocirca"; Lib. III, dist. 1, cap. "Diligenter"; Lib IV, dist. 12, cap. "Institutum". On the other hand, St. Thomas rejects the work as that of Augustine and assigns it to Gennadius in: *Quodlib., 12,* art. 11; and *Catena*, Mat. 1.

34   The full title given in Migne is: *De Ecclesiasticis Dogmatibus* — Liber Gennadio Tributus," although it is placed among the writings of St. Augustine, ML 42, 1213-1222.

35   "Baptizatis tantum iter salutis credimus. Nullum catechumenum, quamvis in bonis operibus defunctum, vitam aeternam habere credamus, excepto martyrio, ubi tota Sacramenta complentur." ML 42, 1220.

36   *S. Bernardi ad Hugonem de Sancto Victore, Epistola 77.* ML 182, 1031.

37   "Sed hoc nimis durum esse videtur. Certe Ambrosius in oratione de obitu Valentiniani disertis verbis affirmat, catechumenos posse salvari, de quorum numero Valentinianus erat, cum de hac vita migraret." *De Ecclesia Militante,* cap. 3.

38   Sed audio vos dolero, quod non accepit sacramena baptismatis. Dicite mihi, quid aliud in nobis est, nisi voluntas, nisi petition ? Atqui etiam dudum hoc voti habuit, ut, et antequam in Italiam venisset, initiaretur, et proxime baptizari se a me velle significavit, et ideo prae ceteris causis me accersendum putavit. Non habet ergo

gratiam quam desideravit ? Non habet, quam poposcit ? Certe, quia poposcit, accepit. Et unde illud est: 'Iustus quacumque morte praeventus fuerit, anima eiuz in requie erit'?" ML16, 402.

39　"Perfecta conversio ac Poepitentia recte Baptismus flaminis dicitur et Baptismum aquae saltem in necessitate supplet ... Non fuisse apud veteres tam certam hanc propositionem, ut erat superior." De *Sacramento Baptismi*, cap. 6.

40　"Nam de martyrio nullus veterum, quod sciam, negavit eo suppleri Baptismum aquae; at de conversione et poenitentia, non desunt, qui id negaverint...At sine dubio dredendum est, veram conversionem supplere Baptismum aquae, cum non ex contemptu, sed ex necessitate sine Baptismo aquae aliqui decedunt." Ibidem.

41　"Nec ego dubito catechumenum catholicum divina Caritate flagrantem haeretico baptizato anteponere. Sed etiam in ipsa intus catholica bonum catechumenum malo baptizato anteponimus; nec ideo tamen Sacramento baptismatis, quo iste nondum, ille iam imbutus est, facimus iniuriam aut catechumeni sacramentum sacramento baptismi praeferendum putamus, cum aliquem catechumenum aliquo baptizato fideliorum meliorumque cognoscimus. Melior enim centurio Cornelius nondum baptizatus Simone baptizato. Iste enim et ante baptismum Sancto Spiritu impletus est, ille et post baptismum immundo spiritu inflatus est...Baptismi sane vicem aliquando implere passionem, de latrone illo cui non baptizato dictum est: hodie mecum eris in paradise (Lc. 23/43), non leve documentum idem beatus Cyprianus assumit. Quod etiam atque etiam considerans invenio non tantum passionem pro nominee Christi id quod ex baptismo deerat posse supplere, sed etiam fidem conversionemque cordis, si forte ad celebrandum mysterium baptismi in angustiis temporum succurri non potest." ML 43, 172-173.

42　"Ab his ergo duabus columnis, Augustinum loquor et Ambrosium, crede mihi, difficile avellor. Cum his, inquam, me aut errare, aut sapere fateor; credens et ipse, sola fide hominem posse salvari, cum desiderio percipiendi sacramentum: si tamen pio adimplendi desiderio more anticipans, seu alia quaecumque vis invincibilis obviarit. Vide etiam ne forte ob hoc Salvator cum diceret: 'Qui crediderit et baptizatus fuerit, salvus erit'; caute et vigilanter nom repetierit: 'Qui vero baptizatus non fuerit,' sed tantum, 'Qui vero,' inquit, 'non crediderit, condemnabitur', Marc. 16/16: nimirum innuens solam interdum fidem sufficere ad salutem, et sine ipsa sufficere nihil. Quapropter etsi martyrium vicem Baptismi posse implere conceditur, non plane hoc facit poena, sed ipsa fides. Nam absque ipsa quid est martyrium, nisi poena?" *Epistola seu Tractatus de Baptismo*, ML 182, 1036.

43　"Inquisitioni tuae taliter respondemus: Presbyterum, quem sine unda baptismatis extremum diem clausisse (litteris tuis) significasti, quia in sanctae matris Ecclesiae fide et Christi nominis confessione perseveraverit, ab originali peccato solutum, et coelestis patriae gaudium esse adeptum (ex auctoritate sanctorum Patrum Augustini atque Ambrosii) asserimus incunctanter. Lege (frater) super octavo libro Augustini de civitate Dei (ML 41, 381), ubi inter cetera legitur: 'Baptismus invisibiliter ministratur, quem non contemptus religionis, sed terminus necessitates excludit.' Librum etiam beati Ambrosii de obitu Valentiniani (ML 16, 1347) idem asserentis revolve. Sopitis igitur quaestionibus, doctorum Patrum sententias teneas, et in ecclesia tua juges preces hostiasque Deo offerri iubeas pro presbytero memorato." ML179, 624. There is some dispute as to which Pope Innocent this letter should be ascribed to. Its full title is: "Apostolicam Sedem", and was addressed to the Bishop of Cremona, date uncertain. According to Migne and Denzinger (DB 388), it belongs to Innocent II, who ruled from 1130 to 1143, and during whose reign the Tenth Ecumenical Council, *Lateranense II*, was held. However, Bellarmine and with him the old *Corpus Iuris Cononici*, Lipsiae (1879-1881), believe it was the composition of Innocent III, who reigned from 1198 to 1216. However, its authenticity is attested to by all the standard sources.

44   "...translatio ab eo statu, in quo homo nascitur filius primi Adae, in statum gratiae et adoptionis filiorum Dei, per secundum Adam Iesum Christum Salvatorem nostrum; quae quidem translatio post Evangelium promulgatum sine lavacro regenerationis aut eius voto fieri non potest, sicut scriptum est: 'Nisi quis renatus fuerit ex aqua et Spiritu Sancto, non potest introire in regnum Dei.'" Sessio VI, *Decretum de Iustificatione*, cap. 4, DB 796. There is a practical question of fact involved, as to the extent of the promulgatio of the Gospel at the present day. Lennerz leaves the question open saying: "Si autem promulgatio in toto mundo nuno iam facta est, sequitur, ut nullae exsistant gentes vel tribus, quae adhuc vivant sub disciplina legis naturae; consequenter absolutae cessavit remedium legis naturae, quo infantes a peccato originali liberari poterant." *De Sacramento Baptismi*, Roma, 1948, p. 93, 94. According to d'Ales, however, a distinction must be made between the lot of children and adults. Moreover, he believes that the Gospel has not yet been universally promulgated. He says: Nunc autem communius distinguunt (theologi) condicionem adultorum et infantium. Adultos negant salvos esse posse sine fide implicita Redemptoris; ad infantes quod attinet, statuunt in unaquaque regione antiqua auxilia tum demum abolita esse cum in illa regione promulgatio Evangelii potuit censeri moraliter facta. Unde sequitur in illis regionibus quae adhuc carent promulgatione Evangelii nullam intervenisse de infantibus mutationem: non enim videtur pertinere ad Dei benignitatem ut condicio illorum infantium per adventum Domini facta sit peior." *De Baptismo et Confirmatione*, pp. 142-143; French edition, Paris, 1928, pp. 109-110.

45   This may be justly inferred from two facts: (1) When Bellarmine speaks of catechumens, he does so without qualification, simply saying they are such as desire Baptism, suggesting that this desire is explicit; (2) The examples which he gives to show that catechumens may be saved are of persons who explicitly ask for Baptism, as Valentinian, or, at least, who explicitly profess the Catholic Faith, as the unbaptized priest on whose case Innocent II pronounced a decision. However, as will be shown later on, Bellarmine also conceived of persons being eligible for salvation who only implicitly desired Baptism.

46   As proof that perfect contrition reconciles a man to God even before Baptism, Bellarmine argues from the following authorities in Christian tradition: St. Ambrose' oration at the death of Valentinian; St. Augustine, *De Baptismo*, lib. 4; cap. 22; St. Bernard, *Epistola 77* already quoted; Innocent III regarding the unbaptized priest; and the Council of Trent, Sess. VI, cap. 4. To the same end, he quotes the text from Ezechiel, 18/21: "If the wicked do penance for all his sins, which he has committed, and keep all my commandments, and do judgment, and justice, living he shall live, and shall not die." His strong argument is that penance, like martyrdom, assimilates a man to the Passion of Christ, and since martyrdom certainly remits sin even before Baptism, so also does since penance. *"Poenitentia configurat hominem Christi passioni, ut facit martyrium: dimittit etiam totam poenam perfecta conversio, ut fuit in conversione Mariae Magdalenae, boni latronis, et aliorum."* However, he is clear on the necessity of having real (vera) conversion of heart to attain this effect. "Neque enim," he says, "dicitur Baptismus flaminis absolute et simpliciter, interna conversio, nisi quando est ita perfecta, et servens, ut omnem

rubiginem peccati tollat. Alioqui enim, si non tollat totam poenam, ut plerumque sit, non est Baptismus, nisi imperfecte." *De Sacramento Baptismi,* cap. 6.

47   This is a regular qualification which Bellarmine makes. Thus: "Sine dubio credendum est, veram conversionem supplere Baptismum aquae, cum non ex contemptu, sed ex necessitate sine Baptismo aquae aliqui decedunt." Ibidem. Again, the Reformers argued that some of the Fathers, notably Augustine, considered catechumens as still burdened with their sins, the conclusion being that charity (which is presumed to exist in catechumens) may co-exist with the state of grave sin. But Bellarmine distinguishes, e.g. on Augustine's text: "Quantumqua catechumenus proficiat, adhue sarcinam suae iniquitatis portat, nec illi dimittitur, nisi cum venerit ad Baptismum." *Tract. XIII in Joan.* "I answer", says Bellarmine, "that he is here speaking of those catechumens who are negligent about approaching Baptism; for such, although they are advanced (in virtue) are never truly justified, since they have not received the sacrament of Baptism either *in re* or *in voto,* nor do they possess true charity. For true charity and a true desire of Baptism do not permit a man to be negligent or contemptuous of Baptism." *De Poenitentia,* lib. 2, cap. 14.

48   Canus, *Loc. Theolog.,* 1, 4, Paris, 1678, p. 187 sqq.

49   "Melchior Canus sit, catechumenos posse salvari, quia etsi non sunt de Ecclesia, quae proprie dicitur Christiana, sunt tamen de Ecclesia, quae comprehendit omnes fideles ab Abel usque mundi consummationem. At non videtur satisfacere. Nam post Christi adventum nulla est vera Ecclesia, nisi illa quae proprie dictitur Christiana; si ergo catechumeni de ista non sunt, de nulla sunt." De Ecclesia Militante, cap. 3.

50   Frequently, in his controversy with the Protestants, Bellarmine had to vindicate the real distinction between the Church of the Old Covenant and the Church of Christ. The Reformers had good reason for making this identification, which permitted them to indulge in Old Testament practices on the plea that the discipline of the Christian Church was no different than that of the Jewish Synagogue, for the simple reason that Synagogue and Church of Christ were one and the same thing. Calvin, for example, took his cue from the mass defection of the Jewish people in the time of Elias, declaring that just as the Church in olden times defected from the service of God, so it defected in the sixteenth century. And just as a universal reformation had to be initiated by the prophets in ancient times, so a reformation by the new prophets, to wit, Calvin and his followers, was in order in modern times. Bellarmine recognizes the force of the argument, once it is conceded that the Church of Christ is really identical with the Mosaic synagogue. So he says: "Non est eadem ratio populi Judaeorum et populi Christianorum. Nam populus Judaeorum non errat Ecclesia universalis, ut est populus Christianorum, sed particularis, et propterea etiam extra illum populum inveniebantur fideles et iusti, ut Melchisedech, Job, et postea Cornelius, Centurio, et eunuchus Candacis reginae, et alii nonnulli. Itaque etiamsi universa synagoga Judaeorum defecisset, non continuo omnis Ecclesia Dei in terries defecisset." *De Ecclesia Militante,* cap. 16. But how could the identification be avoided, if Cano's "Ecclesia omnium fidelium ab Abel ad mundi consummationem," be admitted ?

51   The ultimate basis for the visible unity of the Church of Christ is the submission of all its members to one supreme, visible head, the Roman Pontiff. "Praecipua unitas Corporis," says St. Robert, "consistit in coniunctione membrorum cum capite, et inter se." *De Notis Ecclesiae,* cap. 10. Where, then, would be the common

principle of unity between the Church of the Jews and the Church of Christ, when the Papacy was not established until the time of Christ ?

52   Taking the three types of visibility which guarantee the unity of the Church of Christ (in government, in the means of sanctification, and in harmonious co-operation among its members), all three would disappear if Cano's universal Church of the faithful be admitted. Thus, as Bellarmine argues, "in the very beginning (of the Church of Christ), there were added (to the original number in the Cenacle on Pentecost) in a visible manner, on one day three thousand men, and at another time, five thousand, by their confession of faith and Baptism." *De Ecclesia Militante*, cap. 12. But how could anyone be said to be added to the Church of Christ, and of what significance would visibile profession of faith and Baptism be, if the convert Jews were not really converts at all; if the "new" church which they were entering was only the Old Synagogue with a different name?

53   "Respondeo igitur, quod dicitur, extra Ecclesiam neminem salvari, intelligi debet de iis, qui neque re ipsa, nec desiderio sunt de Ecclesia, sicut de baptismo communiter loquuntur theologi. Quoniam autem catechumeni si non re, saltem voto sunt in Ecclesia, ideo salvari possunt." *De Ecclesia Militante*, cap. 3. It should be noted that he uses the term *voto* and *desiderio* interchangeably. This has considerable significance, as will be seen at length. For while there might be some quibble on the exact meaning of *voto*, there can be none about *desiderio*. The latter term clearly implies all active dynamic, positive act of the will based on cognition. Notice also that he opposes *re ipsa* to *desiderio* and *voto*. The dogmatic value of these terms can scarcely be exaggerated, for they have been formally adopted and approved by the Holy See, in the Encyclical *Mystici Corporis*. Only twice does the Encyclical *ex professo* distinguish the real from the non-real members of the Church; and in one case it uses Bellarmine's terminology relative to the first class, and in the second case, his terminology regarding the second class. Thus, for the actual members we are told; "In Ecclesiae autem membris *reapse* ii soli annumerandi sunt, qui regenerationis lavacrum receperunt veramque fidem profitentur, neque a Corporis compage semet ipsos misere separarunt, vel ob gravissima admissa a legitima auctoritate seiuncti sunt." AAS (35) pg. 202. And for the non-actual members, they are: "...etiamsi inscio quodam *desiderio* voto ad mysticum Redemptoris Corpus ordinentur , tot tamen tantisque caelestibus muneribus adiumentisque carent, quibus in Catholica solummodo Ecclesia frui licet." AAS (35) pg. 243.

54   "Hoc argumentum solum probat, non adesse omnibus auxilium, quo possint immediate converti et credere: non tamen probat simpliciter defuisee aliquibus auxilium sufficiens ad salutem. Possunt enim gentiles quibus nondum est evangelium praedicatum cognoscere per creaturas Deum esse, et proinde possunt a Deo per gratiam praevenientem excitari ad credendum de Deo, quia est, et quod inquirentibus se remunerator sit; et ex tali fide excitari possunt eodem dirigente et adiuvante Deo ad oramdum et eleemosynas faciendas, et eo modo impetrandum a Deo maius fidel lumen, quod Deus per se, vel per angelos, vel per homines facile communicabit." *De Gratis et Libero Arbitrio*, lib. 2, cap. 8. It is difficult to see how Bellarmine makes the elation from the natural knowledge of God among gentiles, to their faith and belief in God supernaturally. He says, indeed, that they begin by knowing from creation that God exists and that by God's grace they attain to a belief in Him. But he makes no reference to the essential element of objective revelation, so that a person might believe, "propter auctoritatem ipsius

Dei revelantis," as the Vatican Council requires, DB 1789, except where he says, "per gratiam praevenientem."

55   Significantly, Bellarmine does not require explicit knowledge of the Church or of the necessity of Baptism for salvation. He does, however, require something beyond the two obvious truths to be believed, namely that God exists and that He is the rewarder of those who seek Him. What this "greater light of faith" specifically is, which pagans may obtain from God if "they pray and give alms," he does not say. The context suggests that it must mean at least the belief in the Trinity and the Incarnation.

56   Bellarmine's reference in to *De Veritate,* q. 14, art. 11, ad 1, where St. Thomas answers the objection that a pagan living in the wilds of a forest, for example, cannot attain to an explicit faith in the truths which are necessary for salvation. He says: "Non sequitur inconveniens posito quod quilibet teneatur aliquid explicite credere, si in silvis vel inter bruta animalia nutriatur: hoc enim ad divinam providentiam pertinet ut cuilibet provideat de necessariis ad salutem, dummodo ex parte eius non impediatur. Si enim aliquis taliter nutritus, ductum naturalis rationis sequeretur in appetitu boni et fuga mali, certissime est tenendum quod ei Deus vel per internam inspirationem revelaret ea quae sunt ad credendum necessaria, vel aliquem fidei praedicatorem ad eum dirigeret, sicut misut Petrum ad Cornelium." Here St. Thomas does not directly touch the question of Baptism, nor does he distinguish between explicit and implicit desire for the Sacrament as a condition for salvation. But elsewhere he does. The two classic passages occur in the Summa, where he says: "De Cornelio tamen sciendum est quod infidelis non erat; alioquin eius operatio accepta non fuisset Deo, cui sine fide nullus potest placere. Habeat autem fidem *implicitam*, nondum manifestata Evangelii Veritate. Unde, ut eum in fide plenius instruitur, mittitur ad eum Petrus." 2/2/10/4, ad 3. The second text is even clearer: "Ante Baptismum Cornelius et alii similes consequuntur gratiam et virtutes per fidem Christi et desiderium baptismi *implicite* vel explicite: postmodum tamen in baptismo maiorem copiam gratiae, et virtutum consequuntur." And this is immediately preceded by the words: "Dicendum quod remissionem peccatorum aliquis consequitur ante baptismum, secundum quod habet *baptismum in voto*, vel explicite vel *implicite*; et tamen cum realiter suscipit baptismum, fit plenior remissio quantum ad liberationem a tota poena." 3/69/4.

57   *De Baptismo,* ML 182, 1032.

58   "Aut puer inter Christianos natus atque educatus, ubi adoleverit, existimabit se esse baptizatum, vel sciet non esse baptizatum. Si baptizatum se esse credat probabile erit, eum fidem divinitus infusam habere. Siquidem approbatio baptismi, quem quis se accepisse, atque habere censet, par est voto baptismi, et ad salutem aeternam perducere potest. De qua re extat rescriptum pontificium capite: Apostolicam, de presbyter. Non Baptiz. Si vero sciat, se non esse baptizatum, et tamen baptismum non postulet, is sine dubio non habet fidem, nisi forte humanam, vel potius nec humanam. Quomodo enim fieri potest, ut aliquis certo credat, sine Baptismo se in aeternum periturum, et tamen Baptismum, rem videlicet factu facillimam, non postulet, neque cupiat? Neque verisimile est, posse aliquem esse inter Christianos institutum, et qui noverit fidem Christianorum, qui tamen de Baptismo nihil unquam audierit, cum inter rudimenta fidei mentio Baptismi, et quotidi in ecclesia receas baptizentur infantes." *De Gratis et Libero Arbitrio*, lib 6, cap. 5.

59   *De Baptismo,* cap. 8.

60   Thus, for example, Tertullian: "Itaque pro cuiusque personae condicione ac dispo-

sitione, etiam aetate, cunctatio baptismi utilior est, praecipue tamen circa parvulos. Quid enim necesse, si non tam necesse est, sponsores etiam periculo ingeri, qui et ipsi per mortalitatem destituere promissiones suas possunt et proventu malae indolis falli....Quid festinat innocens aetas ad remissionem peccatorum *?" De Baptismo*, 18, CV 20, 216. And St. Gregory Nazianzen: "Quid autem de iis dices, qui tenera adhuc aetate sunt, nec aut danum aut gratiam sentiunt ? An eos quoque baptizabimus ? Ita prorsus, si quod periculum urgeat...De reliquis ita censeo, ut triennio exspectato, aut aliquando breviori aut longiori temporis spatio." After which he concludes with several reasons why people should not wait until the age of thirty to be baptized. Oratio 40, nr. 28, MG 36, 399. Even more liberal is Chrysostom who writes: "Nostra autem circumcisio, vel baptismatis, inquam, gratia, medicinam habet citra dolorem, innumeraque bona nobis affert. Spiritus sancti gratia nos implet, et nullum definitum tempus habet sicut illio; sed licet et in prima, et in media et in ultima aetate hanc non manufactam circumcisionem recipere, in qua non sustinetur labor, sed peccatorum deponuntur onera, et remissio invenitur omnium peccatorum, quae per totam vitam gesta sunt." MG 53, 373 sqq.

61   *Institution de la Religion Chrétienne*, Brunsvic, 1865, liv. IV, chap. 14, p. 14.

62   Idem, liv. IV, chap. 15, p. 22.

63   What Bellarmine probably means here by "a faith that is not even human," is giving credence to erroneous doctrine, as, in this case, denying the necessity of Baptism for salvation, from motives which do not spring from even a legitimate trust in human testimony. For what legitimate reason can be given for believing a man, like Calvin, when he preaches a doctrine that goes counter to the obvious testimony of Christian tradition since the time of Christ ?

64   DB 56.

65   *De Ecclesia Militante*, cap. 4.

66   Cum Ecclesia sit multitudo unita (est enim populus quidam, sive regnum, sive corpus unum) et ista unio praecipue in professione unius fidei, et earundem legum ac rituum observatione consistit; nulla ratio permittit, ut eos de Ecclesiae corpore esse dicamus, qui cum eo nullam omnio conjunctionem habent." Ibidem.

67   Bellarmine's phrase, "vel certe esse debent," need not necessarily imply moral censure, as though the Church's jurisdiction extended only to actual members and to those non-actual members who are culpably outside the true Church. Rather the words, "esse debent" may be taken in the objective sense, meaning that the Church's authority extends also to those persons who by reason of their Baptism should be professed Catholics, though actually they are not — prescinding from whether their non-membership is morally blameworthy or not.

68   "Haereticos, licet non sint de Ecclesia tamen debere esse, et proinde ad eam pertinere, ut oves ad ovile, unde fugerunt. Sicut solet dici, ista ovis est illius ovilis, quando tamen vagatur extra ovile. Potest autem Ecclesia iudicare de iis, qui re ipsa intus sunt, vel certe esse debent, sicut pastor revera potest ovem, quae extra ovila errat per montes, cogere iterum ad ovile; et imperator potest desertorem militiae, qui transfugit ad castra hostium, vi cogere ad sua castra, aut etiam suspendere. Apostolus autem loquitur de iis, qui ita foris sunt, ut numquam fuerint intus." Ibidem.

69   Under the general title of: "Posse Haereticos ab Ecclesia damnatos temporalibus poenis, et etiam morte mulotari," Bellarmine declares: "Tres causae sunt propter quas ratio docet homines occidendos esse...Prima causa est, ne mali bonis

noceant…Secunda est, ut paucorum supplicio multi corrigantur … Tertia est, quia ipsis hominibus qui occiduntur, saepe utile est occidi, quando videlicet semper fiunt peiores, et non est probabile unquam eos ad sanitatem mentis reversuros." And he concludes: "Denique haereticis obstinatis beneficium est, quod de hac vita tollantur; nam quo diutius vivunt, eo plures errores excogitant, plures pervertunt, et maiorem sibi damnationem acquirunt." *De Laicis*, cap. 21.

70   *Apologia pro Responsione Sua ad Librum Jacobi, Magnae Britanniae Regis*, cap. 14. In Bellarmine's *Disputationes*, Napoli, 1859, vol. IV, pg 403.

71   *Pro Juramento Fidelitatis, ad Archypresbyterum Angliae,* idem, pg. 441.

72   *De Moribus Haereticorum*, Concio XII, Opera, Napoli, 1861, vol. V, pp. 450-451.

73   *De Lumine Fidei,* Concio I, idem, pg. 401.

74   "At contra objiciunt…potest homo excommunicatus retinere baptismum, fidei professionem, et subjectionem praelatis legitimis, atque adeo esse amicus Dei si nimirum sit iniuste excommunicatus: potest etiam iuate excommunicatus poenitentiam agere, et habere illa tria antequam absolvatur: igitur in Ecclesia erit, etiam manens excommunicatus.

"Respondeo: Talem esse in Ecclesia animo, sive desiderio, quod sufficit illi ad salutem, non tamen esse corpore, sive externe communicatione, quae proprie facit hominem esse de Ecclesia ista visibili, quae est in terris." *De Ecclesia Militante,* cap. 6.

75   Saepe etiam sinit divina providentia expelli de congregatione christiana etiam bonos viros. Quam contumeliam, vel injuriam suam cum patientissime pro Ecclesiae pace tulerint, neque ullas novitates, vel schismatis, vel haeresis moliti fuerint, docebunt hominess quam vero affectu, et quanta sinceritate charitatis Deo serviendum sit. Hos coronat in occulto Pater in occulto videns." *De vera Religione*, cap. 6, ML 34, 128.

PART II
COMPARATIVE ANALYSIS

CHAPTER I
DOCTRINE OF PIUS IX ON NON-CATHOLICS IN BONA FIDE

76   Littera Apostolica, *Providentisimus Deus*, AAS, 23, 433-436, proclaiming St. Robert a Doctor of the Universal Church.

77   Some of the texts most frequently adduced are, for example: "Praescribitur nemini sine baptismo competere salutem, ex illa maxime pronuntiatione Domini, qui sit: 'Nisi natus ex aqua quis erit, non habet vita…'" Tertullian, *De Baptismo*, 12, CV 20, 216. 'Si quis baptisma non recipiat, salutem non habet, solis martyribus exceptis, qui etiam sine aqua regnum accipiunt." S. Cyril of Jerusalem, *Cathecheses*, 3, 10, MG 33, 440. "Nemo ascendit in regnum caelorum, nisi par sacramentum baptismatis." S. Ambrose, *De Abraham*, lib. 2, cap. 11, nr. 79, ML 14, 494. "Ex illo tempore quo Salvator noster dixit: Si quis renatus non fuerit ex aqua et Spiritu Sancto, non potest introire in regnum Dei, absque sacramento baptismatis, praeter eos qui in ecclesia catholica sine baptismata pro Christo sanguinem fundunt, nec regnum caglorum potest quisquam accipere nec vita aeternam." S. Fulgantium, *De Fide ad Petrum*, cap. 3, nr. 41, ML 65, 692.

78   Thus, for example, P. Berruyer, whose *L'Histoire du Peuple de Dieu* was con-

demned by ecclesiastical authorities for at least leaving the impression that faith based on revelation was not absolutely necessary for salvation. "Non satisfait," says Caperan, "de discerner des ames innocentes parmi les infideles, le P. Berruyer a laisse entendre que Dieu pourrait se contenter, en certains cas, de la simple religious naturelle. Par des folrmules specieuses, il a su moins jete le doute sur la necessite de la revelation et celle d'une foi surnaturelle appuyee sur cette revelation. Le doute suggere s'insinue et s'exprime de telle sorte que le lecteur, seduit, est entraine a une affirmation que l'auteur a craint d'enoncer ouvertement a savior que, meme depuis la venue de Jesus-Christ, les homes aux yeux desquels la revelation ne brille pas, et qui, a son defaut, sont prives de la foi, peuvent sans cette revelation at cette foi, en pratiquant, avec le secours de la grace, la religion naturelle, parvequir a la justification. Pour ces motifs, la Sorbonne frappe les propositions du P. Berruyer de la note de captieuses. Elles inspirent, ajcute la *Censure,* un doute heretique." Quoted in Edouard Hugon, *Hors de l'Eglise point de Salut,* Paris, 1927, pp. 22-24.

79   Giuseppe S. Pelczar, *Pio IX e il Suo Pontificato,* vol. I, Torino, 1909, Prefazione, pg. 5.

80   "Errorem alterum nec minus exitiosum aliquas catholici orbis partes occupasse non sine moerore novimus, animisque insedisse plerumque catholicorum, qui bene sperandum de aeterna illorum omnium salute putant, qui in vera Christi Ecclesia nequaquam versantur. Idcirco percontari saepenumero solent, quaenam futura post obitum sit eorum sors et conditio, qui catholicae fidei minime addicti sunt, vanissimisque adductis rationibus responsum praestolantur, quod pravae huic sententiae suffragetur. Absit, Venerabiles Fratres, ut misericordiae divinae, quae infinita est, terminos, audeamus apponere; absit, ut perscrutari velimus arcane cousilia et iudicia Dei, quae sunt abyssus multa (Ps. 35/7), nec humana queunt cogitatione penetrari. Quod vero apostolici Nostri muneris est, episcopalem vestram et sollicitudinem et vigilantiam excitatam volumus, ut, quantum potestis contendere, opinionem illam impiam aeque ac funestam ab hominum mente propulsetis, nimirum quavis in religione reperiri posse aeternae salutis viam. Ea qua praestatis sollertia ac doctrina demonstretis commissis curae vestrae populis, miserationi ac justitiae divinae dogmata catholicae fidei neutiquam adversari.

"Tenendum quippe ex fide est, extra apostolicam Romanam Ecclesiam salvum fieri neminem posse, hanc esse unicam salutis arcam, hanc qui non fuerit ingressus, diluvio periturum; sed tamen pro certo pariter habendum est; qui verae religionis ignorantia labrent, si ea sit invincibilis, nulla ipsos obstringi huiusce rei culpa ante eculos Domini. Nunc vero quis tantum sibi arroget, ut huius nodi ignorantiae designare limites queat iuxta populorum, regionum, ingeniorum aliarumque rerum tam multarum rationem et varietatem? Enimvero cum soluti corporeis hisce vinculis videbimus Deum sicuti est (I John. 3/2), intelligemus profecto, quam arcto pulchroque nexu miseratio ac iustitia divina copulentur; quamdiu vero in terris versamur mortali hac gravati mole, quae hebetat animam, firmissime teneamus, ex catholica doctrina unum Deum esse, unam fidem, unum baptisma (Eph. 4/5); ulterius inquirendo progredi nefas est." Allocutio *Singulari quadam,* Dec. 9, 1854, Codicis Iuris Canonici Fontes, vol. II, Roma, 1924, pg. 894.

81   Atque hic, Dilecti Filii Nostri et Venerabiles Fratres, iterum commemorare et reprehendere oportet gravissimum errorem, in quo nonnulli catholici misere versantur, qui hominess in erroribus viventes et a vera fide atqua a catholica unitate alienos ad aeternam vitam pervenire posse opidantur. Quod quidem Catholicae

doctrinae vel maxime adversatur. Notum Nobis vobisque est, eos, qui invincibili circa sanctisimam nostram religionem ignorantia laborant, quique naturalem
legem eiusque praecepta in omnium cordibus a Deo insculpta sedulo servantes
ao Deo obedire parati, honestam rectamque vitam agunt, posse, divinae lucis et
gratiae operante virtute, aeternam consequi vitam, cum Deus, qui omnium mentes,
animos, cogitationes, habitatusque plane intuetur, scrutatur et noscit, pro summa
sua bonitate et clementia minime patiatur, quempiam aeternis puniri suppliciis,
qui voluntariae culpae reatum non habeat. Sed notissimum quoque est catholicum
dogma, neminem scilicet extra catholicam Ecclesiam posse salvari, et contumaces
adversus eiusdem Ecclesiae auctoritatem, definitions, et ab ipsius Ecclesiae Unitate at que a PETRI successore Romano Pontifice, qui vineac custodia a Salvatore
est commissa, portinaciter divisos aeternam non posse obtinere salutem." Litterae
Encyclical, *Quanto Conficiamur Moerore* ad Episcopos Italiae, Aug. 10, 1863,
Codicis Iuris Canonici Fontes, vol. II, pg. 972.

82   Lamennais, *Essai sur l'indifference en matiere de Religion,* Paris, 1823, t. III, ch.
     26, pg. 345.

83   Idem, t. IV, ch. 29-30.

84   Idem, t. III, ch. 27, pg. 362 sqq.

85   Ibidem, pg. 206-207.

86   Ibidem, pg. 29-30.

87   Ibidem, pg. 483-484.

88   This will be recognized as a condemnation also of Cano's theory of a church of
     the faithful, from Adam to the end of the world. For if Cano's theory were sustain-
     able, that merely faith in general, and not the Christian Faith as embodied in the
     Catholic Church were necessary for salvation, then Lamennais' thesis would at
     least have some probability, since he also did not completely rule out revelation
     from the scheme of salvation, but only the Christian revelation.

89   Jurie, *Le Vrai Système de l'Eglise*, pg. 79, quoted in Acta Concilii Vaticani, C.L.,
     VII, pg. 583b.

90   It will be recalled that the original context in which the metaphor of the Ark oc-
     curs, is in St. Cyprian's *De Catholicae Ecclesiae Unitate.* This work was writ-
     ten as a protest against the current divisions among the communities of Carthage
     and Rome, during the schism of Felicissimus and Novatian. Cyprian recommends
     unity in and with the true Church of Christ, outside of which no one can attain to
     salvation. For, he says, Christ purposely founded the Church upon Peter, that is,
     the one visible basis of unity, to manifest to us that His Church would be recog-
     nized and its existence assured by this mark of unity. Clearly when Cyprian says
     that outside the Church there is no salvation, he is referring to the palpably visible
     unity of the Roman Catholic communion, founded on the successors of St. Peter.
     Thus, Rauschen, *Patrologie*, Paris, 1906, pg. 111.

CHAPTER II
VATICAN COUNCIL

91   "Nota Ecclesiae christianae est, quod sit catholica, comprehendens et omnes an-
     gelos coeli et omnes electos et lustos terrae et omnium saeculorum." *Corpus Iuris
     Canonici*, Richter, Lipsiae, 1836-1839, II, 140 sqq., from the Dogmatic Constitu-
     tion, *Unigenitus*, Sept. 8, 1713; DB 1422.

92   "Quid est Ecclesia, nisi coetus filiorum Dei manentium in eius sinu, adoptatorum

in Christo, subsistentium in eius persona, redemptorum eius sanguine, viventium eius spiritu, agentium per eius gratiam, et exspectantium gratiam future saeculi?" Ibidem, DB 1423.

93   "Ecclesia sive integer Christus incarnatum Verbum habet ut caput, omnes vero sanctos ut membra." Ibidem, DB 1424.

94   "Nihil spatiosius Ecclesia Dei: quia omnes electi et iusti omnium saeculorum illam component." Ibidem, DB 1426.

95   Doctrina quae proponit Ecclesiam consideranam velut unum corpus mysticum coagmentatum ex Christo capite et fidelibus, qui sunt eius membra per unionem ineffabilem, qua mirabiliter evadimus cum ipso unus solus sacerdos, una sola victima, unus solus adorator perfactus Dei Patris in spiritu et Veritate; intellecta hoc sensu, ut ad corpus Ecclesiae non pertineant nisi fideles, qui sunt perfecti adoratores in spiritu et veritate: --haeretica." Errores Synodi Pistoriensis, Damnati in Constitutione, *Auctorem Fidei*, Aug. 28, 1794, Propositio damnata 15, in *Bullarii Rom. Continuatio*, Prati, 1835-1856, vol. VI, pg. 2709; DB 1515.

96   Epistola Encyclica, *Nostis et Nobiscum*, Dec. 8, 1849, in Codicis Iuris Canonici Fontes, Vol. II, pg. 839.

97   "Docemus autem et declaramus, Ecclesiae in esse omnes verae societatis qualitates. Neque societas haec indefinita vel informis a Christo relicta est; sed quemadmodum ab ipso suam existentiam habet: ita eiusdem voluntate ac lege suam existendi formam suamque constitutionem accepit. Neque eadem membrum est sive pars alterius cuiuslibet societatis, nec cum alia quavis confusa aut commiscenda; sed adeo in semetipsa perfecta, ut dum ab omnibus humanis societatibus distinguitur, supra eas tamen quam maxime evehatur. Ab inexhausto enim misericordiae Dei Patris fonte profecta, per incarnati ipsius Verbi ministerium operamque fundata, in Spiritu sancto constituta est, qui in Apostolos primum largissime effusus, abunde etiam iugiter diffunditur in filios adoptionis, ut iidem lumine eius collustrati una mentium fide et Deo adhaereant et inter se cohaereant; ut pignus haereditatis in cordibus suis circumferentes, carnis desideria ab eius, quae in mundo est, concupiscentiae corruptione avellant, et beata una communiqué spe firmati, concupiscant promissam aeternam Dei gloriam, atque adeo per bona opera certam suam vocationem et electionem faciant. Quum autem his bonorum divitiis in Ecclesia homines per Spiritum sanctum augeantur, atque his eiusdem sancti Spiritus nexibus in Unitate cohaereant: Ecclesia ipca spiritualis societas est, atque ordinis omnino supernaturalis." Acta et Decreta Concilii Vaticani, in *Collectio Lacensis*, Vol. VII, 1890, col. 568.

98   Absit tamen, ut quis credat, Ecclesiae membra nonnisi internis ac latentibus vinculis iungi, et abditam inde societatem ac prersus invisibilem fieri. Aeterna siquidem Dei sapientia ac virtus voluit, spiritualibus et invisibilibus vinculis, quibus fideles supremo ac invisibili Ecclesiae capiti per Spiritum sanctum adhaerent, externa quoque ac visibilia respondere, ut spiritualis illa ac supernaturalis societas extrinsecus appareret, et conspicua patesceret. Hinc visible magisterium, a quo credenda interius exteriusque progitenda fides publice proponitur; visibile quoque ministerium, quod visibilia Dei mysteria, quibus interior sanctificatio hominibus et debitus Dei cultus comparator, munere publico moderator ac curat; visibile regimen, quod membrorum inter se communionem ordinat, externamque omnem et publicam fidelium in Ecclesia vitam disponit ac dirigit; visible demum totum Ecclesia corpus, ad quod non iusti tantum aut praedestinati pertinent , sed etiam peccatores, professione tamen fidei et communione cum eo coniuncti. Quibus fit,

ut Christi Ecclesia in terries deo lavisibilis nec latens sit; sed in manifestatione posita, veluti civitas excelsa et illustris in monte, quae abscondi non potest, ac veluti lucerna super candelabrum, quae sole justitiae illuminata, mundum universum luce suae veritatis illustrat." Ibidem.

99   "Si quis dixerit, divinarum promissionum Ecclesiam non esse societatem externam ac conspicuam, sed totam internam ac invisibilem, anathema sit." Idem, col. 577.

100   "At vero quum societas contineatur potestate et auctoritate, si haec invisibilis sit, conspicua esse illa nequit. Quare statuitur, in Ecclesia esse *visibile, magisterium, visibile ministerium, visibile regimen,* a Christo Domino institutum, per quam triplicem potestatem externam ac conspicuam vera Ecclesia Christi cohaeret triplici exterdo nexu, qui nexus externi internis respondeant, eorundem partialis causa exsisunt, totumque Ecclesiae corpus visibile et conspicuum redunt ita ut, Quicumque triplici illo visibili nexu cum Ecclesiae Corpore cohaereat, uti membrum verae Christi Ecclesiae deprehendatur. 'Hoc enim, ait Bellarminus *De Ecclesia Militante*, 1., III, c. II, interest inter sententiam nostram et alias omnes, quod omnes aliae requirunt internas virtutes ad constituendum aliquem in Ecclesia, et propter ea Ecclesiam veram invisibilem faciunt; nos autem, etsi credimus in Ecclesia inveniri omnes virtutues, fidem, spem, caritatem, et ceteras, tamen ut aliquis aliquo modo dici posit pars verae Ecclesiae, de qua Scripturae loquuntur, non putamus requiri ullam internam virtutem, sed tantum externam professionem fidei, et sacramentorum communionem, quae sensu ipso percipitur, et (quod praemiserat) regime legitimorum pastorum ac praecipue unius Christi in terries vicarii Romani Pontificis. Ecclesia enim est coetus hominum ita visibilis et palpabilis, ut est coetus populi Romani, vel regimen Galliae, aut respublica Venetorum." Idem, col. 585.

101   "Cum eiusmodi sit vera Christi Ecclesia, declaramus, hanc visibilem conspicuamque societatem esse illam ipsam divinarum promissionum ac misericordiarum Ecclesiam, quam Christus tot praerogativis ac privilegiis distinguere et exornare voluit; eandemque ita plane in sua constitutione esse determinatam, ut quaecumque societates a fidei Unitate vel a communione huius Corporis seiunctae nullo modo pars eius aut membrum dici possint; neque per varias Christiani nominis consociations dispersam atque diffusam, sed totam in se collectam penitusque cohaerentem, in sua conspicua unitate indivisum ac indivisibile corpus praeferre, quod est ipsm corpus mysticum Christi. De quo Apostolus inquit, unum corpus mysticum Christi. De quo Apostolus inquit, unum corpus, et unus spiritus, sicut vocari estis in una spe vocationis vestrae. Unus Dominus, una fides, unum baptisma. Unus Deus et Pater omnium, qui est super omnes, et per omnia et in omnibus nobis. (Ad Ephes. 4/4-6)." Idem, col. 569.

102   "Si quis dixerit, veram Ecclesiam non esse unum in se corpus, sed ex variis dissitisque Christiani nominis societatibus constare, per easque diffusam esse; aut varias societates ab invicem fidei professione dissidents atque communione seiunctae, tanquam membra vel partes unam et universalem constituere Christi Ecclesiam; anathema sit." Idem, col. 577.

103   "Hinc ait Bellarminus, loc. cit., cap. 2, 'ipsi duas Ecclesias fingunt. Unam veram, et ad quam pertinent privilegia, quae narrantur in Scriptureis, et hanc esse sanctorum congregationem, qui vere credunt et obediunt Deo, et hanc non esse visibilem, nisi oculis fidei. Alternam externam, quae nomine tantum est Ecclesia, et hanc esse congregationem hominum convenientium in doctrina fidei et usu sac-

ramentorum, et in hac bonos et malos inveniri." Idem, col. 585.

104   Idem, col. 631. As a modern example of the Latitudinarism which the Vatican Council condemned, we have the following report on the first Assembly of the Ecumenical Council of Churches gathered at Amsterdam from August 22 to September 4, in
1948. Forty three nations were represented at the Assembly, covering 148 denominations, with over 1500 delegates in attendance. Significantly, the delegates were
satisfied with "agreement only in the confession of Christ... but on the Church, on
the Priesthood, on the Sacraments, on the veneration of the Saints, on the conception
of the future life, the fundamental divergences remain and the divisions are openly
avowed. In the message delivered by the Assembly 'to our brothers in Christ, and to
all who are willing to hear us,' unity is affirmed solely in the confession of Christ.
'We bless God our Father, and our Lord Jesus Christ Who gathers together in one
the children of God that are scattered abroad. He has brought us here together at
Amsterdam. We are one in acknowledging Him as our God and Savior.' They do
not ignore their divisions, but avow that these exist 'in matters of faith, order and
tradition.' This is the attitude which was adopted by the Ecumenical Assembly when
it wished to define its proper nature and its role: 'The World Council of Churches is
composed of Churches which acknowledge Jesus Christ as God and Saviour. They
find their unity in Him. Unity is not for them to create; it is the gift of God. But they
know that it is their duty to make common cause in the search for the expression of
that unity in work and in life. The Council desires to serve the Churches, which are
its constituent members, as an instrument wherby they may bear witness together to
their common allegiance to Jesus Christ, and cooperate in matters requiring united
action.... It is the earnest desire of the Council that the Churches may be found
closer to Christ and therefore closer to one another.' (EPS no. 40, 1948)" Boyer,
Unitas, Rome, Jan.-Mar. 1949, pgs. 9-10.

105   "Hinc omnes intelligant, quam necessaria ad salutem obtinendam societas sit
Ecclesia Christi. Tantae nimirum necessitatis, quantae consortium et coniunctio
est cum Christo capite et mystice eius corpore, praeter quod nullam aliam communionem ipse nutrit et fovet tanquam Ecclesiam suam, quam solam dilexit et
seipsum tradidit pro ea, ut illam sanctificaret, mundans lavacro aquae in verbe
vitae: ut exhiberet ipse sibi gloriosam Ecclesiam, non habentem maculam aut ru-
gam, aut aliquid huiusmodi, sed ut sit sancta et immaculata. Ideirco docemus,
Ecclesiam non liberam societatem esse, quasi indifferens sit ad salutem, eam sive
nosse sive ignorare, sive ingredi sive relinquere; sed esse omino necessariam, et
quidem necessitate non tantum praecepti dominici, quo Salvator omnibus gentibus eam ingrediendam praescripsit; verum etiam medii, quia in instituto salutatis
providentiae ordine communication sancti Spiritus, participatio veritatis et vitae
non obtinetur, nisi in Ecclesia et per Ecclesiam, cuius caput est Christus." Acta
Concilii Vaticani, op. cit., col. 569. "What deserves to be noted is the phrase,
"communicatio sancti Spiritus... non obtinetur, nisi in Ecclesia," which clearly
brings out the necessity of somehow belonging to the true Church in order to
receive the Holy Spirit in sanctifying grace.

106   "Si quis dixerit, Ecclesiam Christi non esse societatem ad aeternam salutem con-
sequendam omnino necessariam; aut homines per cuiusvis religionis cultum salvari posse; anathema sit." Idem, col. 577.

107   "Porro dogma fidei est, extra Ecclesiam salvari neminem posse. Neque tamen,
qui circa Cristum eiusque Ecclesiam invincibili ignorantia laborant, propter hanc
ignorantiam poenis aeternis damnandi sunt, cum nulla obstringantur huiusce rei

culpa ante oculos Domini, qui vult omnes hominess salvos fieri et ad agnitionem
veritatis venire, quique facienti quod in se est non denegat gratiam, ut iustificationem et vitam aeternam consequi possit: sed hanc nullus consequitur, qui a fidei
unitate vel ab Ecclesia communione culpabiliter seiunctus ex hac vita decedit."
Idem, col. 569. Evidently the conciliar theologians recognized the contrary possibility of a person leaving this life who was not culpably separated from the true
Church, and yet who died as an adult non-Catholic.

108   "Si quis dixerit, intolerantiam illam, qua Ecclesia Catholica omnes religiosas sectas a sua communione separatas proscribit et damnat, divino iure non praecipi;
aut de veritate religionis opinions tantum, non autem certitudinem haberi posse;
ideoque omnes sectas religiosas ab Ecclesia tolerandas esse; anathema sit." Idem,
col. 577.

109   "Adiectum hoc Caput fuit ob particulares difficultates, quae praemisso effato
dogmatico obmoventur, ad eiusdemque sensum accuratius explicandum. Quod ad
primum attinet, haec iterum loc. cit. pg. 54, scribit M. Jurieu: 'Le papisme est
cruel au souverain degrè, et il s'engage en mille absurditès en soutenant, comme
il fait, qu'entre toutes les sociètès qui divisent le christianisme, il n'y en a qu'une
qui soit la vraie èglise, dans l'enceinte de laquelle suele se trouvent les elus et les
vrais fidèles, qui sont les membres de Jésus-Christ, hors de laquelle il n'y a point
de salut.'" Idem, col. 589.

110   *"Cui...invincibili ignorantia.* His indicator, fieri posse, ut quid ad *visibilem externamque Ecclesiae communionem* non spectet, et tamen iustificationem vitamque
eternam consequatur. Complexio verborum, quibus ea doctrina effertur, expressa
est ad haec, quae auctor *Vocat. Omn. Gent.* , lib. II, cc. 1, 29, scribit de Deo,' qui
vult omnes homines salvos fieri et ad agnitionem veritatis venire, quique nullum
indebite condemnat, sed multiplici at que inefabili bonitate consuluit semper et
consulit, ut nulli pereuntium excusatio suppetat de abnegato sibi lumine veritatis.'
Ne tamen inde videretur consequi, extra Ecclesiam salvum fieri aliquem posse, in
alia forma Schematis, dicebatur: *Quam* (iustificationem et vitam aeternam) *si consequuntur, non ideo extra Ecclesiam salvantur; omnes enim justificati ad Ecclesiam sive re sive voto pertipent.* Verum quoniam formula, *sive re sive voto,* pluribus
Consultoribus non arridebat, visum est sufficere, si declaretur explicite, nullum
fieri salvum, qui ob propriam culpam ab Ecclesia Seiunctus ex hac vita decedit,
dum implicite significatum intelligatur, non posse penitus vel simpliciter, ut aiunt,
extra Ecclesiam esse, quicumque salvus fiat. Quum id disertius exprimendum esse
quidam censerent, hanc suggerebant formam Capitis: 'Dogma fidei est... Licet
enim qui circa Christum eiusque Ecclesiam invincibili ignorantia laborant, propter hanc ignorantiam poenis aeternis demnandi non sint, cum nulla obstringantur
huiusce rei culpa ante oculos Domini, qui vult omnes homines salvos fieri et ad
agnitionem veritatis venire, quique facienti cum auxilio divino, quod in se est,
non denegat gratiam, ut iustificationem et vitam aeternam consequi possit: hanc
tamen nullus consequitur, qui ad Christi Ecclesiam nullatenus pertinet, et a fidei
unitate vel ab Ecclesiae communione culpabiliter seiunctus ex hac vita decedit'
: *qui nullatenus,* inquiebant, *ad Ecclesiam pertinet,* id est, qui *neque spectat ad
Ecclesiae corpus, neque ad Ecclesiae animam;* ideoque nullo modo pertinet ad
Ecclesiam, videlicet *necue re necue voto.* Haec explicantur praeclare a Bellar-
mino, 'De Ecclesia Militante, lib. III, cap. 3, De non baptizatis,' qui postquam
cap. 2, exposuit, catechumenos esse de anima, sed non de corpore Ecclesiae, intel-
ligendo corpus Ecclesiae de visibili fidelium communione, ad quam 'actu et pro-

prie' tantum pertinent, qui 'profitentur fidem, et in Sacramentis communicant sub regimine pastorum,' interrogat: 'Quomodo igitur salvantur catechumeni, si sunt extra Ecclesiam?' Tum respondet: 'Quod dicitur extra Ecclesiam neminem salvari, intelligi debere de iis, qui *peque re ipsa, nec desiderio* sunt de Ecclesia, sicut de baptismo communiter loquuntur theologi. Quoniam autem catechumeni si non re, saltem voto sunt in Ecclesia, ideo salvari possunt. Neque repugnant similitudo arcae Noe, extra quam nemo salvabatur, etiam si voto in ea fuisset; nam similitudines non in omnibus convenient.' Idem docet Suarez, De Fide, Disp. XII, sect. 4, no. 22 scribens: 'Quod vero tandem additur, quia extra Ecclesiam non est salus, aliqui, ut videre licet in Cano, de Loc. rel. de Sacram. p. II, dicunt, propositionem illam intelligendam esse de generali Ecclesia, prout fuit semper, et non de sola Ecclesia, prout specialiter est a Christo instituta; sed non placet responsio, tum quia Ecclesia simper est una; tum etiam, quia Concilia revera loquuntur de hac Ecclesia Christi, et de illa oportet in aliquo sensu verificari, quod extra illam nemo salvetur. Melius ergo respondendum iuxta distinctionem datam *de necessitate in re vel in voto;* ita enim nemo salvari potest, nisi hanc Christi Ecclesiam vel in re vel in voto satem et desiderio ingrediatur. Ita respondet Bellarmin. lib. III, de Eccl. cap. 3. Estque manifestum, quia nullus est in re ipsa intra hanc Ecclesiam, nisi baptizatus sit, et tamen salvari potest, quia sicut illi sufficit votum baptismi, ita etiam votum ingrediendi Ecclesiam; idem ergo nos dicimus de quocumque fideli vere poenitente qui baptizatus non sit, sive pervenerit ad fidem explicitam Christi, sive tantum ad implicitam: nam per illam habere potest votum saltem implicitum, quod satis est respectu baptismi, ut div. Thom … docet.'" Idem, col. 591, 592.

111   Worth noting is the consistency with which Papal documents before and after the Vatican Council use terms equivalent to *nullatenus* to indicate that salvation is impossible only for those who *in no way whatsoever* belong to the true Church. Thus Pius IX says: "qui in vera Christi Ecclesia *nequaquam* versantur"; (Allocutio, *Singulari Quadam*). And again: "qui nobiscum *minime* coniuncti sunt"; (Encyclica, *Quanto Conficiamur Moerore*). And Pius XII: "membra tamen, a Corpore *omnino* abscissa," (Encyclica, *Mystici Corporis*). The importance of these qualifying terms lies in two facts: first, that the Popes recognize some other kind of membership than real, actual and visible which *per se* is sufficient for salvation; and secondly, that the context in which the terms *nequaquam, minime,* etc. are used, indicates rather a quality of membership than a quantity or degree. In other words, if a non-Catholic is saved, it is not because he belonged to some quantitiative *part* of the true Church, say its soul, but because he possessed some kind of Catholic membership, other than actual and real.

112   It was not without reason that the Vatican consultors added the gloss to Bellarmine, "understanding the body of the Church to mean the visible communion of the faithful." For in so doing, they cleared up the following points:

1.   The body of the Church is constituted by the visible communion of the *faithful*, i.e., of those who believe. This eliminates the inconventient, and unnecessary, speculative point raised by Bellarmine's using *corpus Ecclesiae* in two senses, once as a living body, to which only those belong who have real, internal faith; and again as more of a corpse than a body, when he allows even occult infidels and heretics to belong to the body of the Church.

2.   Membership in this living body of the Church is constituted by having the faith internally, *and* professing the same visibly and externally. This eliminates from its actual membership those sincere non-Catholics who have the

faith, indeed, but who do not profess it in visible communion with the Catholic Church.

113   The voto membership of catechumens, therefore, describes their relation to the whole Church, its body and soul, and not its body alone. So that sincee non-Catholics, even when they are in the state of grace, are still only voto in the soul of the Church; obviously, since they are only voto members of the Church, which is a composite of body and soul; they cannot have a higher membership in a part, i.e., the soul, than they have in the whole, i.e., both body and soul.

114   Thus Hurter: "Iusti qui vitam iam vivunt supernaturalem, immediate, per se et formaliter spectant ad Ecclesiae animam; secundo veluti gradu et inchoative omnes illi, qui iam alique interioris gratiae donno potiuntur, quo disponuntur ad vitam gratiae habitualem." And again: "Extra Ecclesiam, nulla salus, in toto suo rigore verum est, si sermo est de Ecclesia anima: si quis enim *re* ad illam non spectat, caret vita supernaturali." *Theologiae Dogmaticae Compendium*, Oeniponte, 1893, pg. 246, 248, Vol. I.

115   Again the stress on pertaining to the *Church*, either *re* or *voto*, and not merely to either the body or the soul, *re* or *voto*. P. Hugon sees an unwarranted distinction between real and votive membership in either the soul or body of the Church. "Three conclusions," he says, "are derived from ecclesiastical documents, and on which there cannot be any doubt:

1.   The necessity of means for pertaining to the soul of the Church, not merely in desire, but in reality: the *votum* or desire of faith, the *votum* or desire of grace, are not enough, in themselves to give justification.

2.   Necessity of means for pertaining at least in desire to the body of the Church. The visible society instituted by our Lord, being the unique supernatural economy, to which have been confided all the instruments of salvation, to desire salvation efficaciously is to wish, implicitly and necessarily, to be united to her as to the source of life.

3.   Necessity of means for pertaining in reality to the body of the Church in the measure in which it is known and as far as a person can fulfill this obligation. The *votum*, which is a necessity of means, would not have solidity, would not be sincere, and, consequently would lack all efficacy for salvation, if a person neglected to put it into effect, when this execution is possible." Op. cit., pgs. XV-XVI.

However, only the first of the above three statements may be open to criticism, namely, that there is a necessity of means to belong *re* and not just *voto* to the soul of the Church, whereas the Vatican theologians clearly say that *re* or *voto* membership in the whole Church, body and soul, is enough to be saved. What P. Hugon has done is to use "soul of the Church" in a different sense. Certainly no mere desire for grace or faith is enough to be saved. But even a mere desire, and this even implicit, to receive the Holy Spirit Who animates the Mystical Body — coupled, of course, with other necessary dispositions — is enough to be justified. In other words, a person does not have to belong actu to the Holy Spirit *prouti est anima Ecclesiae,* enough that he be attached voto to the Spirit of Christ in this capacity *as* the Soul of the Church. If this *votum* is sincere and adequate, such a person will be rewarded with receiving the Holy Spirit *actu* indeed, but *not* as the Soul of the Church; rather, he will receive the Spirit of Christ, Who also animates the Catholic Church. Schematically, we may say that a non-Catholic in the state of grace belongs to the Soul of the Church, i.e., the Holy Spirit with His gifts, simultaneously

both *re* and *voto*, viewing the Spirit of Christ in two different ways. Thus:
Non-Catholic Membership in the Soul of the Church:

- *voto* — possession of the Holy Spirit in His formal capacity *as* the soul of the Church.
- *re*—possession of the Holy Spirit, *Who is* also the Soul of the Church.

116   *De Fide*, Disputatio XII, sect. 4, n. 22.

CHAPTER III
LEO XII

117   Litterae Apostolicae, *Apostolicae Curae*, Sept. 13, 1896, ASS 29, pgs. 193-203.

118   Pius XII makes the same reference to the 'munera' and 'adiumenta' which only actual members of the Church enjoy, in *Mystici Corporis,* AAS 35, pg. 243.

119   "Hoc restat, ut quo ingressi sumus Pastoris magni nomine et animo veritatem tam gravis rei certissimam commonstrare, e odem adhortemur eos qui Ordinum atque Hierarchiae beneficia sincera voluntate optent ac requirant. Usque adhuc fortasse, virtutis christianae intendentes ardorem, religiosius consulentes divinas litteras, pias duplicantes preces, incerti tamen haeserunt et anxii ad vocem Christi iamdiu intime admonentis. Probe iam vident quo se bonus ille invitet ac velit. Ad unicum eius ovile si redeant, tum vero et quaesita beneficia assecuturi sunt et consenquentia salutis praesidia, quorum administram fecit ipse Ecclesiam, quasi redemptionis suae custodem perpetuam et procuratricem in gentibus. Tum vero haurient aquas in gaudio de fontibus Salvatoris, sacramentis eius mirificis: unde fideles animae in amicitiam Dei, remissis vero peccatis, restituuntur, caelesti pane aluntur et roborantur, adiumentisque maximis affluunt ad vitae adeptionem aeternae. Quorum bonorum revera sitientes, utinam Deus pacis, Deus totius consolationis faciat compotes atque expleat perbenignus. —Hortationem vero Nostram et vota eius maiorem in modum spectare volumus, qui religionis ministry in communitatibus suis habentur. Homines ipso officio praecedentes doctrina et auctoritate, quibus profecto cordi est divina gloria et animorum salus, velint alacres vocanti Deo parare in primis et obsequi, praeclarumque de se edere exemplum. Singulari certe laetitia eos Ecclesia mater excipiet omnique complectetur bonitate et providentia, quippe quos per arduas rerum difficultates virtus animi generosior ad sinum suuz reduxerit. Ex hac vero virtute dici vix potest quae ipsos laus maneat in coetibus fratrum per catholicum orbem, quae aliquando spes et fiducia ante Christum iudicem, quae ab illo praemia in regno caelesti! Nos quidem, quantum omni ope licuerit, eorum cum Ecclesia reconciliationem fovere non desistemus; ex qua et singuli et ordines, id quod vehementer cupimus, multum capere possunt ad imitandum. Interea veritatis gratiaeque divinae patentem cursum ut secundare contendant fideliter, per viscera misericordiae Dei nostri rogamus omnes et obsecramus." AAS 29, 202-203.

120   *De Ecclesia Militante,* cap. 18.

121   *De Poenitentia*, Lib. II, cap. 14.

122   *De Poenitentia*, Lib. II, cap. 13.

123   "Itaque Spiritus sancti et praesentia conspicua super Christum et virtute intima in anima eius, duplex eiusdem Spiritus praesignificatur missio, ea nimirum quae in Ecclesia Manifesto patet, et ea quae in animis iustorum secreto illapsu exercetur." Epistola Encyclica, *Divinum Illud*, May 11, 1897, AsS 29, 649.

124   "Atque noc affirmare sufficiat, quod quum Christus caput sit ecclesiae, Spiritus Sanctus sit eius anima." "Et quoniam populorum salus, ad quam nata est Eccle-

sia, plane postulat ut haec munus idem in perpetuitatem temporum persequatur, perennis idoirco vita atque virtus a Spiritu Sancto suppetit, quae Ecclesiam conservat augetque… Ab ipso namque episcopi constituuntur, quorum ministerio non modo filii generantur, sed etiam patres, sacerdotes videlicet, ad eam regendam enutriendamque eodem sanguine quo est a Christo redempta." Idem. pg. 650.

125   There is a statement of Newman on this point which may serve as a commentary on Leo XIII's exhortation to the Anglicans to be faithful to their present lights, and thereby, may hope to obtain the greater light of the Catholic Faith. Says Newman: "Is it not one's duty… to throw oneself generously into that form of religion which is providentially put before one? Is it right or is it wrong to begin with private judgment? May we not, on the other hand, look for a blessing through obedience even to an erroneous system, and a guidance even by means of it out of it ? Were those who were strict and conscientious in their Judaism, or those who were lukewarm and skeptical, more likely to be led into Christianity when Christ came ? … Certainly I have always contended that obedience even to an erring conscience was the way to gain light, and that it mattered not where a man began, so that he began on what came to hand and in faith; and that any thing might become a divine method of truth." Letter of April 3, 1844, quoted in *Apologia Pro Vita Sua*, London, 1890, pg. 206.

CHAPTER IV
BENEDICT XV

126   "Itaque, invocato divinae gratiae auxilio, Beatorum Petri et Pauli Apostolorum auctoritate confisi, motu proprio, certa scientia atque Apostolicae, qua aucti sumus, potestatis plenitudine, Constitutione hac Nostra, quam volumus perpetuo valituram, praesentem Codicem, sic digestus est, promulgamus, vim legis posthac pro universa Ecclesia decernimus, vestraeque tradimus custodiae ac vigilantiae servandum." Constitutio Apostolica, *Providentissima Mater Ecclesia*, Codex Iuris Canonical, Friburgi Brisgoviae, 1926, pgs. XXXII-XXXIII.

127   "Baptismate homo constituitur in Ecclesis Christi persona cum omnibus christianorum iuribus et officiis, nisi, ad iura quod attinet, obstet obex, ecclesiasticae communionis vinculum impediens, vel lata ab Ecclesia censura." *Codex Iuris Canonici*, Can. 87.

128   #1 Christus Dominus fidei depositum Ecclesiae concredidit, ut ipsa, Spiritu Sancto iugiter assistente,

doctrinam revelatam custodiret et fideliter exponeret.

#2 Ecclesiae, independenter a qualibet civili potestate, ius est et Officium gestes omnes evangelicam

doctrinam docendi: hanc vero rite ediscere veramque Dei Ecclesiam amplecti omnes divina lege

tenentur." C.I.C. Can. 1322.

129   "Fide divina et catholica ea omnia credenda sunt quae verbo Dei scripto vel tradito continentur et ab Ecclesia sive sollemni iudicio sive ordinario et universali magisterio tanquam divinitus revelata credenda proponuntur." C.I.C., Can. 1323.

130   #1 Fideles Christi fidem aperte profiteri te nentur quoties eorum silentium, tergiversatio aut ratio agendi secumferrent implicitam fidei negationem, contemptum religionis, iniuriam Dei vel scandalum proximi. #2 Post receptum baptismum si quis, nomen retinens christianum, pertinaciter aliquam ex veritatibus fide divina et catholica credendis denegat aut de ea dubitet, haereticus; si a fide christiana totali-

ter recedit, apostate; si denique, subesse renuit Summo Pentifici aut cum membris Ecclesiae ei subiectis communicare recusat, schimaticus est." C.I.C., Can. 1325.

131   "Leges ecclesiasticae intelligendae sunt secundum propriam verborum significationem in textu et contextu consideratam." C.I.C., Can. 18.

132   Si quis dixerit, baptizatos liberos esse ab omnibus sanctae Ecclesiae Praeceptis, quae vel scripta vel tradita sunt, ita ut ea observare non teneantur, nisi se sua sponte illis submittere voluerint: anathema sit." Sessio VII, Canones de Sacramento Batismi, Can. 8, DB 864.

133   Thus Arregui, in common with moralists: "Tenentur legibus Ecclesias generalibus, omnes et soli baptizanti, explete septennio nisi aliud expresse caveatur; rationis habitualiter compotes I.C. 12, unde etiam excommunicati; et per se haeretici ex I.C. 87, pro his tamen, si in secta nati et educati fuerint, Ecclesia probabiliter non urget leges quae directe animarum sanctificationem respiciunt, v.c. leges ieiunii, communionis paschalis, etc.; certe alias quae bonum sociale immediatius respiciunt, ut leges de impedimentis matrimonialibus." *Summarium Theologiae Moralis*, Westminter, 1944, pg. 30.

134   Cappello, *Summa Iuris Canonici*, Roma, 1928, vol.I, pgs. 166-167.

135   Thus Canon Law clearly distinguishes between censures and excommunication, indicating a gradation in the degree to which a guilty person may be deprived of the rights which are due to a faithful Catholic. Censure is defined as: "poena qua homo baptizatus, delinquens et contumax quibusdam bonis spiritualibus vel spiritualibus adnexis privatur, donec a contumacia recedens absolvatur." C.I.C., Can. 2241, #1. And excommunication is: "censura qua quis exclutitur a communione fidelium inferens quosdam effectus ab invicem inseperabiles." Can. 2257, #1.

136   "Revelatio, obiectum fidei catholicae constituens, non fuit cum Apostolis completa." Decretum S. Off., *Lamentabili*, ASS 40, 470, sqq.; July 3, 1097; DB 2021.

137   Pius X, Encyclica *Pascendi Dominici Gregis*, Sept. 8, 1907, ASS 40, 593 sqq.; DB 2075.

138   "Quoniam vero 'sine fide…impossibile est placere Deo,' et ad filiorum eius consortium pervenire, ideo nemini unquam sine illa contigit iustification, nec ullus, nisi in ea 'perseveraverit usque in finem', vitam aeternam assequetur. Ut autem officio veram fidem amplectendi in eaque constanter perseverandi satisfacere possemus, Deus per Filium suum unigenitum Ecclesiam instituit, suaeque institutionis manifestis notis instruxit, ut ea tanquam custos et magistra verbi revelati ab omnibus posset agnosci." Sessio III, cap. 3, *De Fide*, DB 1793.

139   *Summa Theologica*, IIa IIae, (q. 2, a. 2) ad 1.

140   Vermeersch-Creusen, Tom. I, Vol. I, Pgs. 107-108, Mechlina-Roma, 1949. Thus also Lercher: "Unde intelligitur, our baptismus sacramentum fidei dicitur, et cur homo demum *per se* ut membrum Ecclesiae incoporetur.) Dico *per se*; quum homo adultus in coetu catholico valide baptizatur, ob defectum professionis verae fidei non incorporator Ecclesiae ut membrum, tametsi eius iurisdictioni subiicitur; sed hoc fit per accidens propter impedimentum suscipiente positum.)" *Institutionee Theologiae Dogmaticae,* I pg. 417, Oeniponte, 1937.

141   Lercher, loc. cit. In fact, Bellarmine logically concludes that even given the hypothetical case of a person who admits all the doctrines contained in the Catholic Creed, yet refuses to be subject to ecclesiastical authority and/or live in communion with the rest of the faithful, he is, ipso facto, outside the visible Church of Christ. "Non possunt," he says, "vera membra Ecclesiae vocari Lutherani et

Calvinista, etiamsi in symbolo nobiscum convenirent; nam praeter illam fidem requiritur subiectio ad legitimum caput Ecclesiae a Christo institutum, et communicatio cum aliis membris; Ecclesia enim est unum corpus visibile, et proinde caput et membra habet visibilia, neo potest dici membrum, quod a capita et corporo relinque separatum est." *De Laicis*, lib. III, cap. 19.

142   *De Baptismo*, cap. 8.

143   de Guibert, *De Christi Ecclesia,* Roma, 1928, pg. 146, quotes, Billot and Wilmers who assume that Bellarmine held that putative baptism made a person a real, actual member of the Church. Understood in this sense, they say, the doctrine is untenable.

144   Loc. cit.

145   "Ad hoc, ut aliquis sit de corpore Ecclesias, (respondeo) non requiri characterem, sed externum baptismum; neo externum baptismum requiri, ut quis cenceatur et sit de Ecclesia, sed tantum ut admittatur. Si quis enim petit admitti ad Ecclesiam, id non fiet sine baptismo. Tamen si quis dicat se baptisatum, et non constet contrarium, admittetur ad sacramenta caetera et per hoc erit de corpore Ecclesiae. Et signum huius est, quia si postea innotescat, illum non fuis se baptizatum, siquidem culpa ipsius id sit factum, expelletur de congregatione, nec recipietur, nisi post poenitentiam baptizetur. At si non culpa eius, non repelletur, sed perficietur in eo, quod de erat, nec iudicabitur non fuisse in Ecclesia, sed iudicabitur intrasse aliunde, quam per ordinariam portam. Unde Innocentius III. Cap. *Apostolicam*, de presbytere non baptizato, iudicavit presbyterum vere fuisse in Ecclesia, et iussit pro eius anima offerri sacrificium,ut pro aliis fidelibus. Et Dionysius Alexandrinus, ut habemus lib. 7, cap. 8, Hist. Eccl. iudicavit quemdam fuisse vere in Ecclesia, quem constabat non vere baptizatum, sed tantum percepisse alia sacramenta ut baptizatum." *De Ecclesia Militante*, cap. 18.

146   Louvain, 1533, 1543, 1550; Lib IV, cap. 2, pars 2.

147   "Haec videtur fuisse sententia Joan. Driedonis.....*De Script et Dogma Ecclesiae*.... ubi sic loquitur: 'Omnes qui habentur, tamquam sacramento fidei visibiliter adscripti Ecclesiae, secundum pacem quamdam corporaliter cum christiano populo conversantes, dicunt esse in Ecclesia, doneo vel iudicio Ecclesiae separentur, vel sua sponte exeant, ipsam Ecclesiamam contemnentes et persequentes.' Haec ille. Qui matis aperte scribit, in Ecclesia esse non solum omnes baptizatos, sed omnes etiam illos, qui habentur, pro baptizatis. Posset tamen etiam responderi, et tur pro Baptizatis. Posset tamen etiam responderi, et melius, eos qui non sunt baptizati, et tamem habentur pro baptizatis, esse de Ecclesia secundum apparentiam exteriorem tantum, idest, putative, non vere. Neo tamen inde sequitur, ut Ecclesia fiat invisibilis: non tametsi non possint aliqui probare se esse baptizatos, tamen plurimi probare possunt: et baptismus natura sua visibilis est." *De Ecclesia Militante*, cap 10.

148   Thus, for example,"Haereticos et apostates baptizatos, Alphonsus ae Cstro... docet esse membra et partes Ecclesiae, etiam si palam falsam doctrinam profiteantur. Quae sententia...est aperte falsa." *De Ecclesia Militante*, cap. 4. "Constat...haereticos nullo modo esse fideles." And again: "Haereticos, licet non sint de Ecclesia, tamen debere esse." Ibidem.

149   Ibidem.

150   Ibidem.

151   *De Ecclesia Militante*, cap. 2.

152   *De Laicis,* cap. 19.

153   "Obiiciunt primo, fundamentum et quasi formam Ecclesiae esee fidem… Respondeo: Formam Ecclesiae non esse fidem internam (nisi Ecclesiam invisibilem habere velimus) sed externam, idest, fidei confessionem. Id quod apertissime docet S. Augustinus lib. 19. contra Faustum, cap. 11, et experientia idem testatur; illi enim admittuntur ad Ecclesiam, qui profitentur fidem. In locis autem allegatis fides non dicitur forma, vel fundamentum Ecclesiae, sed fundamentum iustitiae, vel doctrinae, quae est in Ecclesia. Adde quod Scripturae, sicut in Ecclesia ponunt fidem, ita etiam ponunt charitatem, et omnia dona Spiritus Sancti, et tamen namo catholicorum docet, non esse de Ecclesia eos qui charitate et conis Spiritus Sancti carent." *De Ecclesia Militante,* cap. 10.

CHAPTER V
PIUS XII TO PRESENT

154   "In Eclesiae autem Membris reapse ii soli annumerandi sunt, qui regenerationis lavacrum receperunt veramque fidem profitentur, neque a Corporis compage semetipsos misere separarunt, vel ob gravissima admissa a legitima auctoritate seiuncti sunt. 'Etenimin uno Spiritu, ait Apostolus, omnes nos in unum Corpus baptizati sumus, sive ludaei, sive gentiles, sive servi sive liberi. Sicut igitur in vero christifidelium coetu unum tentummode habetur Corpus, unus Spiritus, unus Dominus et unum Baptisma, sic haberi non potest uisi una fides; atque adeo qui Ecclesiam audire renuerit, iubente Domino habendus est ut ethnicus et publicanus. Quamobrem qui fide vel regimine invicem dividuntur, in uno eiusmodi Corpore, atque uno eius divino Spiritu vivere nequeunt." Litterae Encyclicae, *Mystici Corporis*, June 29, 1943, AAS, 35, 202-203.

155   "Mystici Corporis Christi, quod est Ecclesia, ex ipsius Redemptoris labiis primitus excepta doctrina." Ibid. p. 193.

156   "Iamvero ad definiendam describendamque hanc veracem Christi Ecclesias — quae sancta, catholica, apostolica, Romana Ecclesia est — nihil nobilius, nihil praestantius, nihil denique divinius invenitur sententia illa, qua eadem nuncupatur 'mysticum Iesu Christi Corpus'; quae quidem sententia ex iis effluit ae veluti efflorescit, quae et in Secris Litteris et in sanctorum Patrum scriptis orebro proponuntur." Ibid. pg. 199.

157   "… in arbore Crucis denique sibi suam acquisivit Ecclesiam, hoc est omnia mystici sui Corporis membra, quippe quae per Baptismatis lavacrum mystico huic Corpori non coagmentarentur, nisi ex salutifera virtute Crucis, in qua quidam iam plenissimae Christi ditionis facta essent." Ibid. pg. 206.

158   Ibid. pgs. 247-248.

159   "Ecclesia…integrum quoddam et pulcherrimum corpus est, cuius caput est Christus Deus et homo." Concio 42, *De Nativitate B. Mariae Virginis*, Opera, Vol. V, Napoli, 1861, pg. 298.

160   "In hoc autem consistit similitude panis, et Ecclesiae, ut Cyprianus explicat epist. 6, lib. 1, *ad Magnum*, et Irenaeus lib. 3, cap. 19, quod sicut ex multis granis per aquam sit unus panis, ita ex multis hominibus per aquam baptismi, vel per Spiritum Sanctum…sit unus populus; nemo enim est in Ecclesia, qui non sit baptizatus, et non participet aliquod donum vel internum vel externum Spiritus Sancti." *De Ecclesia Militante,* cap. 9. This last phrase is significant, namely, where Bellarmine defines a member of the Church as one who; 1) is baptized, and 2) participates in some gift of the Holy Spirit, internal or external.

For it gives us a clue to the importance which he attaches to *external* profession of faith, participating in the sacraments and union with ecclesiastical authorities. The point being that this so-called external profession is *also* a gift of the Holy Spirit, and is, therefore, in Bellarmine's mind, external only in its effects, not in its inspiring Cause, which is the grace of the Holy Ghose operating internally, though *ad extra*, in the souls of those who belong to the Mystical Body. This may also serve as another explanation to Bellarmine's much criticized theory of membership by external profession only; which would mean that a person is a member of the Church, although he has no internal virtue; internal, that is, in its effects, but only external profession of the faith; external, that is, only in its effects, but internal, nonetheless, in its generating Cause, which is the Holy Spirit.

161   Ibid., cap. 7.

162   *De Sacramento Eucharistiae*, Lib. I, cap. 10.

163   AAS 35, 217-218.

164   *De Peccatorum Meritis et Remissione*, ML 44, 144-145.

165   *De Romano Pontifice*, Lib. I, cap. 8.

166   The most recent statement of the Holy See in this connection is the Encyclical Letter of Pope Pius XII, *Humani Generis*, in which the erroneous opinion is once condemned which seeks to extend the concept of the Mystical Body outside the limits of the Roman Catholic Church, in the sense of including others than professed Catholics in its earthly membership. "Quidam consent," says the document, "se non devinciri doctrina paucis ante annis in Encyclicis Litteris exposita, ac fontibus 'revelationis' innixa, quae quidem docet corpus Christi mysticum et Ecclesiam Catholicam Romanam unum idemque esse (cfr. Litt. Enc., *Mystici Corporis*, AAS vol. XXXV, p. 193 sq.)." *L'Osservatore Romano*, 21-22, Agosto, 1950.

167   ASS 28, p. 710.

168   "…. Quapropter a divina veritate ii aberrant, qui Ecclesiam ita effingunt, ut neque attingi neque videri possit, sitque tantum 'pneumaticum' aliquid, ut aiunt, quo multae christianorum communitates, licet fide ab se invincem seiunctae, inter se tamen haud adspectabili nexu coniungantur." AAS pg. 199-200.

169   "Ac praeterea sicut in natura rerum non ex qualibet membrorum coagerie constituitur corpus, sed organis, uti aiunt, instructum sit oportet, seu membris, quae non eundem actum habeant ac sint apto ordine composita: ita Ecclesia ea maxime de causa Corpus dicenda est, quod recta consentaneaque coalescit partium temperatione membris congruentibus instructa. Nec aliter Apostolus Ecclesiam describit, cum ducit: "Sicut … in uno corpore multa membra habemus, omnia autem membra non eundem actum habent, ita multi unum corpus sumus in Christo, singuli autem alter alterius membra." Id., pg. 200

170   "Nostra autem, quae in Christo est et cum Christo compages, primo loco ex eo constat, quod cum christiana respublica ex Conditoris sui voluntate sociale exsistat perfectumque Corpus, idcirco in ea copulatio insit oportet membrorum omnium ob eorum in eundem finem conspirationem… Quoniam vero, ut supra diximus, sociale eiusmodi Christi Corpus ex Conditoris sui voluntate adspectabili esse debet,

conspiratio illa membrorum omnium extrinsecus etiam esse manifestet opus est, cum per eiusdem fidei professionem, tum per eorundem communionem sacrorum, per eiusdem participationem sacrificii, tum denique per actuosam earundem legum observantiam. Idque praeterea omnio necessarium est, ut in oculis omnium conspicuum adsit supremum Caput, a quo mutual invicem adiutrix omnium opera ad propositum assequendum finem efficienter dirigatur: Jesu Christi dicimus in terris Vicarium." Id. pgs. 226-227.

171 "Quamvis enim iuridicae rationes, quibus Ecclesia etiam innititur at que componitur, ex divina oriantur a Christo data constitutione, ad supernumque finem assequendum conferant, id tamen, quo christiana societas ad gradum evenitur, qui omnem naturae ordinem prorsus evincit, Redemptoris nostril Spiritus est, qui ceu fons gratiarum, donorum, ac charismatum omnium, perpetuo et intime Ecclesiam replet et in ea operatur. Siquidem, quemadmodum mortalis nostri corporis compages mirificum utique est Creatoris opus, sed quam logissime distat ad excelsa animi nostri dignitate: sic socialis christianae republicae structura, quamvis divini Architecti sui sapientiam praedicet, aliquid tamen inferioris omnino ordinis est, ubi cum spiritualibus donis comparatur, quibus autem ornatur ac vivit, cum eorumque divino fonte." Id., pg. 223.

172 "Huic autem Christi Spiritui tamquam non adspectabili principio id quoque attribuendum est, ut omnes Corporis partes tam intersese, quam cum excelso Capite suo coniungantur, totus in Capite cum sit, totus in Corpore, totus in singulis membris; quibus pro diversis eorum muneribus atque officiis, pro maiore vel minore, quo fruuntur spiritualis sanitatis gradu, diversis rationibus praesens est atque adsistit. Ille est, qui caelesti vitae halitu in omnibus corporis partibus cuiusvis est habendus actionis vitalis ac reapse salutaris principium. Ille est, qui licet per se ipse in omnibus membris habeatur, in iisdemque divinitus agat, in inferioribus tamen etiam per superiorum ministerium operatur; ille denique est, qui dum Ecclesiae nova semper in dies, sua afflante gratia, incrementa parit, membra tamen, a Corpore omnino abscissa, renuit sanctitatis gratia inhabitare. Quam quidem Iesu Christi Spiritus praesentiam operationemque sapientissimus Decessor Noster imm. mem. Leo XIII Encyclicis Litteria *Divinum Illud*, per haec verba presse nervoseque significavit: "Hoc affirmare sufficiat, quod cum Christus Caput sit Ecclesiae, Spiritus Sanctus sit eius anima.' (ASS 29, 650)." Id., pgs. 219-220.

173 "Si vero vitalem illam vim virtutemque, qua tota Christianorum communitas a Conditore suo sustentatur, iam nom in semet ipsa, sed in creatis, qui inde oriuntur, effectibus spectamus, in caelestibus ea muneribus consistit, quae Redemptor noster una cum Spiritu suo Ecclesiae impertit, unaque cum Spiritu suo, supernae lucis datos sanctitatisque effector, operator." Id., pg 226.

174 Bellarmine is not to be understood to deny the objective pre-eminence of *internal* over *external* faith, no more than does Pius XII. The question here is not one of relative values, but of definition and formality. In other words, given internal faith, what formally constitutes a person a member of the Mystical Body is his profession of this faith, beginning with Baptism.

175 "Ecclesiam esse corpus saepe Sacra Eloquia praedicant…suodsi corpus est Ecclesia, unum quiddam et indivisum sit oportet secundum illud Pauli: 'Multi unum corpus sumus in Christo.' Rom. 12/5. Nec solummodo unum quiddam et indivisum esse debet, sed aliquid etiam concretum et perspicibile… Quapropter a divina veritate ii aberrant, qui Ecclesiam ita effingunt, ut neque attingi neque videri posit, sit que tantum 'pneumaticum' aliquid, ut aiunt, quo multae Christiamorum communitates, licet fide ab se invicem seiunctae, inter se tamen haud adspectabili nexu coniungantur." id., pgs. 199-200.

176 Id., pg. 227.

177 The Pope is not saying that anyone who is not an actual member of the Church

by actual profession of the faith is actually united to the Mystical Body, *in facto esse.* But he clearly allows that the same Holy Spirit who actually unites the real members of the Church, is also uniting sincere non-Catholics, *in fieri,* in the sense that He is drawing them towards the Church's unity in which, *hucusque,* they do not have an actual part.

178   Thus, for example, Pope, *The Church,* St. Louis, 1928, pg. 86. Later on we shall see that while this distinction is admissible, it cannot be divorced from member-ship in the body of the Church, *re* or *voto* as the case may be.

179   AAS (39), pg. 226.

180   "… quibus (membris) pro diversis eorum muneribus atque officiis, pro maiore vel minore, quo fruuntur spiritualis sanitatis gradu, diversis rationibus praesens est atque adssistit. Ille est, qui caelesti vitae halitu in omnibus corporis partibus cuius-vis est habendus act ionis vitalis ad reapse salutaris principium." id. pg. 219.

181   "Neque ab iis omnis vita recedit, qui licet caritatem divinamque gratiam peccando amiserint, atque adeo superni promeriti iam non capaces evaserint, fidem tamen christianamque spem retinent, ac caelesti luce collustrati, intimis Spiritus Sancti suasionibus impulsionibusque ad salutarem instigantur timorem, et ad precandum suique lapsus paenitendum divinitus excitandur." Id., pg. 203.

182   *De Ecclesia Militante,* cap. 2.

183   His membership in the *anima ecclesiae,* however, will be *actu* or *voto,* depending on whether he professes the true faith or not.

184   Grabowski, *Theological Studies,* March, 1945, pgs. 76 sqq. This writer does not concede that Bellarmine even considers the Holy Ghost Himself as the soul of the Church. His criticism is that St. Robert regards only the gifts of the Holy Spirit as the *anima ecclesiae.*

185   AAS 35, pg. 220.

186   Ibid.

187   While theologians are unanimous in accepting the doctrine of the personal in-dwelling of the Holy Ghost in the just, as clearly contained in Sacred Scriptures and Tradition, they differ in explaining the manner in which He dwells in the soul. The great majority hold that the Holy Ghost can not dwell in the soul, as the human soul dwells in the body, *per modum informationis,* and still less by a kind of hypostatic union, as Godhead and manhood dwell together in the Person of Christ; and that consequently His indwelling is the whole Trinity, which is appropriated to the Third Person merely because the Holy Ghost is "Hypostatic Holiness" or "personal Love." This view is based on "the fundamental law of the Trinity," namely, "In God all things are one except where there is opposi-tion of relation." Pohle-Preuss, *Grace, Actual and Habitual,* St. Louis, 1924, pg. 374.

188   However, as we saw, when Bellarmine comes to describe the "membership" of such a person in the Church, he speaks of it as "secundum apparentiam exteriorem tantum, idest, putative, non vere." *De Ecclesia Militante,* cap. 10.

189   AAS pg. 203.

190   Id., pg 202.

191   DB 696.

192   *De Ecclesia Militante,* cap. 6.

193   "Censura punitur tantummodo delictum externum, grave, consummatum, cum

contumacia coniunctum." CIC, Can. 2242, ≠1.

194 "Ac vehementer cupimus, ut eis quoque communes hae preces incense Caritate prospiciant, qui vel mondom Evangelii sint Veritate collustrati, heque in secura Ecclasiae caulas ingressi; vel a Nobis, qui licet immerentes iesu Christi personam hisoe in terris sustinemus, ob miserum fidei unitatisque discidium seiuncti sint." AAS pg. 242.

195 "Hos etiam, qui ad aspectabilem non pertinent Catholicae Ecclesiae compagem, ut profecto nostris, Venerabiles Fratres, inde ab inito Pontificatu, supernae Nos commisimus tutelae supernoque regimini, sollemniter adseverantes nihil Nobis, Boni Pastoris exemplum sequentibus, magis cordi esse, quam ut vitam habeant et abundantius habeant. Quam quidem sollemnem adseverationem Nostram per Encyclicas has Litteras, quibus 'magni et gloriosi Corporis Christi' laudes praedicavimus, imploratis totius Ecclesiae precibus, iterare cupimus, eos singulos universos amantissimo animo invitantes, ut internis divinae gratiae impulsionibus ultro libenterque concedentes, ab eo statu se eripere studeant, in quo de sempiterna cuiusque propria salute securi esse non possunt; quandequidem, etiamsi inscio quodam desiderio ac voto ad mysticum Redemptoris Corpus ordinentur, tot tamen tantisque caelestibus muneribus adiumentisque carent, quibus in Catholica solummodo Ecclesia frui licet. Ingradiantur igitur catholicam unitatem, et Nobiscum omnes in una Iesu Christi Corporis compagine coniuncti, ad unum Caput in gloriosissimae dilectionis societate concurrant. Numquam intermissis ad Spiritum dilectionis et veritatis precibus, eos Nos elatis aperisque manibus exspectamus, non tamquam alisnam, sed propriam paternamque domum adituros." Ibid., pgs. 242-243

196 "At si cupimus non intermissam eiusmodi totius mystici Corporis comprecationem admoveri Deo, ut aberrantes omnes in unum Iesu Christi ovile quam primum ingrediantur, profitemur tamen omnio necessarium esse id sponte libenterque fieri, cum nemo credit nisi volens. Quam ob rem si qui, non credentes, eo reapse compelluntur ut Ecclesiae aedificium intrent,ut ad altare accedant, sacramentaque suscipiant, ii procul dubio veri christifideles non fiunt; fides eaim sine qua 'impossibile est placare Deo' liberrimum esse debet obsequium intellectus et voluntatis.'" Ibid., pg. 243.

197 Id., pg. 242.

198 Ibid.

199 Ibid., pg. 243.

200 Id., pg. 199.

201 Id., pg. 42.

202 Id., pg. 243.

203 The two correlatives, *re* and *voto*, are are separated in the text of the Encyclical. The first occurs in the phrase, "In Ecclesiae autem membris reapse ii soli annumerandi sunt, qui regenerationis lavacrum receperunt, etc." AAS pg. 202; the second occurs in the present context, AAS pg. 243.

204 *Mystici Corporis*, n. 117

205 Thus, for example, in St. Thomas: "Ad hoc quod aliqua sint ordinata, duo requiruntur: primo quidem quod aliqua ordinentur ad debitum finem, qui est principium totius ordinis in rebus agendis…Secundo oportet quod id quod est ad finem sit proportionatum fini." *Summa Theologica*, la ae, q. 102, a. 1, corpus.

206   *De Ecclesia Militante*, cap. 3.

207   AAS pg. 243.

208   Ibid.

209   Sic humani generis servitor ex infinita bonitate sua Corpori suo mystico mirum
      in modum prospexit, illud sacramentis ditando, quibus membra quasi per non in-
      termissos gratiarum gradus, ab incunabulis ad extremum usque halitum sustentar-
      entur, itemque socialibus totius Corporis necessitatibus uberrime provideretur."
      Id., pg. 201.

210   Id., pg. 243.

PART III
CRITICAL COMPARISON

CHAPTER I
INTRODUCTION

211   AAS 42, 1950, pgs. 142 sqq.

212   AAS pg. 142.

213   AAS pgs. 143-144.

214   AAS, pg. 146.

215   AAS, pg. 144.

216   Thus, for example, Leo XIII in, *Longingua Oceani*, Jan. 6, 1895, Fontes CIC, Vol.
      III, pgs. 460-468. And Pius XII in the Encyclical, *Sertum Laetitiae*, AAS (1939)
      51, pgs. 635-644.

217   The opinion which conceives adult non-Catholics as outside the friendship of God,
      almost without exception, will be considered in the last chapter of this study.

CHAPTER II
FIRST THEORY: "NON-CATHOLICS ARE ENTIRELY OUTSIDE THE CATHOLIC CHURCH"

218   Gurden, John C., *The Mystical Christ,* St. Louis, 1936.

219   Id., pgs. 175-176.

220   Id., pg. 167.

221   Id., pgs. 174-175.

222   Id., pg. 175.

223   Id., pg. 176.

224   Ibid.

225   DB 430.

226   DB 469.

227   Op. cit., pgs. 173-174.

228   Ibid.

229   *De Ecclesia Militante,* cap. 2.

230   Chapters I and II.

231   AAS (35), pg. 220.

232   Op. cit., pg. 175.

233   Ibid.

234   Id., pgs. 176-177. The author quoted to this effect is Bainvel. However, it is do-
      ing Bainvel an injustice to suggest that he juxtaposed membership in the Church

as the ordinary means of salvation, and non-membership as the extra-ordinary means. For he clearly recognizes the necessity of some kind of membership as an indispensable condition for salvation. Thus he says; after describing the various types of actual members of the Church, "Reliqui viatores potentia omnes, non actu, membra sunt. Quamquam eorum etiam aliqua est cum Eclesia coniunctio. Nam catechumeni, ut pueri in utero matris Ecclesiae, ad eam voto vel merito… pertinent." And he adds, "… ad eius (Ecclesiae) animam… iusti omnes pertinent, at que ita de eius vita vivunt, ut voti impliciti ad eam pertinendi, eius intuitu et influxu objectivo, ut de Christo dicitur, omnem gratiam accipiant." *De Ecclesia Christi*, Paris, 1925, pg. 112-113.

235   *De Sacramentis in Genere*, cap. 22.

236   This applied properly only to adults, i.e., to those who in place of *actual*, can have *voto* membership in the Church; a possibility which is absent in the case of infants who must be actually baptized in order to be in the Church and therefore to be saved.

237   DB 1677.

238   Op. cit., col. 569.

239   The only authority cited is Tanquerey, *Synopsis Theologiae Dogmaticae*, III, nos. 228-230. However Tanquerey is not quoted. On examination, we find that he most emphatically does not teach that God gives infants dying without baptism the proximate means of salvation, which is Gruden's implication. Says Tanqueray: "Deus paravit parvulis etiam iis qui in sinu matris moriuntur antequam baptizari possint, media ex se sufficientia ad salutem. Ita communiter. Certum est Deum remote saltem omnibus illis parvulis media salutis paravisse, dum instituit medium ad originale peccatum delendum, quale est baptismus. Aliquae aliae solutiones propositae sunt, sed parum tutae." After detailing some of these opinions which claim salvation for infants without baptism, whether before or after birth, he concludes, "Remanet igiturut dicamus hos infantes in limbum descendere." Op. cit., Roma, 1930, pgs. 166-167.

240   Op. cit., pg. 176.

241   Sermo 323, 324. Cf. *Anonymus de Miraculis S. Stephani*, I, 15, 1.

242   *Summa Theologica*, Pars 3a, q. 68, a. 11, ad 1.

243   The work of Cajetan in which this occurs in his Commentary on St. Thomas. The edition is that of Rome, 1570; the section are the articles 2 and 11 of the Commentary.

244   d'Ales, Bapteme et Confirmation, Paris, 1927, pgs. 122-124.

245   DB 102.

246   ML 20, 592.

247   ML 54, 685.

248   DB 410.

249   DB 712.

250   DB 796.

251   DB 1470.

252   *De Sacramento Baptismi*, cap. 8.

253   Op. cit., pgs. 176-177.

254   DB 1677.

255   DB 1647.

256   DB 1677.

257   Ibid.

CHAPTER III
SECOND THEORY: "SINCERE HERETICS ARE FORMAL MEMBERS OF THE CATHOLIC CHURCH, BUT LACK JURIDICAL COMMUNION WITH THE FAITHFUL"

258   Homiletic and Pastoral Review, New York, 1949, pg. 821. (Dr. Joseph P. Donovan).

259   Chapter IV supra.

260   "De excommunicatis, quod in Ecclesia non sint, docent, Catechismus Romanus in explication. symboli; Thomas Baldensis, tom.1, lib.2, cap.9… Joannes de Turrecremata lib.1, cap.3, *Summae de Ecclesia*; Joannes Driedo, lib.4, cap.2, part 2, et alii … *De Ecclesia Militante*, cap. 6.

261   Bellarmine quotes the following passage, "Canonica instituta, et Sanctorum Patrum exempla sequentes, Ecclesiarum Dei violators, auctoritate Dei et judicio sancti Spiritus, a gremio sanctae matris Ecclesiae, et a consortio totius christianitatis eliminamus." (Ex Jure Canonico, 11, q. 3). *De Ecclesia Militante,* cap. 6.

262   Among the Fathers quoted are: Epiphanius, Hilary, Chrysostm, Jerome and Augustine. The following is a passage from Augustine: "Omnis Christianus, qui a sacerdotibus excommunicatur, eatanae traditur. Quomodo quia scilicet extra Ecclesiam diabolus eat, sicut in Ecclesia Christus." Ibid.

263   The three reasons given by Bellarmine are: 1. Through excommunication the guilty are separated from excommunication with the rest of the faithful, which members of the Church enjoy. 2. Excommunication holds the same place in the Church which death held in the Old Testament. 3. Where is no worse penalty which the Church can impose. Ibid.

264   Ibid.

265   "Restituo te unitati Ecclesiae et membrorum participationi." To which Bellarmine adds: 'Quod signu est persicuum, excommunicatum separatum fuisse ab Ecclesiae Unitate." Ibid.

266   AAS (35) pg. 6.

267   Anscar Vonier, *Key to the Doctrine of the Eucharist,* London, 1931, pgs. 5-7.

268   AAS (35), pg. 203.

269   AAS (35), pg. 224.

CHAPTER IV
THIRD THEORY: "ACTUAL CATHOLICS ARE MEMBERS OF THE BODY OF THE CHURCH; NON-CATHOLICS ARE MEMBERS OF THE SOUL OF THE CHURCH"

270   Paul J. Glenn, *Apologetics*, St. Louis, 1931, pgs. 283-284.

CHAPTER V
FOURTH THEORY: "NON-CATHOLICS ARE NOT MEMBERS OF THE CHURCH IN ANY SENSE, THEREFORE, WITH RARE EXCEPTIONS, THEY CANNOT ATTAIN TO SALVATION"

271   DB 621.

272   DB 1677.

273   Ibid.

274   Raymond Karam, *From the Housetops*, Cambridge Massachusetts, 1949, Vol. III, no. 6, pgs. 17-18.

275   Id., pgs. 20-21.

276   Id., pg. 21.

277   Bainvel, *Is There Salvation Outside the Church?,* English translation by Weidenhan, II Ed. 1923, St. Louis, pg. 37.

278   Id., pg. 54.

279   Ibid.

280   Louis Caperan, *Le Problème du ...des infidèles, Toulouse, 1934,* (_ssai Theologique), Vol. II, pg. 102.

281   Caperan, *Union Missionnaire du Clerge'*, Oct. 1945, Jan. 1946.

282   *De Ecclesia Militante*, cap.18.

283   *De Ecclesia Militante*, cap.1; also *De Poenitentia*, Lib II, cap. 14. However, on examination of the reference cited, we find that Bellarmine merely denies that catechumens have actual membership in the Church; so far from denying that they are *voto* in the Mystical Body, he positively affirms it, as will be seen.

284   Op. cit., pg. 24.

285   Op. cit., pg. 24.

286   *Epistola* ML 33, 160.

287   The quotation is wrongly attributed to St. Augustine, whereas it belongs to St. Thomas, in the *Summa*, where he says: "Haereticus est qui falsas vel novas opiniones vel gignit vel sequitur." Ila Ilae, q. 11, a.l.

288   Karam, op. cit., pg. 46.

289   Karam, op. cit. pgs. 54-55.

290   Karam, op. cit., pgs. 55-56.

291   Id., pgs. 57-58.

292   *De Baptismo*, Lib. IV, cap.21, num.28., ML 43, 173.

293   Id., Lib. IV, cap.22, num.29., ML 43, 173.

294   MG 56, 658.

295   *De Ecclesia Militante*, cap. 2.

296   Karam, op. cit., pgs. 58-60.

297   *De Baptismo*, Lib., cap. 6.

298   *In Joannem*, cap. III, Lectio I, pars 4.

299   Karam, op. cit., pgs. 60-62.

300   Karam, op. cit., Vol. III, no. 2, pgs. 11-18.

301   Karam, op. cit., Vol. III, pg. 85.

302   *De Ecclesia Militante*, cap. 4.

303   *De Ecclesia Militante*, cap. 8.

304   Karam, op. cit., pg. 61.

305   For example, Benedict XIV's Encyclical, *Maximum Illud*, November 30, 1918; and Pius XI's, *Rerum Ecclesiae,* February 28, 1926.

306   DB 796.

307   Karam, op. cit., pgs. 57-58.

308 Introductory letter of recommendation to the *Opera* of St. Alphonsus, Roma, 1905.

309 *Osservatore Romano*, June 1, 1950.

310 *Opera*, Roma, 1905, Vol. I, *De Baptismo*, pg. 75.

311 *Opera*, Roma, 1905, Vol. I, *De Praecepto Fidei*, pgs. 295-296.

312 Id. Pg. 298.

313 Karam, op. cit., pg. 59.

314 DB 796.

315 DB 799.

316 "In nominibus poenitentibus ante sacramentum absolutionis et in catechumenis ante baptismum est vera justificatio, separata tamen a remissione peccatorum." DB 1043.

317 Besides the evidence already given, we may add that Bellarmine was too familiar with the mind of St. Thomas, to have departed from the clear statement of the latter on the sufficiency of an implicit desire for Baptism as a condition for salvation. Thus in the *Summa*, "Ante Baptismum Cornelius et alii similes consequuntur gratiam et virtutes per fidem Christi et desiderium baptismi *implicite* vel explicite." Pars 3a, q. 69, a. 4.

318 *De Ecclesia Militante*, cap 8.

319 *De Ecclesia Militante*, cap. 9.

320 *De Poenitentia*, Lib. III, cap. 14.

321 Karam, op.cit., Vol. III, pg. 59.

322 Loc. cit.

323 The reference should be to St. Thomas, *Summa Theologica*, lla llae, q. 11, a.1.

324 Karam, op.cit., pg. 24.

325 DB 1647.

326 DB 1677.

327 Op.cit., col. 591.

328 Op.cit., col. 569.

329 DB 1793.

330 Op.cit., col 73.

331 Op.cit., col. 177-178.

332 AAS (35), pgs. 242-243.

333 Id., pg. 219.

BIBLIOGRAPHY

The following is a list of those works and authors which are actually cited in the thesis.

I.   COLLECTED WORKS

Acta Apostolicae Sedis

    Benedict VI, Litterae Encyclicae: *Maximum Illud*, Vol. II, 1919.

    Pius XI, Litterae Encyclicae: R*erum Ecclesiae*,
                                          Vol. 18, 1926.

    Litterae Apostolicae: *Providentissimus Deus*,
                                          vol. 23, 1931.

    Pius XII, Litterae Encyclicae: S*ertum Laetitiae*,
                                          Vol. 31, 1939.

    Litterae Encyclicae: *Mystici Corporis*,
                                          Vol. 35, 1943.

Instruction of the Holy Office on the *Ecumenical Movement*,
                 vol. 42, 1950.

Acta et Decreta Concilii Vaticani, *Collectio Lacensis*, Friburgi Brisgoviae, vol. VII, 1692.

Acta Sanctae Sedis

      Pius IX, *Syllabus Errorum Modernorum*, Vol. 3, 1867.

      Leo XIII, Litterae Encyclicae: S*atis Cognitum*, Vol. 28, 1896.

            Litterae Apostolicae: *Apostolicae Curae*, Vol. 29, 1896.

Litterae Encyclicae: *Divinum Illud*. Vol. 29, 1897.

            Pius X, Decretum S. Officii, *Lamentabili*, Vol. 40, 1907.

            Litterae Encyclicae: *Pascendi*, Vol. 40, 1907.

Bellarminus, S. Robertus

    Opera Omnia, Milano, 1857, sqq.

        De Controversiis Christianae Fidei, Vol. I — IV.
        De Ecclesia Militante, Vol. II.
        De Gratia et Libero Arbitrio, Vol. IV.
        De Laicis, Vol. II.
        De Notis Ecclesiae, Vol. II.
        De Poenitentia, Vol. III.
        De Romano Pontifice, Vol. I.
        De Sacramentis in Genere, Vol. III

De Sacramento Baptismi, vol. III.

De Sacramento Eucharistae, vol. III.

Opera Omnia, Napoli, 1856, sqq.

Apologia ad Librum Jacobi Regis, vol. IV.

Pro Juramento Fedelitatis, vol. IV.

De Lumine Fidei, vol. V.

De Moribus Haereticorum, vol. V.

De Nativitate B.M.V., vol. V.

Codex Iuris Canonici, Friburgi Brisgoviae, 1920.

Corpus Iuris Canonici, Lipsiae, 1879-1881.

Corpus Scriptorum Ecclesiasticorum Latinorum, Vindobonae, 1866, sqq.
Tertullianus, De Baptismo, vol. 20.

Fontes Codicis Iuris Canonici, Roma, 1924.
Pius IX, Litterae Encyclicae: *Nostis et Nobiscum,* Vol. II, 1849.
Allocutio: *Singulari Quadam*, vol. II, 1854.
Litterae Encyclicae: *Quanto Conficiamur Moerore*, Vol. II, 1863.
Leo XIII, Litterae Encyclicae: *Longingua Oceani*, Vol. III, 1895.

Mansi, *Sacrorum Conciliorum Collectio*, Florentiae, 1759 sqq., Vol I, XXII, XXXI.

Migne, J.P.

Patrologia Graeca, Paris, 1886 sqq.

S. Cyrillus Hierosolymitanus, *Catecheses*, MG 33.

S. Gregorius Nazianzenus, *Oratio 40 in Sanctum Baptism*, MG 36.

S. Joannes Chrysostomus, *Homilia 4 in Matthaeum*, MG 36.

Patrologia Latina, Paris, 1878, sqq.

S. Cyprianus, *De Catholicae Ecclesiae Unitate*, ML 4.

S. Ambrosius, *De Abraham*, ML 14.

De Obitu Valentiniani Consolatio, ML 16.

S. Hieronymus, *Epistula 1 ad Damasum*, ML 22.

S. Augustinus, *Epistula 43*, ML 33.

De Vera Religione, ML 34.

Tractatus XXII in Joannem, ML 35.

Sermo 267, 268, in die Pentecostes, ML 38.
Breviculo Collationis, ML 38.
De Ecclesiasticis Dogmatibus, ML 42.
De Baptismo, ML 43.
De Gratia et Libero Arbitrio, ML 44.
De Peccatorum Meritis et Remissione, ML 44.
S. Fulgentius, De Fide ad Petrum, ML 65.
S. Bernardus, Epistula 77 ad Hugonem de S. Victore, ML 182.

Suarez, Francisus, Opera Omnia, Paris, 1856, sqq., Vol. XII, Disputatio XII,
De Fide.

II. AUTHORS

S. Alphonsus Liguori, Opera, Roma, 1905.
    De Baptismo, Vol. I.
    De Praecepto Fidei, Vol. I.

Arragui, Summarium Theologiae Moralis, Westminster, 1944.
Bainvel, De Ecclesia Christi, Paris, 1925.
    Is There Salvation Outside the Church?, St. Louis, 1923.
Bellarminus, S. Robertus, Dichiarazione Piu Copiosa della Dottrina
Christiana,
 Roma, 1824.
Billot, De Ecclesia, Roma, 1921.
Calvin, Jean, Institution de la Religion Chrétienne, Brunsvic, 1865.
Cano, De Locis Theologicis, Paris, 1678, Vol. I.
Capetran, Le Problème du Salut des Infidèles, Toulouse, 1934.
Cappello, Summa Iuris Canonici, Roma, 1945, Vol I — III.
D'Alès, Baptême et Confirmation, Paris, 1928.
de Guibert, De Christi Ecclesia, Roma, 1928.
Denzinger-Bannwart, Enchiridion Symbolorum, Friburgi, 1942.
Glenn, Apologetics, St. Louis, 1931.
Gruden, The Mystical Christ, St. Louis, 1936.
Hugon, Hors de l'Englise point de Salut, Paris, 1927.
Hurter, Theologiae Dogmaticae Compendium, vol. I, Oeniponte, 1893.
Lamennsia, Essai sur l'Indifférence en Matière de Religion, Paris, 1823.
Le Bachelet, Bellarmin Avant Son Cardinalat, Paris, 1911.
Lennerz, De Sacramento Baptismi, Roma, 1948.
Lercher, Institutiones Theologiae Dogmaticae, vol. I, Oeniponte, 1927.
Newman, Apologia Pro Vita Sua, London, 1890.
Palczar, Pio IX e il Suo Pontificato, Torino, 1909.
Pohle-Preuss, Grace, Actual and Habitual, St. Louis, 1924.
Pope, The Church, St. Louis, 1928.
Rauschen, Patrologie, Paris, 1906.

Tanquerey, *Theologiae Dogmaticae Compendium*, Oeniponte, 1893.

St. Thomas
  Catena Aurea, Parma, 1860.
  De Veritate, Taurini, 1927.
  In Joannem, Taurini, 1925.
  Quaestiones Quodlibetales, Taurini, 1924.
  Summa Theologica, Roma, 1894.

Vermeersch-Creusen, *Epitome Iuris Canonici*, Tom. I, vol. II, Mechlina-Roma, 1949.
Von Frentz, *Vita di S. Roberto Bellarmin*, Isola del Liri, 1930.
Vonier, Anscar, *Key to the Doctrine of the Eucharist*, London, 1961.

III.   PERIODICALS

From the Housetops, Vol. III, Cambridge, 1949.
Homiletic and Pastoral Review, New York, 1949.
L'Osservatore Romano, Roma, 1 Giugno, 21-22 Agosto, 1950.
Theological Studies, New York, March, 1945.
Unitas, Rome, January-March, 1949.